Carl Boyer

THE CONCEPT OF DUTY IN SOUTH ASIA

The Concept of Duty in South Asia

Edited by

WENDY DONIGER O'FLAHERTY
J. DUNCAN M. DERRETT

Published in the USA for the School of Oriental and African Studies by

SOUTH ASIA BOOKS

ISBN 0-8364-0025-9

LC 77-089488

Printed in India

Contents

Preface vii

Introduction xiii

Contributors xxi

PART I: THE ANCIENT PERIOD: DUTY AND *DHARMA*

ARNOLD KUNST: *Use and Misuse of Dharma* 3

J. DUNCAN M. DERRETT: *The Concept of Duty in Ancient Indian Jurisprudence: The Problem of Ascertainment* 18

FRIEDRICH WILHELM: *The Concept of Dharma in Artha and Kāma Literature* 66

J.C. HEESTERMAN: *Veda and Dharma* 80

WENDY DONIGER O'FLAHERTY: *The Clash between Relative and Absolute Duty: The Dharma of Demons* 96

RICHARD F. GOMBRICH: *The Duty of a Buddhist according to the Pali Scriptures* 107

ALEX GUNASEKARA: *Rājakāriya or the Duty to the King in the Kandyan Kingdom of Sri Lanka* 119

PART II: THE MEDIEVAL AND MODERN PERIOD: MUSLIM, BRITISH AND NATIONALIST CONCEPTS OF DUTY

P. HARDY: *The Duty of the Sultan (in the Sultanate Period) to Further the Material Welfare of his Subjects* 147

T.G.P. SPEAR: *Stern Daughter of the Voice of God: Ideas of Duty among the British in India*

KENNETH A. BALLHATCHET: *British Rights and Indian Duties: The Case of Sir William Lee-Warner* 190

DAVID TAYLOR: *Concepts of Duty held by Indian Nationalist Thinkers* 205

SIMON WEIGHTMAN and S. M. PANDEY: *The Semantic Fields of Dharm and Kartavy in Modern Hindi* 217

S.C. DUBE: *Changing Norms in the Hindu Joint Family* 228

Index 237

Preface

It is high time that the peoples of South Asia polished their mirror. The clash between modernity and tradition has intrigued, now, two generations of scholars and lined a wall in many a university library. While historians and anthropologists discuss the emergence of Pakistan, India, Bangladesh and Sri Lanka into the nuclear age, the populations who harbour them are locked in conflict with themselves and with each other.

Our understanding of them is not so immediately relevant. Their conception of themselves is all important. Herein tradition is made and remade, and the dramatic events in India during the last three years stress the vital importance of discovering what is DUTY.

Before we come to those events, let us study the dedication by A. S. Altekar of his *Position of Women in Hindu Civilisation* (*sic*) *from Pre-historic Times to the Present Day* (first ed., 1938). The life of his father, a pleader in Maharashtra, is described as 'a beautiful synthesis of Dehakārya, Deśakārya, and Devakārya'. All three are fictitions terms. 'Duty to the body', which presumably recalled *mens sana in corpore sano*, was a notion dear to Maharashtrian self-dedication, a preparation for the 'Freedom Struggle'. It figures still in Hindu extremist movements. The concept of physical fitness as a 'duty' is wholly western and India's authentic notions, such as the alleged need to retain *retas*, are in no sense a counterpart. *Deśakārya* makes us think of the Servants of India Society, and comes from the same milieu. 'Duty to one's country' is wholly foreign, and is not yet acclimatised to the population of the sub-continent at large. *Devakārya*, 'duty to the devas' was, presumably, a surrogate for 'religion'. This half-conscious assimilation of foreign or foreign-inspired ideals as if they were (laudably) traditional is characteristic of India, and here we find it on the very threshold of Independence. Imitation of the West, masquerading as a redefinition of the ancient past, interests the foreign observer and confuses the subjects of this mental process.

Altekar was a Bachelor of Laws as well as a Master of Arts, a professor of ancient Indian history and culture. Nearly half a century of dedicated revelation by him and by his colleagues, of the glories of the ages before foreign rule has led us to this present year in which the following developments are to be noted. Criticism of the government's measures to control 'subversion' and develop the economy is controlled by a form of censorship, and in acute cases by preventive detention. Amendments of the Constitution, which have cascaded during the last decade, have reached a point where constitutional protection of the individual has become checkered, or is confined to relatively undramatic areas. The government's proceedings strive for legality, while necessity knows no law. The courts, which were never tired of applying elaborate, expensive, even luxurious techniques in *certiorari* proceedings to check illegality by the executive, have been handicapped, and some of the individual judges have felt it might have been altogether better to sacrifice some of the Rule of Law (as a girl might sacrifice some of her virginity) at a much earlier stage in this conflict.

The draconian measures, which exasperate lawyers and public men who were trained in the West or whose minds are in tune with common-law traditions, still make a marvellous contrast with 'detention without trial' (with or without torture) as known in the other underdeveloped countries watched jealously by Amnesty or the International Commission Jurists. What restrains the executive whom no Constitution can restrain? Only the innate sense of propriety (not 'fairness') which is called *dharma*! Uganda, South Africa, South America and Iron Curtain countries have no *dharma*: and one of the consequences is notorious. India's *dharma* owes nothing to freedom movements or Independence.

Those same draconian measures to control acts allegedly prejudicial to internal security and to prevent smuggling are, like the constitutional changes, constantly under attack from the very same élite that obtained Independence. The cooperation between the transmitters of the indigenous culture, patriots, lawyers, and politicians that existed at the time of Independence has come to this, that the atavistic, post-mediaeval India has finally pulled up our cosmopolitan, modern man, saying 'Stop!' And he does not recognize where he is.

Law, as we understand it in countries of the Anglo-American world, does not have deep roots. It is a luxury, part of the elegant furniture of the élite. As teachers like Altekar were never tired of reminding their pupils, ancient Indian ethics knew nothing of *rights*, only duties. When pressed to say what these were, they turn out mostly to be duties towards mankind (e.g. mildness, absence of anger and lust), or in particular towards parents or one's husband, towards the ethics and *mores* of the sub-caste, and towards that sub-caste itself. In 1898 Japan adopted a western-styled Civil Code, and we are told that the first professors of civil law, who studied in England and/or in Germany, never really comprehended what 'law' was. Duty they understood perfectly. As in India, it is the psychological obligation-stance of a junior towards his senior. When the word 'right' had to be translated into Japanese difficulties arose. A word had to be invented, and it was found by M. Tsuda in 1868. Indian ideas are perhaps not so very sharp-focused as this, but the intrusion of legal, i.e. 'contract' (rather than 'status') concepts into India in the late eighteenth century was as grave a disturbance to the psyche and the peace of the sub-continent as it subsequently became essential for the development of an entrepreneurial and all-Indian élite class.

This class, with a sigh, suffers in the interests of an organization for which no traditional ideas and no traditional methods make any provision. That is, after all, a higher good. It is no wonder that the very same class is unable to understand why its famous Constitution has not worked smoothly. The imported, even Victorian liberal notions are unworkable with a population which on the one hand admits that the achievements of its cosmopolitans are gratifying, and on the other insists that its concept of duty, to one's parents, one's kindred, one's sub-caste, far outstrips, when resources are scarce or undependable, any claims by so unvisualizable an entity as the State. The élite, who cannot understand how village machinery for dispute-settlement works, branding it as corrupt and non-legal, long for an imaginary system of 'people's justice' which will link New Delhi and the 'grass-roots' in ineffable harmony. But the villagers' concept of harmony is very different and is timeless.

The villager knows that if a Muslim handles Hindu matters, or *vice versa*, some disturbance of unseen harmonies will occur. The élite deny it, and assert the cosmopolitan ideal that any judge may dispose validly of any contest, even with words prejudicial to the quiet enjoyment of their culture by another community. The villager, for example, would not see how we could allow a Jew to dispose of Christian matrimonial matters, whereas the élite could not see how anyone could object to it. The Indian judiciary scouts the concept of, for example, the 'Hindu husband', who could conceivably have different duties towards his wife than a Muslim husband could have. To them a couple is just a couple, and their duties can be finally decided by Parliament with the intervention of an educated judicial mind. In May 1976 the Marriage Laws (Amendment) Act put an end to all function, in law, of the age-old concepts of the wife's loyalty to her husband which had been, till then, the backbone of Hindu culture. Even arranged marriages can now be frustrated if a girl bride who has passed the age of 15 but not yet reached the age of 18 repudiates the match! Such a development, entirely intelligible to readers of *Yojana* or similar high-grade English magazines, is part of the rapid stride of the élite towards tommorrow's world in which individualism will be so pervasive that only two duties will need to be considered, towards oneself and towards one's country. It is not an accident that some ladies of that same élite, in their Report to the Ministry of Education and Social Welfare called *Towards Equality* (1974), demand abolition of the *Mitakshara* joint family, which feeds and encourages many mercantile and agricultural communities, but has no genuine role in the government-servant and professional classes. We have seen already how prepared the population at large is for 'duty to oneself' and 'duty to one's country'. The former is not easily translated into regional languages. If the ideas can be received at all this will depend on, not cooperative effort by kindred and mutual-support groups, but the Rule of Law—that very entity which has wilted in the Supreme Court and the High Courts in high constitutional matters after two centuries of sincere dedication to the métier of lawyer, just as the Hindu marriage has bowed itself out after two millenia of missionary activity in the *dharmaśāstra*.

Not content with their headlong motion, the élite wish to eliminate from the arena of law all rules based on conscience. Had the Supreme Court not scotched it some time ago, the Bombay High Court's idea that religion (as protected by the Constitution) was a purely personal affair of the individual would have secularized the Constitution in spirit as well as form. Abdicating the Victorian concern for the morals of the nation, in particular of the young; over-sensitive to the manifestations of hypocrisy in which the previous regime had excelled; aiming now at a lowest common denominator of regulatable behaviour; the same élite, heirs to Independence, forgetting nothing but remembering nothing, chafes visibly at the political hindrances to reforming forcibly the religious laws of Muslims and Christians. Yet these reforms are overdue, and perhaps only just around the corner. And then, having established on paper, with the educational motive that so much Indian legislation has, the limits within which courts must define and effectuate the rights of individuals, they will sit back, and let time do its work, if it can, as they hope, uniting the nation.

How the Constitution of 1950, or for that matter the penal code of 1860, has succeeded in the realms of smuggling and food-adulteration recent news shows. As for the Child Marriage Restraint Acts, 1929-1949 and the Dowry Prohibition Act, 1961, the élite's chagrin is pitiful indeed; *Towards Equality* provides tables concerning the marriage age of girls in numerous classes: vast numbers are married still at 12, or even 10 and under. That tells us where *duty* actually lies, and who responds to it.

What is said about India can be said, *mutatis mutandis*, of the other territories. It could have been better if a sympathetic and honest study of *dharma* and its counterparts had been fostered, and continued even after it was found as a fact that the colleges at Calcutta and Benares lacked original inspiration. For Hinduism, Islam and Buddhism are equipped, unlike non-Buddhistic elements in China and Japan, with a rich apparatus of perceptual sources, ancient, mediaeval and modern, supplying an abundance of casuistical illustration on all aspects of duty. If their authors knew nothing of bicycles and television that does not mean that they had not experienced, collectively, all human problems. It might have been better to invest actively in indigenous education, and not to be too easily discouraged by defensive developments. If originality had been stimulated and indigenous scholars and adepts had been well remunerated to provide answers to new problems in traditional terms, we might have seen an accommodation to modernity which has taken place in some parts of the Jewish and Moslem world. To give, in effect, *carte blanche* in all matters of leadership to an alienated and élitist group who, by definition, outstripped and outfaced the bulk of the populations that fed them has turned out to be a very dubious investment. The better education of that élite's children may possibly be an acceptable and appropriate reparation.

Introduction

Superfluous as the academic world is in general, there are few academic pursuits more frivolous than the academic conference. It is always good to see one's colleagues from abroad, and occasionally useful to have a forum for work one has had stashed away for a rainy day, but seldom is one inspired to produce an original piece of scholarship tailored for the specific occasion; either the garment, pre-cut, does not fit the model, or it fits and has no style or quality of its own. The actual conference, apart from pleasant gossip, often sounds rather like nursery-school conversation, everyone saying his own piece without listening to the others: 'I have a new train'; 'My father is bigger than yours'; 'I cut my knee yesterday'.

Firmly convinced of this as I have always been, it was with some considerable trepidation (and largely in deference to my mentor) that I allowed myself to be 'volunteered' to chair the conference on the concept of duty in South Asia. To my delight, all of the participants had something to say which was both relevant and original; and to my greater astonishment, at the conference it became evident that the participants had actually read one another's papers and were able to respond with genuine interest, perspicacity and good will. As a result of this remarkable interplay, most of the papers were radically modified on the basis of comments arising at their original presentation; and the gratified chairperson, furiously taking notes at the final conference, had little to do but call a regretful halt when discussions—spirited but never malicious—threatened to run over into valuable drinking and banqueting time.

On the basis of those pages of notes, I have constructed this introduction. I have not attributed specific remarks to specific contributors, nor can I blame anyone but myself for their formulation here, but I must thank my colleagues for supplying all of the basic ideas. Participants in the discussion included, in addition to the thirteen authors of the essays in this collection, other members of the faculty of the School (Professor Christoph von Fürer-Haimendorf, Major John Harrison, Mrs Audrey Hayley), an emeritus scholar (Dr N. S. Junankar), students (including Dr David Shulman), and visitors (Professor Alex Wayman).

Although we all tried to stick to the central topic of duty, most of the scholars dealing with the ancient period gravitated, *volens nolens*, toward the intersecting but by no means synonymous category of *dharma*; exceptions to this were the studies of *karaṇīyam* (Gombrich), *rājakāriya* (Gunasekara), and *itikartavyatā* (Derrett). Yet this centripetal pull was exerted on the Indians themselves as much as on scholars of India, which may justify at least some of the lopsided emphasis of these essays; *dharma* appears to be central because it *is* central. Unfortunately, no one is quite sure what *dharma* is; those who think they are sure clash with others equally convinced of quite different definitions. Each of the scholars at this conference saw a different part of the elephant of *dharma*—the tail, the trunk, the legs — yet we all agreed that the elephant did exist.

Dharma is a problem rather than a concept, vague, indeterminable, impossible to define without broadening it into useless generality or narrowing it to exclude valid instances. Ultimately, it must be accepted as an ambiguous concept; even in modern instances, attempts to define it too precisely have led to serious problems for nationalist thinkers. It is clear from Derrett's essay that *adharma* has the backing of *dharma*, just as the study of demons' *dharma* and gods' *adharma* demonstrates the interdependence of the polar categories. Kunst demonstrates that *ṛta* involves both *dharma* and *adharma*; and one is reminded of a similar formulation: *summa ius, summa iniuria*. In the Ṛg Veda, *ṛta* is hidden in the netherworld; later it is said to be *guhyanīta*. Yama, the protector of *dharma*, is king of the underworld; demons steal the *dharma* (the Vedas) and carry it below the sea to the underworld; Yudhiṣṭhira, the human embodiment of *dharma*, goes to hell because there is no *dharma* in heaven. Thus an attempt is made to incorporate evil into the realm of *dharma*, an attempt which determines the enduring ambiguity of the concept.

Since *dharma* is hidden, it must be found and activated by a dialectic process, by a context, by each new situation. It must be activated by dispute, by battle, even as, in Europe in the Middle Ages, God and Law became manifest only in battle. *Dharma* must be wrested away from the demons, the revilers, the opponents; and in order for this to occur, *dharma* can never be pinned down. The enunciation of explicit absolute rules is a sin, as is evident from Ballhatchet's description of British attempts to deal with 'moral education' in India; there is always opposition against instruction in *explicit* rules of behaviour, resistance against explicit codification. Thus the inconclusiveness of our investigation is not a problem but a tentative solution : it places *dharma* where the ancient Indians placed it, squarely upon the horns of a dilemma.

This ambiguity is heightened by an enduring conflict between theory and fact, a conflict evident on one level in the materials themselves and on another level in different scholarly approaches to the material. On the first level, one sees a contrast (and occasionally a conflict) between texts composed by theologians and texts composed by politicians; Wilhelm demonstrates this in his comparison of *Dharmaśāstra* and *Arthaśāstra* views of *dharma*, and it is also germane to Hardy's study of the Sultanate concept of duty. There is a tension between the duty to the gods and the needs of the day, and each faction wants to use the other for the promotion of its own special subjects. In the British period, there is a similar tension between the official in India who championed Indian interests and the administrator in England who had 'higher' interests, as well as a further tension between district commissioner and central authority; both of these may be seen as structural parallels to the contrast in views of *dharma* held by pragmatic thinkers and abstract thinkers. And finally, again in the British period (as well as in ancient Ceylon), there is the ultimate dichotomy—between the concepts of duty held by the ruler and by the ruled.

On the secondary level, we find a division between scholars inclined to let the texts reveal the theory and those who search instead for the injunctions implied by actions; the second approach by and large characterizes the sociologists and anthropologists (Gunasekara, Dube), in contrast with the Indologists, while the historians span both groups. In contemporary Indian society there is little discussion about rules, but statements are made from which we can reconstruct the rules; this is evident from the linguistic study provided by Weightman and Pandey, a study of one dialect (the 'Russell Square' dialect, which has a semantic structure, albeit no regional standards). Non-explicit rules may be extrapolated from myths (O'Flaherty) or texts (Heesterman, Wilhelm), as well as from behaviour. Anthropologists do not deny the usefulness of textual data, but they emphasize that the texts do not necessarily represent reality; one must also have knowledge of the social context. It might be argued that since most Indians have not read the texts, anthropologists need not know them; but it might then be countered that many illiterate Indians behave in a way that shows a tacit acceptance of the norms enunciated in the classical texts. Moreover, since many modern Indians *think* (often wrongly) that they are acting on the basis of the classical texts, it behoves students of their behaviour to know what these texts say.

Folk literature often incorporates the classical tradition, and people use the texts to justify what they are doing. Classical literature often shows breaches with traditional theory (in the *Mṛcchakaṭika*, for example, the king is dethroned in violation of the *Arthaśāstra* rules); though fictional, these instances reveal much about the actual application of theoretical texts. Literary texts such as the *Pañcatantra* apply the teachings of the *Dharmaśāstras* and *Arthaśāstra* in ways that filter down to villagers (as in the tale of the crow who follows one minister and thus overpowers the owl who follows the majority, a relevant example of the problem of majority discussed by Derrett). Indeed, the practical power of this text was tacitly admitted by the British, who tried to suppress the *Pañcatantra* because it showed how cunning could bring success (though they did find it preferable to the *Arabian Nights* as an Indian parallel to Aesop's *Fables*).

Classical ideas of duty are, therefore, present in the field. A member of the conference cited as an instance of unintended field work an encounter with an Indian garage mechanic who refused to repair a car properly until formally (albeit sarcastically, and in some heat) reminded of his *dharma* to do so, at which time there occurred an almost Pavlovian reaction to the magic word; the garageman's nature (his *svabhāva*) allowed him to cheat, but the concept of *dharma* made him react as a member of a class (a garageman) rather than an individual (a cheat). Since *dharma* is weak and nature is strong, we need to be reminded of our *dharma*, and this is the function of the texts. Yet it cannot be denied that there is a need for more pragmatic observation of Hindus in the field facing moral problems; even in the ancient and Muslim periods, there is a need for a gloss put upon the hypotheses by the actions, if not the words, of the rulers themselves; in the British period, too, one may see concepts of duty visible in action. The present collection of essays tends to emphasize the concept of duty and Indian attempts to make sense of the universe, rather than to explore how Indians form rules for actual behaviour.

It may also be argued that this approach emphasizes the so-called Great Tradition and a static view of *dharma* while ignoring the many other traditions and the dynamic aspect of *dharma*; there is an assumption that there is a monolith continuous over time and space. Yet Derrett's paper points out the legal attention paid to local divergences from the 'Great' tradition, and, at the other end of the chronological scale, Ballhatchet shows how the British attempted to universalize and impersonalize the Indian sense of duty, to extend the horizon from the village to the wider, national scale (a task first attempted, with equally small success, by the great emperor Aśoka, perhaps the first to publish a formal re-definition of the term *dharma*). Taylor shows some personal and divergent aspects of *dharma* in the thinking of Vivekananda, Aurobindo and others, while Kunst points out some of the dangers of this divergence in the hands of such political reformers as Gandhi. Apart from these remarks, however, there is scant discussion here of the numerous important movements of dissent and reform which have challenged the injustice (the *adharma*) latent in the social system. Though these movements were eventually absorbed, they did change the social ethos and values of society, causing ferment that changed the 'unchanging' *dharma*.

Yet, though the Maharashtra saints and the Lingayats are often depicted by historians as social reformers, this may not have been the case; it is hard to determine the actual content of, for example, the work of Kabir. There is constant interplay between the great and local traditions, and divergent sects supply the internal history of Hinduism in such a way that there is an endless scale of intermediate traditions, very important, but very hard to grasp. There is dissent, but more in the realm of intellectual history than in the realm of social history; there is dissent, but there is no revolution. This may be because traditional Indian society insisted upon what Frits Staal has called 'orthopraxy' and tolerated extreme divergences from 'orthodoxy' (while the power of the sects stems from their toleration of deviations from 'orthopraxy', at the cost of a more dogmatic emphasis upon 'orthodoxy').

Moreover, although the Indian tradition allows for dissent through the institution of the sect, and the sect begins with a renouncer, a reformer, he must then decide whether or not to go back to the world; if he decides not to return, we never hear of him; if he returns, he establishes a sect of lay followers. Though the founder of a sect may reject caste, the sect itself must eventually become imbedded in Indian society, must, in effect, become a caste. The *bhakti* movements provide their own texts, but they changed so thoroughly that the ideas of their founders were no longer truly represented. If *dharma* appears then to be treated here as if it were static, perhaps this is because, ultimately, it *is* static. Or, rather, the *ideal* of *dharma* was static, though formulated in such a way as to allow constant change and development of that *soi-disant* static ideal.

In later concepts of duty, however, one can see a more clear-cut periodization; here it is a pity that the present volume includes no material to bridge the Hindu and Sultanate periods, that is to cover the Mughal period, for which there is much interesting data. (It would also have added a useful dimension to have considered the implications of duty in Jainism, where the inflexible ideal of non-injury provoked many interesting pragmatic adjustments.) In the medieval period, it is possible to see much interaction between different bodies of practice and different ideas of duty. The Mughals were influenced by Persian imperialist ideas, and the danger of Mongol invasion was the bogey that kept kings from being too free-thinking. By the eighteenth century, Hindu ideas filtered through to the British, through Persian translations, and Warren Hastings and Sir William Jones were determined to rule Hindus and Muslims by their own laws, to inculcate in them their own native sense of duty. By the nineteenth and twentieth centuries, in return, Western ideas came to influence Hindu ideas of duty (as is evident from the essays of Taylor and Kunst); Gokhale and Surendranath Banerjee were consciously influenced in this direction, as was Gandhi. Rammohun Roy, Bankim Chandra Chatterji, and Vivekananda all deviated sharply from classical *dharma* in seeing God in the Untouchable, the *Mleccha*, and the atheist, and here we may see the influence of Christian moralism (although there are also classical antecedents for this in the incorporation of evil, demonic *adharma* into divine *dharma*). A static or absolutist vision denies the relativism of the concept of duty as it develops and changes; yet, in spite of the more discernible periodization of the post-classical eras, there is nevertheless an equally discernible enduring view of duty.

One aspect that seems to characterize this typically South Asian view of duty is the attitude to nature. Traditional India regards duty as emanating from one's nature—one can't help doing it—while the Western idea of duty requires a struggle against oneself, and the idea of 'glad concurrence' is far less prominent in Western attitudes to duty than is the image of bitter medicine. Also, in India duty is enmeshed in social circumstances, while in the West it is internalized, individualized, a matter of choice and contest. Among the British in India, this tendency to internalize duty resulted in a conflict between obedience to constitutional authority and to the 'inner voice'. What, then, prompted the Westerner in India to do his duty? Fear of disgrace, perhaps, an emotional mediating between public and private views of duty, an internalized pressure but underpinned by social obligations. And what a far cry this is from the complex of forces that compelled the Indian to carry out what he regarded as *his* duty. Indeed, just as the ancient *dharma* had no meaning unless framed in the oppositional context of *adharma*, just as the gods could not exist were there no demons, so too, perhaps, can we only focus upon the elusive South Asian concept of duty by seeing it in contrast with what it is *not*—our own concept of duty.

The Editors would like to express their thanks to the Publications Committee of the School of Oriental and African Studies for its assistance in meeting the cost of publication.

Contributors

KENNETH A. BALLHATCHET
Professor of the History of South Asia at the School of Oriental and African Studies, University of London.

J. DUNCAN M. DERRETT
Professor of Oriental Laws at the School of Oriental and African Studies, University of London.

S. C. DUBE
Director of the Indian Institute of Advanced Study, Simla.

RICHARD F. GOMBRICH
Boden Professor of Sanskrit, University of Oxford.

ALEX GUNASEKARA
Lecturer in Sociology and Anthropology in the Department of Management and Social Science at the Oxford Polytechnic, Oxford.

PETER HARDY
Reader in the History of Islam in South Asia at the School of Oriental and African Studies, University of London.

J. C. HEESTERMAN
Professor of Languages and Cultural History of South Asia at the State University of Leiden.

ARNOLD KUNST
Lecturer in Indian Religions at the School of Oriental and African Studies, University of London (retired).

WENDY DONIGER O'FLAHERTY
At the time of this conference was Lecturer in the Ancient History of South Asia at the School of Oriental and African Studies, University of London. Now Visiting Associate Professor at the Graduate Theological Union, Berkeley.

PERCIVAL G. SPEAR
Fellow of Selwyn College, Cambridge, University Lecturer in History at the University of Cambridge (retired).

DAVID TAYLOR
Lecturer in Politics with reference to South Asia at the School of Oriental and African Studies, University of London.

SIMON WEIGHTMAN
Lecturer in Hindi at the School of Oriental and African Studies, University of London.

FRIEDRICH WILHELM
Privatdozent für Indologie und Tibetologie at the University of Munich.

S. M. PANDEY
Formerly Lecturer in Hindi at the School of Oriental and African Studies, University of London.

PART I

THE ANCIENT PERIOD: DUTY AND *DHARMA*

Use and Misuse of Dharma

ARNOLD KUNST

It is inevitable that, whatever the vast scope the concept of duty comprises, it will be primarily *dharma* which will come under scrutiny as the closest approximation to what has been understood in India under this concept.

The question of scope does not end here. A glance at the very recent bibliography on the subject of *dharma* and *artha* by L. Sternbach[1] will remind us that hardly any topic has been more lavishly treated in books and articles than that of *dharma*. In his bibliography, which lists over 2,200 items, Sternbach stipulates that it is incomplete as, apart from other reasons, it includes primarily works connected with law, politics and economics, but as a rule excludes entries on cosmogony, social sciences and other germane topics.

Furthermore, at the risk of repeating what has been said often before, *dharma* is alleged to denote so many concepts and to convey so many meanings that it might be considered proper to specify and closely determine that particular function of the *dharma* which is to be the subject of the discourse. The pinpointing of the sense and, if one may say so, intention of *dharma* is the most difficult task; this for a variety of reasons.

The first is what one may call an historico-traditional reason. As has been suggested by Professor van Baumer in her as yet unpublished article on *The Reinterpretation of Dharma in Nineteenth-century Bengal*, 'an examination of the various views of *dharma* in chronological sequence would provide a fascinating study of the expansion of social, religious and political ideas by Hindu scholars'.

It is, however, my conviction that the concept of *dharma* which from the beginning included the concept of duty has, despite diverse interpretations, retained its essential continuity in meaning. What has to a larger or lesser extent changed, is the object towards which the fulfilment of duty is directed but not the principle guiding the *sense* of duty. Whether in its Vedic garb or that of the Vedānta, Mīmāṃsā or other schools of ancient origin, the fundamentals of *dharma* can be brought to a common denominator while the variants of its function and meaning need not be deprived of their *ad hoc* relevant interpretation suited to the context in hand. I shall try to elaborate the point in the following parts of the paper. It is true (and this is said with deference to some historians and social anthropologists) that the meaning of *dharma* has been not infrequently bent beyond recognition; there are cases when this term could be replaced by any other expressing the intention of the author better than the arbitrarily chosen '*dharma*'. I shall try to produce some examples of this apparent misuse, for which Indian writers are as equally responsible as writers in the West. The misuse can be especially annoying when the authenticity of the arbitrary use or even definition of the *dharma* is claimed to conform with the definition originally and traditionally conceived.

Another type of difficulty arises from the fact that both the concept and the term, while basically unitary in intent and purpose, have been often treated in such a way as to convey the impression that *dharma* in its religious, philosophical, legal, ethical or even epistemological sense, forms in each case an independent denotation with no, or at best, very loose, interaction. There is no denying that the changes postulating different interpretations of the concept (especially by commentators and, even more so, translators) require certain adjustments to the context; nor must we overlook the proclivities of the Indian scholiast towards categorizations and overclassifications; we have, among others, such categories of *dharma* as *sanātanadharma*, *svadharma* and *varṇāśramadharma*, but these overlap so closely as to sometimes render such distinctions almost meaningless.

An article by Dr Walpola Rāhula on *The Wrong Notions of Dharmatā*[2] mentions a twelfth-century Pāli dictionary (*Abhidhānappadīpikā*) which lists fourteen meanings of the word *dhamma*. The list ends with *ādo*, i.e., 'and so forth'. The article, as Dr

Rāhula says, was prompted by a statement of an American scholar insisting that in Theravāda Buddhism *dhamma* meant *Grace.* (I do not hesitate to insert in the context of this paper a reference to the Buddhist *dhamma* or *dharma,* as, with some exceptions, the Buddhist concept of *dharma* along with a number of other ideas is of Hindu origin and with some adaptations follows the Hindu tradition.) We need not shun the view that throughout the ages *dharma* constituted a 'monistic' or unitary concept. The various meanings attributed to it by the commentators and translators, suggesting the alleged flexibility of this term, amount to no more than an attempt at the clarification of the *dharma's* function within the specific context, be it of literary, philosophical or mythological nature.[3]

The concept of duty is a part of the totality of the idea of *dharma,* if by the sense and fulfilment of duty is understood such behaviour and series of actions as are inherent in the beings endowed with *dharma.* To perform a duty means what one does, not as an act carried out under pressure, but an act dictated by the nature of one's immanent 'constitution'.

As mentioned before, the definition and principal meaning of *dharma* has already been amply discussed and written about. The purpose of this paper is to attempt to give a very brief survey of this concept, including that of duty, as it has emerged from its oldest references extant in a few Vedic and post-Vedic texts. The *dharma* in its strictly legal sense as represented in the *śāstras,* being a derivative of the general concept, is not treated in this sketch.

The clearly anthropomorphic representation of Dharma accompanying the Aśvins along with Mitra and Varuṇa in *ṚV* 8. 35, 13 (hymn to the Aśvins) does not say much about Dharma's nature, as it presupposes the reader's (or rather listener's) familiarity with his existence. In later Epic and Purāṇic literature Dharma as a person was often the focus of various mythical motifs. To my knowledge, anthropomorphic Dharma (without any genealogy), occurs in the *ṚV* once only, in the passage just quoted.[4] With the reservation that often there is in the *Saṃhitā* quite a narrow margin between anthropomorphic and conceptual representation of what we may call an idea or an abstract noun, other references to *dharma* in the *ṚV* tend to be more enlightening as to its meaning and function. The concept of *dharma* is here quite frequently connected with the twosome of Mitra and Varuṇa. In *ṚV* 5. 63,7, there is an interesting invocation to Mitrāvaruṇā:

dhármaṇā mitrāvaruṇā vipaścitā vratá rakṣethe ... ṛtena viśvaṃ bhúvanam ví rājathaḥ

You, Mitra and Varuṇa, full of wisdom, watch by means of *dharma* the conduct (or observances) [of beings] and rule by *ṛta* the whole world.

Within the assembly of the three expressions in one stanza, *dharma*, *ṛta* and *vrata*, the significance of *dharma* stands out fairly clearly. For Sāyaṇa, whose commentary is often helpful, *dharma* is *jagaddhārakaṃ vṛddhyādilakṣaṇaṃ karman*, while *ṛta* is *nimittam*, and *vrata* is *yajñādikarman*.[5]

As is borne out by many passages in the *ṚV* (for a classical example cf. 1. 65, 3, hymn to Agni: *ṛtásya devā ánu vratā..*) *ṛta* is the primary and rudimentary state of affairs which envelops all beings, divine, human and elemental. Its frequent connection with Agni and the sacrifice is indicative of man's zeal that *ṛta* be properly accommodated and that *dharma* be wisely watched over by the god or gods within that *ṛta*'s irreversible framework.

The context further indicates that by means of the *dharma* the *ṛta* is, as it were, implemented; this leads to the further assumption that the scope of the *dharma* determines the quantity and quality of action engendered by the *ṛta*. In the *ṛta* are enclosed all the elements of existence, while by the *dharma* is understood the urge for action with which *ṛta* has endowed all beings. In relation to *vrata*, *dharma* would seem to constitute a generic concept consisting of a variety of *vratas*, i.e. specific duties performed on specific occasions. References to *vrata* in the *ṚV* are copious, and gods are frequently referred to as *vratapas*, guardians of the specific duties or observances embraced by the *dharma*.

Various kinds of *vrata* are described in considerable detail in *ChU* (II. 11-21), *BĀU* (1. 5,21 and 23) and the *TaittU* (III, 7.1; 8.1; 9.1; 10.1). In the second *prapāthaka* of *ChU* a number of special duties are enjoined. These are generosity, not spitting at the fire, respect for women, not offending the sun or rain or the season. In *BĀU*, the chapter (1. 5,21) begins with *athāto vratamīmāṃsā* ('now let us consider the *vrata*') and later, discussing the permanence of *dharma*,[6] confirms that as long as there is *dharma* there will be *vrata*.[7] *TaittU* repeats a description similar to that in *ChU*.

The identification of *dharma* with action is repeated in the *ṚV* several times, in that the action attributed to the agent (deity) is one resulting from his nature accorded to him in the *ṛta*. So in 5.72,2 Mitrāvaruṇā unite people by *dharma*; in 9. 25,2 Pavamāna is asked to enter Vāyu by the vehicle of *dharma*.[8] In 5. 63,7 Indra is the *dharmakṛt*—acting by means of *dharma*. Geldner translates: 'gehe nach *deiner* Bestimmung' though the text has no *svadharma*. But the expression *svadharma* which in the succeeding tradition has gained so much significance in combination with the *varnṇāśrama*, *does* occur in the *ṚV* to my knowledge once only, as Agni's epithet in 3. 21,2. Here Agni is requested to act according to *his dharma* and to 'give us (do for us) the best and the desired'.[9]

Consequently, to set aside the *vrata* (though not at all insignificant as a term indicating the performance of mainly ritual duties), *dharma* in the *Saṃhitā* literature is the law governing the conduct of the world with all its phenomena established within the *ṛta*. *Ṛta* cannot be changed and any action deviating from *ṛta* would become *adharma*. The logical difficulty arises when we consider that since all phenomena and actions are embraced by the *ṛta*, the *adharma* would also have to come within the category of *dharma*. For instance, Vṛtra's obstructionist acts against Indra's creativity are not outside the realm of *ṛta* and, arising from his inherent nature, are his *dharma*, while ethically it would have to be listed as *adharma*.[10]

In his *Religious Consciousness*, (New York, 1934), T. B. Pratt describes religion as a power or, better, *Schicksalsbestimmer*,[11] a controller of human destiny. Widengren takes this concept up as coterminous with *dharma*. This fatalistic rationale does not, however, suit the description of *dharma*. In all its hypostases, including duty, the *dharma* represents action determined by the *ṛta* or its later equivalents, but in psychological terms it allows man the relative freedom to act in accordance with his desire prompted by his 'nature', i.e., his mental and emotional equipment.[12] This position persists largely unaltered throughout the post-Vedic philosophizing. *Dharma* remains as the intrinsic nature of beings, motivating their conduct.

In the *BĀU* 1. 4, 14 we read that Brahma (neuter) created (*atyasṛjata*) *dharma*, the superior form (*śreyarūpa*), which is the ruler of the ruler (*tad etat kṣatrasya kṣatraṃ yad dharmaḥ*). We further read that nothing is superior to *dharma*, that by *dharma* a weakling can appear as one that is stronger (*abalīyān baliyāṃsam āśaṃsate dharmeṇa*). This is—continues the passage—why *dharma* is being identified with truth.[13] While with this passage we move into the ethical aspect of *dharma*, we must also keep in mind that *satyam* as truth conveys the ontological notion of reality as a true constellation of events. The *TaittU* (1.11) makes, however, some subtle distinctions between the two; the teacher in his farewell speech to his students asks them to *practise dharma* and *speak* the truth (*satyam vada, dharmaṃ cara*). The *dharmas* enumerated in the *TaittU* I. 11 as duties to be performed by man can be understood as the replica of the cosmic *dharma* mirrored in the nature of man. Among these duties and the do's and don'ts are listed in the *TaittU* the study of the Vedas (*svādhyāya*), respect for parents, giving (*dāna*), [14] and following in deed and speech the Brahmins unless their judgement of *dharma* is warped.

In the Upaniṣads, *ṛta* gradually (though not altogether) recedes as the force behind the *dharma* and in its stead emphasis is placed on the *ātman*, a course of development entirely natural for the Upaniṣadic sentiments. In the *BĀU* II. 5, 11 the 'honey-chapter' juxtaposes the individual's well-being against his surrounding world; here *dharma* is 'the honey of all the beings' (*sarveṣaṃ bhūtānām madhu*) and vice versa.

> The person made of light and immortality residing in the *dharma*, and the person who constitutes, with reference to his self, the *dharma*, is the same as *ātman*.[15]

The Upaniṣadic internalization of ontological processes and the emphasis on the individual *dharma* as a reflection of the cosmic *dharma* of the Vedas seem to have contributed to the breakthrough by which the concept of *svadharma* has come to the forefront.

Here we find a greater tendency towards the emphasis on the *svadharma* as a set of duties attributed to an individual as a member of a group rather than as an independent person. These two types of duties, however, largely overlap; the duties of an individual are conditioned by his personal *saṃskāra*[16] evolving from the scope of *karma* peculiar to that *āśrama* or *varṇa* to which he belongs.

In the familiar passage of the *Gītā* (III, 35), Kṛṣṇa says that ineffective *svadharma* is better than *dharma* of another person even if the latter is effective; it is better to die in *svadharma*; the *dharma* of another is fraught with danger.[17] Radhakrishnan's by no means isolated fascination with this recommendation for acquiescence in knowing 'one's own place' in society and not coveting any other position beyond one's station was, to put it mildly, not in keeping with the spirit of our time. It cannot be denied that basically his interpretation of the *Gītā's* understanding of *svadharma* is correct, but his enthusiasm about the passage may not be universally shared.

Among the passages perpetuating the Vedic interpretation of the *dharma*, though transposed into the cosmos of an individual representing his *āśrama* and/or *varṇa* is the passage in the *Maitrayaṇī U* (4, 3.)[18]

> This then is the instruction to counteract the elemental beings (≠gross reality) : to learn the lore of the Vedas, to observe one's own *dharma*, to pursue one's own *āśrama*. One vests [everything] in one's own *dharma*...

A later addition to this passage characteristically inserts a sentence to the effect that 'if one says that a man does not belong to any *āśrama* because he just practises an ascetic life, such a statement is wrong.'[19] This text, inspired by the Sāṃkhya philosophy (cf. *bhūtātmā* = *śarīram* in 3,2), underlines the prevalence of the thesis that *svadharma* applies to a homogeneous class of individuals rather than independent personalities and denies the right of practising austerity to one who exceeds the privileges attributed to a group. It equally lays stress on the soteriological aspect of the practice of *svadharma*. In the earlier Upaniṣads (among which the archetype of *Maitrayaṇīya* probably was one), such crude attempts at limiting the scope of *dharma* to individuals claiming their personal rights to spiritual advancement outside their *varṇas* or *āśramas*, are not usual. It would be of interest to examine the way in which India's social structure in that period tried to intrude into the processes of automaticism so deeply otherwise ingrained in the concept of *dharma*, *karma*, *saṃsāra* and *mokṣa*. We have generally analyzed the social structure of India in the light of her religious proclivities; seldom the other way round.

I have so far attempted to suggest that the function of *dharma* in the context of religion, society or ethics, though giving rise to the selection of apposite denotations fitting each of these areas, does not in fact signify *dharma's* departure from its essential intent and purpose. When Jaiminī's *Mīmāṃsāsūtra*, in the examination of the *dharmajijñāsa*, defines duty as meaning 'any matter enjoined by the Vedas with a view to attaining a useful purpose', the list of these duties is topped by sacrifice,[20] but the urge to fulfil this duty as defined by the Veda comes from the intrinsic desire of a man to attain happiness as he sees it, assisted by the *Jñānaśakti*, the potential of attaining knowledge.[21] For the Mīmāṃsaka there is no deity, whose favours he would hope to obtain by bribing him with sacrifice. *Dharma*, the sense of duty, comes from man himself, as he has recognized the Veda as the doketistic (*apauruṣeya*) voice determining his *dharma*.

While the original interest of the Vaiśeṣikas in the *dharma* seems to be non-existent,[22] the *dharma* doctrine was discussed by Praśastapāda (fifth century) but with a slight twist. In his *bhāṣya* to the *Vaiś. sūtra* he contends that *dharma* is the *quality* of the *ātman*, by the presence of which the *ātman* can attain salvation. *Dharma* in this context is the opposite of the *adharma*, which causes man to suffer. While thus demoting the *dharma* to one of the *ātma*-qualities along with *bhāvanā, adharma* and *adṛṣṭa*, he has not basically deviated from the orthodox import of *dharma* as that factor which is latent in man and underlies his actions and performance of duties leading to the understanding of the world structure.

In the realm of logic and epistemology, *dharma* is used as early as in Gautama's *Nyāyasūtra*, as a specific property of an object. This further leads to the employment of *dharma* as a predicate inextricably connected with the subject (*dharmin*) and reflecting that subject's primary nature (the smokiness of fire; the permanence or, as the case may be, impermanence of sound; the existence of *ātman* or, as the case may be, its non-existence, etc).[23] However a discussion of *dharma* in the sphere of logic would lead us too far astray; but it is not irrelevant.

As has been mentioned before, the Buddhist concept of *dharma* has elements which can be traced to traditional Hinduism. To venture a cliché, many aspects of Buddhism owe as much to

Hinduism, as the Vedānta, Nyāya and Sāṃkhya owe many of their ideas to the impact of Buddhism. The concept of *dharma* in Buddhism, both in the Theravāda and Mahāyāna, went through so many complex stages and was dissipated in so many variants that a casual discussion on the subject would obscure rather than clarify the matter. As a provision for a separate treatment of the concept of duty in Buddhism has been made in this publication, this paper will limit itself to one particular set of references where, *mutatis mutandis*, the Buddhist description of *dharma* appears to be closer to the Vedic tradition than are some appearing in the *āstika* exegeses. I shall of course not touch on the complexity of the Sarvāstivāda *dharmas* and refrain from references to scholars who tried to adapt the function of the seventy-two or seventy-five *dharmas* to the generality of the *dharma* concept. It is only fit to mention that the causal relationship of the Theravāda and Sarvāstivāda *dharmas* as phenomena, later rejected by the Śūnyavādins (though technically used for dialectical purposes), was coordinated in the doctrine of *pratītyasamutpāda* (equally rejected by the Śūnyavādins).[24] The *pratītyasamutpāda*, in its rigorous series of sequences, is essentially not unlike the Vedic combination of *ṛta* and *dharma*.

A characteristic passage occurring in a few Pāli texts (*Saṃyutta*, *Aṅguttara*, a. o.) confirms the description of *dharma* as the uniform norm according to which the world runs its course and according to which the duties of the Buddhas are performed.

Being nature itself, *dharma* controls the behaviour and acts of beings. The text in the *Saṃyutta* II, 25 reads :

> *uppadā vā tathāgatānaṃ anuppadā vā tathāgatānaṃ ṭhitāvā sā dhātu dhammaṭṭhitatā dhammaniyamatā idappaccayata*;
>
> '*Que les Tathāgata apparaissent ou non dans le monde, demeure cette Nature des choses, ce Statut causal, cette Détermination causale, la Relation de ceci par rapport à cela.* (*Should the Tathāgatas appear or not in the world, there remains in the nature of things, this causal law, this causal determination, the relationship of this vis-à-vis that.*)

The French translation has been done by Professor Lamotte.[25] A similar passage in the *Laṅkāvatārasūtra* says :

> *utpādād vā tathāgatānām anutpādād vā tathāgatānāṃ sthitaivaiṣā*[26] *dharmatā dharmasthititā dharmaniyamatā...*

> *Tathāgata or no Tathāgata, [there exists] the dharmatā, the stability of the dharma, and the fundamentality [or unavoidability] of the dharma.*

The setting in motion of the wheel of *dharma* (*dharmacakrapravartana*) by the Buddha or Bodhisattva is not the result of creation, nor is the *dharma* itself created by Buddha. As the *buddhagocara* it is there waiting for him to be realized and activated by his omniscience.

In pursuing further the contention, in the light of the text samples given, that the core of the original Vedic concept of *dharma* has remained the seed and root of the subsequent conceptual derivations, it is logical to conclude that too much freedom in the interpretation of this concept, which divests it of that rudimentary meaning, may lead to a misrepresentation whereby *dharma* can become an X, replaceable by any concept, however remote from its essential notion. The attempts by some students of Hinduism to use the term too freely so as to underline the links between traditional and modern institutions become eventually counterproductive, as the connection with the past is artificially imposed on modern social movements and ethical principles having little or no connection with that past. It is a one-sided and garbled description of *dharma* when Max Weber[27] attributes it to 'those chosen few [aiming at the achievement of salvation who] are required to wander ceaselessly...freed from...ties to family and world, pursuing the goal of mystical illumination by fulfilling the injunctions relating to the correct path (*dharma*)'. The reference concurs neither with the traditional concept of *dharma* nor with that of the eighteenth/nineteenth century reformers, such as Ram Mohun Roy or Bankimchandra, who placed *dharma* primarily on a socio-ethical level. For the latter, *manuṣyatva* (humanitarianism?) was the alpha and omega of the *dharma*. Professor van Baumer (cf. above) has translated a passage from Bankimchandra's *Kṛṣṇacarita* which runs as follows:

> The expression and maturing, the consistency and fulfilment of all our physical and mental faculties in every part is *dharma*. This *dharma* is dependent on cultivation, and cultivation is dependent on action (*karma*). Therefore *karma* is the chief means

of *dharma*. This *dharma* may be called duty (*svadharmapālan*).

In his text, says van Baumer, Bankimchandra has himself inserted in parentheses the word 'duty' in English.

A further modification of the *dharma* concept from duty to God, to duty to country is only too natural with the rise of nationalism in India. *Dharma* has thus become the hallmark of patriotism and a body of all such prescriptions of duties as should lead to India's self-government and independence. A still further expansion of the concept has led to cosmopolitan sentiments, duty to humanity at large with the stipulation that as part of humanity India suffers injustice and has a high priority in the list of objects towards which a citizen's duty should be directed.

This interpretation of *dharma* does not intend to revolutionize the original concept as it continues to associate it with action (*karma*) and as it still derives its authority from the tradition of either the Vedānta for such leaders as Ram Mohun Roy, or the Vaiṣṇava *bhakti* for Bankimchandra. Yet, to continue with the 'institutional' and normative rather than teleological treatment of *dharma*, it is impossible to overlook the fact that this concept has been quite drastically bent by these and other leaders, to suit their intentions. It is difficult to rid oneself of the impression that the appeal to the people through the vehicle of *dharma* is more politic than straight from the heart (despite Bankimchandra's *viśuddhadharma*) and that for national appeal a less orthodox and more practical strategy might have been healthier and perhaps more effective. But who knows? Was it the people of India who needed these stimuli from their leaders or was it the leaders who felt (and possibly believed) that the recourse to *dharma* was the desirable and necessary inducement to rouse people's susceptibilities?

Jawaharlal Nehru seems to have recognized this dilemma when he wrote that *sanātanadharma* 'has been more or less monopolized today by some orthodox sections among the Hindus who claim to follow the ancient faith'.[28] Yet, in his writings, he understood the concept of *dharma* well but preferred to treat it as a precious relic of the Indian tradition without involving it in the performance of duty by an Indian leader or any other citizen. In *The Discovery of India* he called *dharma* religion. In his autobiography (new edition, reprint, London, 1947, p. 378) he wrote:

> It would be far better if it [viz. the word "religion"] were dropped altogether and other words with more limited meanings were used instead, such as theology, philosophy, morals, ethics..., metaphysics, *duty* [my italics], ceremonial, etc.

Nehru's initial resentment of Gandhi's religiosity followed by the apparent acceptance of it seems to have been the result of a mutual acquiescence in the two men's conceptions of ethics and morality. Not perhaps with great enthusiasm did Nehru accept Gandhi's assertion that he (Nehru) was closer to God than he knew. The point of reconciliation lay in the fact that with Gandhi ethics was a gift of God while for Nehru this was a human value separable from religon. Both, however, were aware of the traditional impact of *dharma* as the concept of duty. One wanted to retain its religious significance, while the other preferred to strip it of its religious involvement and keep it within the framework of secularity.

Whether or not the propagation of *dharma* as a religious factor may be considered damaging to society, the misuse of this concept has undoubtedly obscured our understanding of this basic notion, and with it, sometimes, of the whole course of Indian religions and philosophies. Following Max Weber's[29] interpretation of Buddhism, a number of modern writers have condemned the Buddhist conception of duty as hostile to society. In a similar vein, as was intimated in the latest Jordan lecture by Professor Werblowsky, Spiro[30] has declared that the doctrines of 'nibbanic Buddhism' (whatever this means) 'at no point articulate with the secular social order' and 'Dhamma provides no point of articulation of the world' and consequently the same is true for the whole of *triratna*. Elsewhere (p. 441) it is said that 'unlike Hindu *dharma*, which prescribes compliance with one's own caste norms..., Buddhism in no wise adopts such a conservative stance'. The reason for this, it is said, is the Buddhist's strict adherence to the *karma* doctrine. From this might follow that the Hindu *svadharma*, i.e., the set of duties engendered by caste rule, excludes the dependence on karmic factors; this is completely false. The whole argument, as could also be witnessed during the

Jordan lecture, stems from a complete misunderstanding regarding the vast variety of Buddhist approaches to Buddhism; any generalization regarding Buddhism and any inferences drawn from isolated texts or excerpts from texts, especially those dealing with the duties (or their absence) of Arhats or Bodhisattvas, lead of necessity to a complete misinterpretation of the otherwise down-to-earth Buddhist social attitudes.[31] This is particularly apparent when the so-called nibbanic Buddhism and the layman's *triratna* are treated in the same breath.

By *misuse of dharma* signalled in the title of this paper I meant no condemnation of those who apply this concept as freely as it fits their *ad hoc* purpose. The fault lies mainly in the fact that well-meaning philosophers, religiologists and anthropologists tackling problems of India construe ideas and apply terms which often betray an imaginative mind, but at the same time, only a nodding acquaintance with Indian tradition. While this critique may appear conservative, it is not intended to be so. An analysis based on one-sided and limited knowledge of the subject under scrutiny cannot and does not do justice to the true realities, stymies rather than promotes further study, and diminishes the advantages to be acquired from such studies. We come across definitions of *dharma* such as *dharma*='in Hindu thought a person's allotted role in life' (J. Brown, *Gandhi's Rise to Power*) which was perhaps influenced by Pratt's and Widengren's *Schicksalsbestimmer*; *dharma*='grace'; *dharma*='mental contact', 'ideation', 'mental processes', and *Kuśaladhamma*='skilful processes' (R. Johansson, *The Psychology of Nirvana*); *dharma*='conscience' (Lannoy[32] and others), etc.

These and other substitutes for *dharma*, in whatever context they appear, are inadequate and could be replaced by any other term taken from either Indian or Western philosophy, as was hinted at by Nehru. *Dharma* is a powerful concept and should not be arbitrarily tampered with. It is typical of India, her tradition and her genius for inventing terms not easily expressible in one word of another language: nor does it tolerate imprecise definitions. Like Giovanni Papini's God it would probably thank all who have misconstrued it, misinterpreted and misapplied it, if it were allowed to perish and be erased from people's minds. As a concept which has so deeply infiltrated religious, philosophical and social thinking, it merits further constructive examination.

Notes

[1]*Bibliography on Dharma and Artha in Ancient and Mediaeval India*, Wiesbaden, 1973.

[2]L. Cousins, A. Kunst and K. R. Norman (eds), *Buddhist Studies in Honour of I. B. Horner*, Dordrecht-Boston, 1974.

[3]By way of example one can think of the concept of *Jñāna*, knowledge, which in itself remains relatively static and has its function fulfilled according to the object towards which it is directed.

[4]*mitrāvaruṇavaṃtā uta dhármavaṃtā... gacchatho....*

[5]For a more detailed treatment of these concepts see W. Norman Brown, 'Duty as Truth in the Rig Veda', *India Maior, Congratulatory Volume presented to J. Gonda*, Leiden, 1972, pp. 57-67.

[6]I.5,23 : *taṃ devāś cakrire dharmam; sa evādya sa u śvah*, 'It (=the prāṇa) the gods made as *dharma*; as such it is today and as such it will be tomorrow'.

[7]A discussion of *vrata* as a set of duties prescribed in Jaina soteriology is of necessity outside the scope of this paper.

[8]*dhármaṇā vāyúm ā́ viśa.*

[9]*svádharman* (scil. Agne)... *śréṣṭaṃ no dhehi vā́ryam* (*Sāyaṇa* : *svadharman* = *svāyattadharmakaḥ*).

[10]No such expression seems to be known to the *Ṛgveda*. Consistently enough, there only occurs the juxtaposition of *ṛta* against *anṛta* (e.g. 10.124,5).

[11]Cf. Widengren, *Religionsphänomenologie*, Berlin, 1969, p. 4.

[12]For instance, Śaṅkara in his commentary to the *Vedāntasūtra* 3. 1.11 interprets the performance of duty as follows: *yo hi iṣṭādilakṣaṇaṃ... karma karoti taṃ laukikā ācakṣate dharmaṃ carati....*

[13]*asmāt satyam vadantam āhur dharmaṃ vadatīti, dharmaṃ vā vadantaṃ satyaṃ vadatīti, etad dhy evaited ubhayam bhavati.*

[14]Cf. also *ChU* II. 23,1 : *trayo dharmaskandhāḥ* : *yajño, adhyāyanam, dānam.*

[15]*Ibid.*, *yaś cāyam asmin dharme tejomayo 'mṛtamayaḥ puruṣaḥ, yaś cāyam adhyātmaṃ dhārmas... ayam eva so 'yam ātmā....* Cf. however, *KaṭhaU* 2. 14: *anyatra dharmād anyatrādharmāt... yat paśyasi tad vada.* This question coming from Naciketas to Yama would point to a 'higher philosophy' locating *dharma* (and *adharma*) merely within empirical reality and leaving it out of the sphere of immortality.

[16]Cf. Śaṅkara's commentary to *Gītā* III. 34: *prakṛtir nāmā pūrvakṛtadharmādharmādisaṃskāro*: '[man's] nature is the artefact of previous *dharma, adharma*, etc'.

[17]*śreyān svadharmo viguṇah paradharmāt svanuṣṭhitāt, svadharme nidhanaṃ śreyah: paradharmo bhayāvahaḥ.* A similar sentiment is expressed in *Gītā* XVIII. 47, with the 'amendment' that one does not get into mischief when one pursues one's activity based on one's own nature (*svabhāvaniyataṃ karma kurvan nāpnoti kilbiṣam*). See also *Gītā* I. 40 ff.

[18]Here I follow van Buitenen (ed.), *Maitrāyaṇīya Upaniṣad*, 'S-Gravenhage, 1962: *ayaṁ vāva khalv asya pratividhir bhūtātmano yad vedavidyādhigamaḥ svadharmasyānucaraṇaṃ, svāśrameṣu evānukramaṇam; svadharma eva dhatte....*

[19]Left out in van Buitenen's text of the Vulgate (see p. 104).

[20]F. Edgerton, *The Mīmāṃsā Nyāya Prakāśa*, New Haven, 1929, § 3: *vedena prayojanam uddiśya* [scil. Jaiminī] *vidhīyamāno 'rtho dharmaḥ, yathā yagādiḥ.*

[21]Das Gupta (Vol. V, p. 165) quotes Śrī Kumāra who in his commentary to Bhoja's *Tattvaprakāśa* (eleventh century) rejects all traditional theories of *dharma* in defining it as that range of activities which are a special cause of happiness. While Das Gupta's reference to 'Srī Kumāra's objection' is basically correct, the latter's definition is in a way reminiscent of that propounded by the Mīmāṃsaka but it lacks the profundity of the Mīmāṃsā exegesis.

[22]An unpublished article by E. Frauwallner has convincingly proved that the '*dharma* preface' to the *Vaiśeṣikasūtra* was a later addition.

[23]I am grateful to Dr. T. Gelblum for drawing my attention to the fact that in the Navya-Nyāya the *dharma* may also figure as an adventitious property. This does not, however, take away from the *dharma* the value of immanence in the *dharmin*, e.g. the kitchen, the mountain, etc., that is an object where fire occurs. The 'fiery' mountain has thus 'ceded' the *dhūma-vahni vyāpti* to the *vyāpti* of the *dhūma-vahnimān* and has become accidentally and, as it were, vicariously the *dharmin* of the *dhūmavattvam*. (Cf. also C. Goekoop, *The Logic of Invariable Concomitance in the Tattvacintāmaṇi*, Dordrecht, 1967, pp. 3, 85, 88.)

[24]Cf. Nāgārjuna's *Madhyamakakārikā* 1. 9: *anutpanneṣu dharmeṣu nirodhonopapadyate; nānantaram ato yuktaṃ nirudhe, pratyayaś ca kaḥ?* 'With the non-arising of *dharmas* there is also no arising of their extinction. Causal relationship is not possible in the state of extinction. Where then [can there be] dependent orgination?' I find Inada's translation of this passage unconvincing (Kenneth K. Inada, *Nāgārjuna, a Translation of his Mūlamadhyamakakārikā with an Introductory Essay*, Tokyo, 1970, p. 41).

[25]*L'Enseignement de Vimalakīrti*, Louvain, 1962, p. 38.

[26]Bunyiu Nanjio (p. 143) reads in his text *eṣāṃ dharmāṇāṃ* in lieu of *eṣā*. The Tibetan version aptly omits this plural complying with the spirit of a Mādhyamika-Yogācāra text.

[27]*The Sociology of Religion* (English translation), London, 1965, p. 267.

[28]*The Discovery of India*, New York, 1946, p. 64.

[29]*Op. cit.*

[30]Melford E. Spiro, *Buddhism and Society*, London, 1971.

[31]If such generalizations were admissible, what conclusions about Buddhism could be drawn from the Buddha's dining with the harlot Ambapāli, an episode cited more than once in the canon?

[32]Cf. R. Lannoy, *The Speaking Tree*, London, New York, Bombay, 1971. In an otherwise fascinating discourse on the dilemma between *dharma* and *svadharma*, the term 'conscience' as an equivalent of either suggests too much dependence on the Western idea of conflict between good and evil rather than on the Indian concept of norm regulating the nature of phenomena and the ensuing ethical postulates. Cf. also, for the often confusing discussions on this and similar subjects, G. H. Mees, *Dharma and Society*, London, 1935.

The Concept of Duty in Ancient Indian Jurisprudence: The Problem of Ascertainment

J. DUNCAN M. DERRETT

I

Introduction

1. *What is 'duty' and why ascertain it?*

Though we should clear our minds of irrelevant aspects of concepts native to our own environment, we must, to understand Asian phenomena, at least identify the common ground we owe to our humanity, as well as the divergencies which could make the sources, ancient as well as Asian, misleading or even meaningless to us. The word 'duty' is now defined[1] as 'action, or an act, that is due by moral or legal obligation; that which one ought or is bound to do'. Absolutely it means 'moral obligation'. An older meaning is 'the action and conduct due to a superior; homage; reverence; due respect'.[2] Duty once included overt respect to the person and authority of a superior—acknowledgment of what some may irreverently but usefully call 'the pecking order'. It may be a content of duty that one should give in charity, which has (generally) no reference to deference. But who determines whether to give in charity is one's duty? Hierarchy and duty are inseparable ideas, and we may soon see why. 'Hierarchy' lends authority to various sorts of duty, by no means chiefly internal obligation, personal 'conscience'. An ancient society may differ from us in its methods of eliciting authority, but 'duty' will be defined much more widely than we define it.

The notion of *exaction* used to dominate discussions of duty: 'Unless we think that it may be exacted from him, we do not call it his duty' (Mill, 1861). Could one define duty as a prophecy that if a man does certain things he will be subject to disagreeable consequences by way of imprisonment or compulsory payment of money or the like (Holmes, 1897)? Would it still be accurate to equate duty with an acknowledgement of the dominance of the social environment upon the individual, which dominance could be called 'conscience' (Smith, 1937)? The last writer took it, then, as axiomatic that a religious view would see duty derived from without and sanctioned by external pressure: the sense of duty was the last silent witness of a past which the sooner overcome and forgotten the better! In his view the only significant duty today must be 'to be uniformly intelligent'. So optimistic a notion hardly fits the results of psychology or sociology. Yet it is equally unsatisfactory to talk of duty in empirical terms as the minimum contribution to social life, 'required minimal performance'. It is more to the point to speak of the 'is' of a society (not of its 'good') and of its 'ought' as a function of its 'is'. Duty cannot be pegged down to a correlative of censure. Nor is it only the morally incumbent as distinct from the legally incumbent: indeed the 'incumbent' is in need of definition. In the interaction of man with his fellows (including superiors) there are a myriad of occasions when their expectations relate to his capacity for performance, and it seems to be within that area that our phenomenon or group of phenomena passing under the name 'duty', comes to be considered. In what follows no attempt will be made to take as a substratum any results of western philosophers (which conflict).[3]

'Duty' we subdivide into religious (*superstitious* duty, e.g. not to speak ill of the recently dead, is mostly obsolete), moral, social, and legal. We are adjusted to the frequent conflicts between these. A trustee may be under a legal duty to protect his beneficiary's or ward's lands from encroachment, and a religious duty not to molest the encroacher by a lawsuit, a moral duty to warn the ward of his danger, and under no duty whatsoever to associate with the ward socially. An academic may be under a social duty to call his colleague by a given name and to listen to him politely, and under a moral duty not to exploit his work without acknowledgement, but yet be under no duty to announce to him publications he is under a legal or moral duty to discover for himself. A constitution may include Directive Principles, whereby the state's duty infringes or diminishes private rights! The recognition (*i*) that duties are many and may conflict and (*ii*) that legal duties (enforceable by courts) are neither fully expressive of duty at large nor necessarily consistent with it, is a product of a civilization which has, in England, grown steadily more individualistic from the Tudor period until the 1960s, when concern for (for example) the environment and the social as opposed to the economic value of labour has begun consciously to recreate a sense of corporate obligations. Meanwhile our concept of duty is a part of an individualistic world-view and the occasions when a man must ascertain his duty are few and easily analyzed. A fascinating modern development is the growth of reliance upon a single trained referee to solve a complex legal, political or economic conflict: it proves that the cross indications of duties *and their corresponding rights* cannot be resolved (even by compromising them) except by a referee who takes all relevant subjective philosophies seriously and sorts them out, in the context, without personal prejudice.

Where a child or an adult is told his duty the implications are usually twofold: first the duty-teller believes he has the right (an authority or a superiority in this case) to be listened to; secondly, the content of the alleged duty could be verified by reference to a further authority the victim would accept. I say 'victim' not only because his duty is far more often impressed upon him at the other party's option, but chiefly because he suffers a shock, and that too whether he welcomes instruction (usually an unpleasant one) or ultimately defies it. 'Duty' thus carries with it the implication that, irrespective of *compulsion* (which adds nothing to it), the individual's inclinations are guided in deference to standards emanating in some mysterious way from ultimate authorities whose judgement both the duty-teller and his victim would accept. The fictional 'reasonable man' to whom Anglo-Saxon judges refer as a standard of behaviour is quite evidently not an arbiter of duty: he is something much more mundane and less exacting. The acceptance of something more rigorous is itself an abstract hypothesis, and, like harmony itself, a social attitude with a psychological explanation. Deviance and alienation from authority are associated. Instinct and observation confirm that social balance and mutual acceptance are symptoms of individual as well as corporate health. Persons without authority, and those who have a personal interest in the outcome, are not accepted as arbiters of duty; rebellion against those whose precepts suit, mainly or exclusively, their own comfort, is not a breach of duty in a world in which subservience to mere power has not, since the seventeenth century, been systematically internalized.

To this picture of ultimate authority there are apparent exceptions. Duties are often created by contract, e.g. at the time of employment or at marriage, or by an agreement such as that under which pupils are educated. The self-imposed duty is not less capable of being defined than natural or imposed duties; reference to an arbitrator or arbitrators calls forth the same awareness of an obligation to obey a solution discovered by objective research. A further seeming exception is where a man pursues a challenged course of action, justifying it by alleging that his duty requires it. Leaving aside the many detectable cases of hypocrisy, we can see that a feeling of being bound to an otherwise unattractive course by mere duty carries with it the anticipation of *evaluation* by an ultimate authority, for, as the myth of the Last Judgement and similar myths testify, man's nature projects for him a time at which his quality is finally mirrored for him in his deeds. This is an extremely ancient and widespread concept. Even in its decay shadows of it appear in strange places. The need for approbation (e. g. the Honours List) is a human characteristic, and persistence in a course of conduct one knows to be blamed by one's immediate society is rare. Yet self-approval, well documented by memory, is of much more weight than any approbation from human beings as fallible as oneself. Anthropologists have revealed the pathos in a self-approval based on behaviour foreign societies would regard as comical or detestable.

2. *'Duty' and conscience*

It would be difficult to imagine a society in which the balance between the internal judge and public opinion was not delicate. An individualistic culture sees duty (as the dictionary confirms) as primarily a personal matter. A legal duty (e.g. parking) will have no moral content, or it may have much; a moral duty may fall short of the law's demands (e.g. hire-purchase transactions). If duty is confined to personal decision-making our prevalent system of education, with follow-on techniques suitable for advising adults, is bound to align instruction towards personal rather than social aspects of problems. A standardized social answer is not, at least in Western European contexts, tendered as a realistic precept. Modern life enables exploitation of individuals to occur without certainty of detection. The individualistic society provides greater privacy than an Asian, and also greater opportunities for challenge to the personal conscience. India, as we shall see, left, as she still leaves, few occasions for personal decision-making. In all perplexities, amongst us, where the individual (in a genuine doubt) seeks advice from an unbiased adviser, instinct tells him to seek one who is not only trained in investigating the facts but able to diagnose the complaint sympathetically to the complainant, however unpalatable the ultimate prescription might turn out to be.

A case typical of our society illustrates its own limitations, and it adumbrates the advantages, as well as the cost of the traditional set-up we are about to study. A wife consults a doctor about her husband and he identifies him as a deviant; the husband consults a priest who identifies the wife as uncharitable, and counsels patience; the two consult attorneys who independently advise divorce; and the judge, expressing doubt whether either or both spouses were at fault, divides the husband's assets (less fees and costs) between the two of them. Such independent advice-seeking and such dramatic sequels to the advice would be unthinkable in ancient India. In our case a *social* answer to both spouses might have mended their marriage; personal answers did no good and the state's answer is an abdication of pastoral responsibility. The ultimate sanction, public opinion, left (as it tends to leave) to the individual's conscience everything that mattered, but the conscience was ineffectively supported throughout. Because of the damage done to the children, not to speak of the couple themselves, by this policy, a more collective answer is being groped for, which presupposes a solution superior not only to the interests, but also to the feeble consciences of the immediate parties. One feels that an answer must exist *somewhere*. It must be capable of overriding the inevitably handicapped self-judgments of the ostensible complainants, truly the victims of their own want of discrimination between their rights and their desires (usually described by them as 'needs').

3. *Ancient and modern societies; the role of the referee*

No referee who is worth anything will accept a reference unless his own impartiality is accepted by both parties to a dispute, nor unless they undertake to implement his award or precept to the degree, and in the circumstances, he himself has foreseen. An arbitrator's award must be implemented unless it transpires that he has misdirected himself, or misconducted himself. Where the doubt is merely personal, and there is no dispute, the doubters may consult a referee whose answer will not be expected to bind anyone. All referees gain prestige at the expense of those who submit their cases to them; 'wisdom' is therefore an essential qualification. It is a comical, but persistent characteristic of humanity that those who do not agree with your own subjective presentation of your problem are, in your eyes, 'fools' : and whatever may be said of your folly, theirs is 'dangerous', 'irresponsible', etc. He who accepts a reference without qualifications is indeed a fool. Long experience, a sense of humour and certainly self-awareness, knowledge of his own preferences and of their likely effect on his powers of judgment, and the capacity to foresee not only the abstract fitness of a decision but also its suitability in the circumstances and as a precedent; all these point to an old person, and, if a single referee is to be chosen, then to a man. The objectivity of men is commonly superior to that of women, whose sound practicality and common sense all too often fail to rescue them from subjective handicaps, partiality,[4] the sometimes disastrous para-menstrual depression of faculties, and banality.

The judge today, in Western Europe and America, is not guided by religious and ethical considerations so much as by what is practical, what has always been done, and what the legislature has commanded to be done. He abdicates completely the role of adviser to the conscience and a thoroughly unconscionable rule may be perfectly good law. It is possible to speak of public and private acts being 'without conscience', which (except in morons) is impossible. The typical ancient society knew little legislation or none. A decision or settlement against conscience was not accepted, though it might temporarily be acquiesced in. The judge, arbitrator, or director of conscience applied, and, where appropriate, still applies in many Asian territories, his attention to the precepts of ageless wisdom of which his own function is an instant exemplification and continuation. Admittedly this is supremely difficult and both in Islamic and Hindu culture the actual post of judge or referee carries with it the likelihood, or rather certainty of sin,[5] since human conceptions of the just decision must fall short of truth.

A society which does not accept individuality, which sees all rights and duties as subjective phenomena—they are functions of corporate living—can conceive of an individual consulting a specialist in a superstitious, religious or moral quandary; and is bound to accept that the occasional dispute, incapable of internal adjustment (irrespective of abstract right), will ultimately come up for public solution; but cannot understand how justice can involve the gain of one party to the detriment of another. Only where society as a whole cannot arrive at a correct diagnosis of an unabsorbed dispute must the problem be formally identified, clarified, and submitted in the most solemn form to specialists in the relevant wisdom. These can detect the errors of the parties or their predecessors, define how far justice can be done, and provide a practical solution in which all concerned should acquiesce. The decision, essentially *ad hoc*, may well be recorded, but is not a precedent in the sense understood in western legal systems. Each time the referees must go back to the sources of wisdom and work out the problem *ab initio*. Since no two cases are identical this is, though apparently wasteful, not unreasonable.

One can predict referees' qualifications. There is much to be said for a plurality of referees. Where a variety of experience is called for, a single judge is hardly satisfactory. Where a new rule has to be invented, and a new configuration of interests has to be adjusted, different skills are imperatively required. Judges need the support of differently-based judgments by men of equal, but differently matured wisdom. Ancient societies, heavily collective in their approach, view impartiality as almost absurdly remote, and suspicions of partiality and corruption are difficult to rebut. There is the insidious corruption involved in the desire on the part of less prestige-worthy members of any board to obtain the approval of the others; at best this may lead to a compromise against the consciences of the former, so vitiating their function. Numbers do not necessarily increase the probity of a decision, but they will limit the chances that sectional interests or limited viewpoints will go unrepresented. A court combining the power of decision with a multiplicity of advice is an attractive proposition. There are several possible ways of achieving this; the Indian mind favoured several specialist assessors, whose views could be stated without fear or favour and who could avoid the responsibility for the actual outcome, with an informal possibility that, at the hearing, other qualified persons might intervene and give their opinions.[6] The informality of a village or clan dispute-settling would gain from a more or less official reference to abstract criteria, with power to hand down a definitive sentence at the end of the proceedings, however protracted. One cannot underestimate the effect on the appointed assessors and the judge of intelligent local notables' gasps at the depositions of witnesses and applause at the individual assessor's quotation from the ocean of traditional maxims more or less relevant to the subject-matter. The diffusing of responsibilty is always welcome where actual enforcement of any aspect of social discipline is weak. Hence to adopt the practice of reference to a single referee requires very strong arguments.

II
Hindu Theory

4. *When is 'duty' to be ascertained* ?

The subject of our study lies under a cloud in that unprepared observers tend to see *dharma* as a despotic coercive factor restraining the individual from pursuing his own chosen goal. The classical Hindu sources on our subject (the *dharmaśāstra*) contemplate specific situations in which duty has to be defined and pronounced (otherwise than in schools where the subject is taught): (*i*) when a dispute between groups or individuals comes up for disposal, (*ii*) when an abstract proposition must be arrived at for the guidance of ministers, officials, and religious leaders if a question of public and/or social policy is at large, (*iii*) when an individual, under pressure from his conscience or from illness or from his family or other groups able to annoy him or them, seeks (by stages) absolution from sin, whether or not it has led to degradation or loss of caste *de facto* or as the result of a decision by caste authorities. All our texts relate to one or more of these premises. Since it was assumed that judicial administration was likely to be haphazard, and unlikely to be moved without substantial pressure of public opinion, the payment of fees and other gratuities, it was not a matter of course that disputes went before a court of any kind, and internal solution of complaints was preferred. In that context the higher duty of preserving the autonomy and peace of the caste or guild or other unit took precedence over the individual's rights and duties, and compromises must have been very frequent. Formally to ascertain duty was a last resort.

The Sanskrit for 'duty' is *iti-kartavyatā* (that one should act in such-and-such a way), which is one of the possible definitions of *dharma*. The wide spread of meanings of *dharma* is well known.[7] For our purpose it is sufficient to realize that *dharma* was always transcendental, super-substantial, occult, divine rather than created, predicated and enunciated rather than promulgated. The 'ought' of any situation was a question of prudence and convenience only at the moment of a judicial decision, when aspects of policy (*artha*) had to be considered by the judge equally with those of righteousness (*dharma*). The abstract justice of any proposal or opinion offered by a judicial assessor derived from his having been trained in wisdom, which gave to events a supernatural as well as a natural value. That wisdom had been matured by Brahmins only and formed one of the branches of their traditional education. Brahmins alone had the right to say what *dharma* was and their participation was regarded as essential to the discovery and effectuation of the ultimately righteous solution to any problem, however practical in its nature, provided that it came within the traditional scope of the obligations imposed (it was thought) by life itself upon a caste society.

A cynical comment on the task of the referees in all these cases was that *dharma* was unfathomable, and that the right course of conduct amounted, in the ultimate analysis, to that which 'great men' had pursued before. Such cynical or 'realistic' remarks deserve to be given weight in our study. A prime text, though unique, is so apt that it is worth reproducing verbatim :[8]

> *tarko 'pratiṣṭaḥ śrutayo vibhinnā naiko ṛṣir yasya matam pramaṇam. dharmasya tattvaṃ nihitaṃ guhāyām. mahājano yena gataḥ sa panthāḥ.*
> Reason is fickle. The scriptures are discordant. No one sage's

opinion is authoritative. The truth about *dharma* is buried in a cave. The road we must take is that trodden by the great ones!

Without irony Āpastamba says:[9]

Dharma and *adharma* (sin) do not go about saying "Here we are!" nor do gods, Gandharvas or (departed) Fathers say "this is *dharma*, this *adharma*". But that is *dharma* which, when done, *āryas* (twice-born folk, gentlemen) praise, what they reprobate is *adharma*. He shall pursue a course of conduct similar to that which, in all districts, is pursued unanimously by *āryas* who have been thoroughly educated, and are *old*, in control of their selves (*ātmavataḥ*), free from avarice and hypocrisy.

To keep the distinction, at this rate, between *dharma* and actual practice, even custom, is difficult, though it is obvious that custom itself is open to scrutiny, to approbation or the reverse. Samantu says:[10]

Where the path of the *śāstra* is divided, in deeds of all sorts, Bhārata, the wise man should practise the custom (*ācāra*) which has come down to him within his family.

Manu himself lauds family custom, even in the case of a *snātaka* (accomplished student), no doubt a person under a taboo and hypersensitive as to right conduct:[11]

Let him walk in that path of the good by which his fathers went and by which his grandfathers went; walking in that path he will not suffer harm.

One could, evidently, not go wrong if one copied prestige-worthy folk, a self-authenticating standard of behaviour. Naturally this could not help if the problem was new, especially where neither analogy nor inference could produce a solution. Neither party might be aware of unrighteousness in his conduct; and vociferous support for the justice of either position could be had for the asking. An appeal to ultimate, superior values which all could recognize was imperative in many a thorny dilemma; and the application of such principles (often tantalizingly vague in themselves) to the facts, once these have been ascertained, must be convincing.

Ancient Indian ideas about duty are illustrated by the curious story of Draupadī in the *Mahābhārata*.[12] A society which eschewed polyandry could not understand how she became the joint bride of five of India's most celebrated heroes. The epic gives rein to drama, almost up to the style of Sophocles' *Antigone*. It is argued on the one hand that such conduct, though backed by the proximate authority, the boys' mother, lacked authentication in *āryas*' society at large. Sharing a wife had no support in the *dharmaśāstra*, then as now.[13] The reply alleges ancient practice which permitted such a transaction, and the debate closes inconclusively with the characteristically unsolved problem, who is to judge as between precedent and the would-be universal standard of righteousness which can, perforce, be expressed only through a code of behaviour which is far from universal (in fact that of Brahmins of north-central India).

Since the decision, for the individual, depends on who is accepted for the time being as authority, we now turn to the human referees who are the real, as opposed to the ostensible arbiters of duty, taking the three contexts of doubt (above) in turn.

5. *The human referees*

(1) A dispute between individuals or groups is a *vyavahāra* (judicial business) out of which one party must win, and one fail. There almost certainly was a time when official authentication of decisions was unnecessary or even unknown. Characteristically for this culture, however, the decision is made by the king or his deputy or delegate, who may or may not be trained in the *śāstras*. The interrogation of witnesses and conduct of the case may be in his hands or those of a skilled interlocutor (*prāḍvivāka*). The discovery and utterance of *dharma* is in the hands of *sabhyas*, qualified judicial assessors. This does not exclude interventions by persons having a right to express an opinion, obviously commensurate with their prestige and knowledge.[14] The sources of *dharma*, the actual (though not nominal) referees are the *sabhyas*. The word comes from Sabhā, which implies an assembly of Brahmins for ritual purposes, and one can assume with the least amount of doubt that the eliciting of *dharma* in the course of a

vyavahāra was regarded as a solemn act with ritual implications.

The qualifications laid down for them in the *śāstra*[15] can be classified into three categories: (*a*) character, in respect of behaviour, good name, lineage, etc.; (*b*) independence and impartiality, expressed compendiously as freedom from love and anger; (*c*) learning, especially learning relevant to abstract norm-projecting in an *āryan* society. They were, therefore, to belong to the Brahmin caste. It is from Brahmins that men must learn their *dharma*,[16] whether they merely imitate their practices[17] or seek their advice. Whatever other motives lie behind this glorification of the Brahmin it is clear that the policy would tend to reinforce a sense of responsibility which the exacting traditional education already induced in members of this caste. The ancient text of Āpastamba lists the qualifications of a judicial committee as (*i*) learning, (*ii*) good family, (*iii*) advanced age, (*iv*) intelligence, (*v*) adequacy of obedience to their own *dharmas*.[18]

We are still speaking of *vyavahāra*, the judicial process. Though our early texts require the *sabhyas* to be Brahmins a discordant note is heard: Kātyāyana requires merchants (of the *vaiśya* caste presumably) to be part of the court.[19] These represent non-official and non-Brahmin interests. Their presence is to be accounted for by the fact that many financial questions arise, not to speak of problems of accounting, debts and documentary proof in indebtedness (sometimes written in special scripts), wherein a merchant would have more skill than a Brahmin devoted to simple living and high thinking. In a drama of about A. D. 450 a merchant is actually found as a member of the court.[20] The qualifications of such assessors were guild-membership, good family, character, wealth, freedom from malice and being 'well advanced in years'. Few of our texts (we saw one above) require the Brahmin *sabhyas* to be old: unless they were rare in the locality they must usually have been so. A text shared by the *Mahābhārata* and Nārada[21] reads,

> *na sā sabhā yatra na santi vṛddhā*
> *na te vṛddhā ye na vadanti dharmam*
>
> That is not a court where there are no old men: those are not old men who do not speak *dharma*....

The question why merchants are to be appointed, when Manu,

for example, mentions only Brahmins, is answered laconically by Vijñāneśvara and (doubtless following him) Devaṇṇa-bhaṭṭa,[22] 'to placate the common people of the country', not evidently because of anti-Brahmin feeling, but because without such assistance a decision was unlikely to be given much weight, since impartiality alone cannot command the respect due to skill.

A more interesting requirement is the *sabhyas*' number or quorum. The number of merchants required is not specified, but the Brahmins (excluding the judge and/or interlocutor) must not be less than three.[23] The advantage of an odd number is that a faction cannot operate unless all three pertain to it, and unanimity is aided, even though a minority would eventually submit to the majority. The odd number argues, powerfully, for the principle that a single, unanimous opinion (Skt. *vyavasthā*) must be tendered to the judge though, as we shall see, the texts are capable of quite a different interpretation. Jayaswal[24] was, to my mind, right in relating the texts requiring an even number to the majority principle known in India in very ancient times (see below). Bṛhaspati[25] requires the Brahmins to be learned in secular matters (*loka-*), ancillary Vedic sciences and in *dharma*, to the number of *seven*, *five*, or even *three*, whereupon the *sabhā* amounts to a sacrificial session, with the significance of the latter.[26] In an extremity the king may follow the advice of *one* Brahmin *sabhya*,[27] but the number *two* is nowhere found.

(2) An opinion on an abstract question was sought from a *pariṣad* (also *parṣad*), a council of Brahmins, usually such as lived in a centre of learning or pilgrimage. It was a king's duty to settle Brahmins learned in the three Vedas in his capital itself to provide precepts on *svadharma* for his subjects.[28] To such Brahmins might be referred even judicial questions where the *sabhyas* failed to reach agreement or a satisfactory decision.[29] The word *pariṣad* is properly appropriated to an aggregate of members of one *varṇa* (here Brahmins) assembled for a specific purpose: most collective nouns for councils or committees have implications of a similarly definite character.[30] In the ascertainment of duty the *pariṣad* stands very high and its composition and character have rightly attracted interest.[31] The *śāstra's* many divisions, into *varṇa-dharma*, *āśrama-dharma*, and the combination of both, also into *guṇa-*, *nimitta-*, and *sādhāraṇa-dharma* (the last common to all Hindus at all times)[32] gave scope for specialist knowledge of very

diverse kinds, and a large council might be needed to lend weight to a decision which might well be controversial. Nevertheless the text of Manu (XII. 108-9)[33] which is most readily adapted to this context insists that *śiṣṭa*, i.e., fully educated, Brahmins are competent to determine hitherto undeclared, undefined questions of law, and defines *śiṣṭa* in terms of Vedic learning and capacity to represent the very essence of the Veda. *Ten at least* make up such a court (see below), or three or more. So essential is it that trained minds alone should purport to reinterpret or define *dharma* that Manu insists that whereas one learned Brahmin may, in case of need, act as an authority, *no* number of unobservant and unlearned persons (whatever their caste) can constitute a *pariṣad* (XII. 113). Thus the practice of elders cannot make *dharma* here.

(3) If a penance had to be prescribed the general principle was that the culprit should declare his guilt, and the confession was part of his expiation.[34] Since all debate as to the appropriate penance must be within the committee (*pariṣad*), there was never, it seems, any objection to the number being an even one. In their award to the culprit and in their report to the ruler a single voice was heard. The ruler was involved, in theory, and (it seems) often in practice, because he was ultimately responsible for securing that penance was performed and that sinners should not be readmitted to caste-privileges hastily or on terms the community might afterwards dispute.[35] A full committee would consist of ten or more, made up (ideally) of Brahmins of various qualifications, prescribed so that no relevant skill should be wanting to apply occult principles to the case before them.[36] In one view seven, five or three would suffice.[37] Four traditional texts permit a *pariṣad* of four members.[38] In exceptional, ostensibly less approved cases[39] a single learned Brahmin would serve as a one-man *pariṣad*.[40]

The alleged usurpation of important disciplinary powers by the Śaṅkarācāryas does, however, have an ancient support. Aṅgiras, quoted by Aparārka (on Yājñ. 1.9), says that even a single man may be a *pariṣad* provided he belongs to a group of ascetics of true penance, whose minds are equipped with *jñāna* and *vijñāna* (mystic knowledge and discrimination, realization), and who have bathed (i.e. been initiated) with the *śirovrata* (an ascetic's initiation involving, *inter-alia*, shaving the head). A text of Yama quoted by Kullūka on Manu XII. 113 reads,

> *eko dvau vā trayo vāpi yad brūyur dharma-pāṭakāḥ* |
> *sa dharma iti vijñeyo netareṣaṃ sahasraśaḥ* ||
> What one, two or even three reciters of *dharma* utter, that must be known as *dharma*, and not (what is uttered by) others by the thousand.

The verse seems vaguely modelled on Manu VII. 108. It is of interest that the Pāñcarātra work called *Sanatkumāra-saṃhitā*, which has been placed before A. D. 900 (Yama can hardly be later), reads (at IV. 33),

> *traya vā dvau tathaiko vā yad brūyur vaiṣṇavā narāḥ* |
> *sa dharma iti vijñeyo netareṣaṃ sahasraśaḥ* ||
> What three, or two Vaiṣṇava men utter or even one that must be known as *dharma*, and not (what is uttered by) others by the thousand.

The latter text is somewhat more attractive, since we can take for granted that the elders of the community would have superior and realistic authority, and a sectarian work would be bound to announce its adepts as arbiters. But the most agreeable feature is that, commencing with the more traditional figure of three it descends, unlike Yama, progressively to one, which is a more characteristic way of projecting such developing norms.

Śaṅkarācārya's own idea was that a single distinguished referee could serve as a leader of a *pariṣad*, which seems euphemistic.[41] When unlearned and unenlightened men prescribe penances, says Manu (XII. 115), the sin of the penitent recoils upon them a hundredfold—almost certainly because the want of capacity, training, and personal example encourages light penances and so indirectly increases the total of sin in the world. That kings made provision for *pariṣads* in the districts is proved by inscriptions.[42] The ruler presided, by deputy, over the deliberations of a large *pariṣad* and authenticated its acts.[43] Number was highly valued where the problem was difficult and the penance might be severe, sympathy might be excited, and evasion or faction evoked: numbers were evidently a refuge here, a *pariṣad* of a thousand being mentioned by Vijñāneśvara somewhat fancifully.[44] The decision must be unanimous, for welfare (or spiritual benefit) is furthered by the council's speaking with one voice: even a minority of respectable referees could indirectly undermine the authority of the whole.[45]

In short the *śāstra* provided against the public's violating *dharma* with the connivance of interested parties, and attempted to set up authorities of unimpeachable integrity, whose expertise could safely be relied upon, as much in fields for which practice and traditional learning did not make adequate provision as for fields in which they did. It is unfortunate that the authors of *śāstric* scriptures, though not consciously bowing to the whims of majorities, gradually, even from very early times, began to admit into tradition alternative propositions regarding duty and the ways of repairing breaches in it, which steadily diminished the rigidity of the system in the interests of non-observant, lax groups, and individuals. The process has gone on into our own day so that when a single referee is approached for an opinion and gives an orthodox answer[46] the public are more astonished than depressed by it.

6. *The referee's sources and the role of the śāstra*

Śāstra is 'teaching', impersonal. The literature of the *dharmaśāstra*,[47] of which some two thousand specimens survive, is the unprejudiced source *par excellence*, impartial except as to the ultimate spiritual welfare of the individual, whose attainment of *svarga* (heaven), avoidance of unpropitious metempsychoses, or even total avoidance of rebirth, is an express object of the study.[48] Further, the welfare of the kingdom itself depends on the king's upholding every aspect of *dharma* (as defined above, I, 5(2)) which it is within his power to foster.[49] Two *śāstras* come within our view, the *arthaśāstra*, politics, and the *dharmaśāstra* itself: any judge in what we should nowadays call a civil or criminal action must apply his mind to both.[50] His assessor, however, is an expert, *śāstrī* or pandit. This fact takes us at once to the *śāstra's* own definition of the sources to which the referee, as in all other cases the individual applicant himself, must resort in order that society may be satisfied that a valid and righteous judgment, one consistent with *dharma* (*dharmya*), has been reached. Our texts reveal a development in favour of the practice of respectable (i. e. superior) classes, but a convenient mid-point of *śāstric* exposition is already present in Manu. Practice as such, indeed, is no authority, for it must be the practice of specially qualified classes. As Gautama had put it,

> The Veda is the (real) root of *dharma* and the tradition (*smṛti*) and practice (*śīla*) of those who know it: transgression of *dharma* (e.g. Draupadī's marriage) and violence occurred on the part of great men, but the current (Kali) Age cannot stand this.[51]

Baudhāyana placed the Veda, *smṛti*, and the practice of *śiṣṭas* in order of priority, the assembly of ten functioning only in the absence of the latter as a clear guide.[52] We take up the position as seen by Manu:

> *vidvadbhiḥ sevitaḥ sadbhir nityam adveṣa-rāgibhiḥ*
> *hṛdayenābhyanujñāto yo dharmas taṃ nibodhata.*[53]
>
> The *dharma* practised by the learned, the good who are perpetually free from hatred and attachment (i.e. impartial) fully internalized in their hearts (or minds)—that *dharma* you should (now) learn.
>
> *vedo 'khilo dharma-mūlam smṛti-śīle ca tad-vidām*
> *ācāraś caiva sādhūnām atmanas tuṣṭir eva ca*[54]
>
> The entire Veda is the root of *dharma* and the tradition and conduct (i.e. tradition-sanctioned conduct)[55] of those that know it (the Veda). Also the custom of the good, and even (in the last resort?) the approval of one's own self (i. e. conscience).[56]
>
> *śruti-smṛty uditam dharmam anutiṣṭhan hi manāvaḥ*
> *iha kīrtim avāpnoti pretya cānuttamaṃ sukham*[57]
>
> When men practise *dharma* declared in the revelation and in *smṛti* they achieve fame in this world and after death unsurpassable bliss.

Mediaeval scholars were satisfied that by *smṛtī* was meant our known *smṛitis*, the authority of which, in spite of their being written by human authors,[58] was high because of their compilers' superior learning in Vedic material, much of which has subsequently been lost.[59]

śrutis tu vedo vijñeyo dharma-śāstram tu vai smṛtiḥ
te sarvārtheṣv amīmāṃsye tābhyāṃ dharmo hi nirbabhau[60]

'Revelation' is the Veda, and the *smṛti* is the *dharmaśāstra.* In all matters these two are indisputable, for through them *dharma* shone forth.

vedaḥ smṛtiḥ sadācāraḥ svasya ca priyam ātmanaḥ
etac caturvidhaṃ prāhuḥ sākṣād dharmasya lakṣaṇam[61]

The Veda, *smṛti*, the custom of the good and what is agreeable to one's own self (i.e. conscience), this, they say, is the fourfold open sign of *dharma* (or means whereby *dharma* is recognized).

tasmin deśe ya ācāraḥ pāramparya-kramāgataḥ
varṇānāṃ sāntarālānāṃ sa sadācāra ucyate[62]

That custom which has come down, in the case of the *varṇas* and mixed castes respectively, in that country (previously specified)[63] from generation to generation, is what is meant by custom of the good.

etad deśa-prasūtasya sakāśād agrajanmanaḥ
svaṃ svaṃ caritraṃ śikṣeran pṛthivyāṃ sarva-mānavāḥ[64]

Each individual on earth should learn his own course of conduct from one of the highest birth (a Brahmin) born in that country.

We have already noticed that qualified Brahmins are to be looked to as sources of that intangible thing, duty. A Vedic text, presupposing a doubt as to *dharma*, is cited by Mitra-miśra: [65]

ye tatra Brāhmaṇāḥ sama-darśino yuktā ayuktā arūkṣā dharma-kāmāḥ
syuḥ yathā te tatra varteran tathā tatra vartethāḥ

In such (a quandary) you should behave exactly as in similar cases those Brahmins behave who are impartial, concentrated, devoted, free from harshness, desirous of *dharma.*

Baudhāyana qualified the *śiṣṭas* whose custom is the third source of *dharma* as being free from envy, pride, hoarding, covetousness; hypocrisy, arrogance, greed, perplexity and anger—

as having studied the Veda and its appendages, and able to reason from the Vedic texts.[66] Now it is a fact that Brahmins were imported during the early centuries of this millennium from the North to be settled in settlements (*agrahāras*) of the South, no doubt in order to bring such a standard of conduct within the grasp of Southerners. The obvious question—what, at that rate, was the authority of *customs* other than those of Brahmins from such a locality—cannot be given a definite answer (pending further research) since the *śistra* gave an incoherent and ambiguous picture. The possibility of a circular definition, that men are *śiṣṭas* when they practise customs of the good, and customs of the good are those practised by *śiṣṭas*, is expressed forcibly by the *Nṛsiṃhaprasāda*,[67] whose answer is that customs are authoritative if *śiṣṭas* practise them deliberately as *dharma* (which leaves room for some *śiṣṭas* to be better informed about their *dharma*!) Rationally, and in the uncompromising view of the *mīmāṃsakas*,[68] no custom was valid which contradicted the *śāstra*. This was accepted by the commentators on *smṛtis* who, by preference, illustrate *ācāra* (custom) by relatively insignificant and uncontroversial practices,[69] whilst claiming that customs contrary to the *śāstra* are illegal.[70]

Similarly some of the hardier of them are prepared to hold royal orders devoid of moral authority and void from the *śāstric* standpoint if they contradict *śāstric* injunctions of the *varṇāśrama* (i.e. not *vyavahāra*) category.[71] Yet on the other hand, despite the recommendation that customs should be tested by the king and abolished if they conflict with *dharma* (and registered if they do not),[72] the basic proposition of Manu that custom is paramount law (which we now probe) correctly represents the path which the culture took. Indeed the seemingly late text of Pitāmaha[73] says that whatever the *śreṣṭha* (person of highest prestige) practises *whether it be dharmic or not* (!) is called *caritra* (equivalent to *ācāra*) because it is in use in a family, etc., in a particular country. It may be set aside, as we shall see, if a judge regards it as overruled by *dharma*, etc., but, there again, it may not be, for the recognized order of priority required *dharma* to be overruled by *ācāra/carita*. Moreover it would be wrong to ignore the equally definite proposition of the *śāstra* that inhabitants of regions known to practice aberrant (even abhorrent) customs may safely practice them and will be liable to no moral or legal penalty for doing so.[74]

Adharma thus has *de facto dharmic* backing, which understandably puzzled some authors.[75] Consequently it must be remembered that in all practical contexts, in which marriages were contracted, wages earned, taxes exacted, and the like, popular concepts of justice and right received a sympathetic, if persistent and crucial testing.

ācārāḥ paramo dharmaḥ śrutyuktaḥ smārta eva ca
tasmād asmin sadā yukto nityaṃ syād ātmavān dvijaḥ[76]

Custom[77] is the highest *dharma*, stated in the *śruti* and in the *smṛti* too. Therefore a twice-born who is in control of his self must perpetually attach himself to it.

jāti-jānapadān dharmāñ śreṇi-dharmāṃs ca dharma-vit
samīkṣya kula-dharmāṃs ca sva-dharmaṃ pratipādayet[78]

He (the king) who knows *dharma* must inquire into the laws (or norms) of castes, districts, (mercantile) guilds, and even (important) families and thus settle the particular *dharma* for each.

svāni karmāṇi kurvāṇā dūre santo 'pi mānavāḥ
priyā bhavanti lokasya sve sve karmaṇy avasthitāḥ[79]

Men who perform their peculiar occupations, each remaining attached to his own duty, though they be far off, become dear to the people.

sadbhir ācaritaṃ yat syād dhārmikaiś ca dvijātibhiḥ
tad deśa-kula-jātīnam aviruddhaṃ prakalpayet[80]

That which has been practised by the good and by the best of twice-born attached to *dharma*, that he shall establish—provided it be not repugnant for countries, families, and castes.

The following refers to the aftermath of a conquest of territory :

pramāṇāni ca kurvīta teṣāṃ dharmyān yathoditān
ratnaiś ca pūjayed enaṃ pradhāna-puruṣaiḥ saha[81]

And the *dharmic* rules (or authorities) obtaining amongst them he shall render authoritative in the form represented to him, and he shall honour him (i.e. their ruler) with jewels in the company of his chief officers.

On the basis of the point of view thus charmingly revealed by Manu in spite of the prevailing *mīmāṃsā* ideology, it was in order for Vijñāneśvara (12th century) to found his law of property on 'popular recognition' (*loka-siddhi*),[82] and for an important successor, Mādhava (14th century) to say boldly that *śruti*, *smṛti*, and (not *sadācāra* but) *loka-prasiddhi* are the roots of dharma.[83] The individualist Āpastamba had long previously identified the *dharma* which he taught as *sāmayācārika* (part of the customs of daily life) and added that the (moral ultimate) *authority* (*pramāṇam*) was the agreement of those that knew *dharma* and, almost as an afterthought, the Vedas.[84] This is taken up by Vijñāneśvara without hesitation, if with subtle modification (having Manu I. 107 in mind, doubtless):[85] the two kinds of *dharmas* which an expert administrator must know are those derived from the scriptures (*śruti* and *smṛti*) and from the decisions or imputed decisions of popular bodies.[86] The ultimate roots of 'duty' in practice were the scriptures which embody age-old wisdom tested in the fire of the practice of the 'good' of long ago, and modern usages and customs which can be traced back to a consensus of authorized bodies of rule-makers. On this a great deal could be said. Our mediaeval commentators give examples of royal ordinance-making (administrative rules, evidently) and our inscriptional evidence abundantly documents decision-taking, local legislation, often with the royal sanction, concerning a host of matters including caste and village discipline—many of which are backed with superstitious sanctions.[87] The village was bound as a matter of duty in conscience as in law to obey those rules, arrived at with the royal sanction or by mere public consent.[88]

With this background it is easy to understand the controversial stanza which I now quote :

dharmaś ca vyavahāraś ca caritraṃ rājaśāsanam
catuṣpād vyavahāro 'yam uttaraḥ pūrva-bādhakaḥ[89]

Dharma, practice, usage and the royal decree : this is the Litigation, having four feet; each bars those earlier (in the series).

Notwithstanding the opinion of Lingat to the contrary,[90] the natural interpretation is the best: in a *vyavahāra* context, in which we know from elsewhere that *artha* considerations must figure, the judge (as opposed to the *sabhya*) must regard as overruled the precepts of *dharma*, etc., in the order stated. The four items are not means of proof, as Kātyāyana's gloss suggests[91] but sources of law,[92] as Bṛhaspati's gloss makes abundantly clear.[93] Kātyāyana urges the king to follow the *śāstra* in preference to custom where possible (e.g. where a text exists) for superstitious reasons.[94] He sensibly adds that the *śāstra* is *not* to be referred to when disputes arise between those who are bound by the same conventional usages (*samaya*), but only in disputes between those and strangers.[95] There was, after all, no other source for a 'righteous' principle which he could apply.

It is of interest that, though the king could not decide what was *dharma* in the sense of what was the purport of the *śāstra*, he could cut the Gordian knot when ascetics and others were in bitter conflict (*vivadatām mithaḥ*) about *dharma*. In such cases it was politic for him to bring them to a cool frame of mind and, with the aid of others, viz. Brahmins, find their solution for them in a deferential spirit: Manu VIII. 390-1 with the commentary of Kullūka.

It might well be asked at this rate whether the *śāstra*'s actual power was not very qualified when vital decisions had to be taken. In conscience it sat high as a source, whoever sought the opinion of the learned; yet when it came to a practical decision at least three sources of law, by no means necessarily subservient to *dharma*, took, or could take precedence over it. To make matters worse, the *śāstra*, though it signals the point rather inconspicuously, frankly acknowledged that no rule of *dharma* was to be followed, let alone enforced, if it were opposed by the public's censure : that which is *lokavidviṣṭa* (hated by the people) is not be be practised.[96] The illustrations of this[97] are not numerous, but the principle is undoubted.[98] This brings us to the ambiguous role of the *śāstra* itself in the hands of its manipulators.

7. *Inerrancy of scriptures and the price paid for it*

The *śāstric* sources admitted the impracticability and therefore impropriety of applying civil and criminal justice by an overarching theoretical standard (such as the *śāstra* itself provided) to peoples or groups whose customs did not conform to it, and whose deviations from it had not been subjected to formal and notorious royal censure. Yet all lay down that the ultimate criterion of rightness is the settled and consensual practice of persons, e.g. elders, qualified by virtues prescribed by the *śāstra* including knowledge of the Veda and its ancillary sciences of which the *śāstra* forms a part. A Hindu needing his duty to be defined must refer himself ultimately to the Veda and derivative or nominally derivative scripture. Actually the Veda comprises prayers and mystic and sacrificial formulae, and the derivative literature arranged and classified norms which had been recovered by observation of practice and were thereafter purged by a refining process by which, applying ethical values and calling upon 'righteous' objectives, non-conducive matter was eliminated and congruent data organized, trimmed, and justified. The intellectual effort required for this work,[99] and the emotional satisfaction procured through it, especially after proselytism had enlarged the bounds of the dominant culture, created the phenomenon well known to Judaism, Islam, and pre-Reformation Western Europe, the *inerrancy of scripture.*

The scriptures, *smṛtis* as well as Vedas, were memorized and thus passed from generation to generation by word of mouth. The rule sought for, and where to seek it, were thus at the command not only of the referee's memory, fitfully and tardily aided by manuscripts, but of his motives. Hence the intense interest in the ideal referee's qualifications. The *interpretation* and application of the rule was likewise his, and in a myriad of cases both were conjointly transmitted by way of oral learning. A result, found in all the cultures mentioned above, was to enhance the value of the 'text' far above its literal worth. Since the spirit of the interpretation was more or less obviously human and transient, unconscious forces placed the accent overwhelmingly upon the latter, the verity and sufficiency of which was not allowed to be called in question (Skt. *amīmāṃsya*). Subtle and even novel questions of ethics and law were referred to jointly or commonly accepted referees on the basis that their authority should be indisputable. In the nature of things that authority must appear to bind them and be incapable of being manipulated by them. If this were denied there was no further authority to which one might regress and the result would be chaos. Consequently the prestige of the arbiter-class, the Brahmins, was tied up with their authorities, and they alone might state, define, express and interpret them. A historical and literal interpretation of the actual 'original' meaning of a Vedic or *smṛti* text was not permitted. The texts meant what, at any time or place, the referees said they meant. Their personal signature certified that they had applied their minds to the authorities and that the latter required the solution (and only that solution) which purported to be based upon them.

In moments of frankness this state of affairs is disclosed without shame. M. K. Gandhi is known to have re-used the concept of *dharma* and re-modelled its content to suit his own political purposes, and he had no difficulty in internalizing his own reinterpretations of scripture. On one occasion, speaking of the *Bhagavadgitā*, he said,[100]

> The seeker is at liberty to extract from this treasure any meaning he likes so as to enable him to enforce in his life the central teaching.

An analogous situation in the Islamic world is known for long to have frozen social, political and legal advance. Since interpretation of the Qur'ān and the Sunna was not confined to a hereditary class which drew financial and social advantage from keeping the scripture and its interpretation permanently and exclusively in its own hands, reform movements have lacked an attractive human target for rebellion. The position in the Western Church until approximately 1520, feelingly and appositely explained by G. G. Coulton, was that scripture was cited as absolute and final authority for purposes which it could not justify rationally or historically.[101] To question publicly the authenticity of the traditional interpretations placed upon it by the church was likely to cause the doubter to be burnt at the stake. It followed that the *text* of scripture itself was consistently withheld from the people,[102] since if they knew the literal meaning and the context of the passages quoted by the authorities tendentiously and inaccurately, they would expose the organization as a fraud. The coming of good vernacular bibles and the collapse *pro tanto* of the traditional moral authority, which claimed secular and spiritual jurisdiction, were inter-connected.

To return to India, we find that the Brahmins perpetually

denied the right to hear, let alone study, the Veda and *smṛtis* to the bulk of the population, the Śūdras, whose spiritual duty to learn from the Brahmins we have already encountered.[103] As soon as orthodox pandits are told that the correct interpretation of the *Mitākṣarā*, for example, leads to a conclusion different from that which they place upon it, they reply, 'Even if the author himself were to re-appear and assure us of it, we should not believe him!'[104]

The real advance came about through the discovery that duty had its secular, practical side, which was as real objectively as its moral, superstitious side, in terms of which, for many centuries in every evolved civilization,[105] all duties had been expressed. This discovery was made possible in turn by the actual co-existence and interdependence of social elements which could not share the same referees in all matters of duty. At the critical moment men woke up to the fact that a system which had worked well—namely one that allows 'authorities' to select their own texts and attribute to them any meaning they choose (in defiance of context and often even of grammar)—was too open to be manipulated to the advantage of one party in a dispute, often one in which the 'authorities' were themselves interested. But this awakening by no means abolished at once the old method of argument. The same inerrant scripture, whose truth no one was allowed to question and survive, was interpreted, for long, in other, not necessarily more accurate senses.[106]

The ridicule, however, which modern educated man, child of the 'blessed freedom' of the Reformation, has been able to pour, first upon European obscurantists, and in due course upon their Asian counterparts, must itself yield to a counter-ridiculing critique. It was naive to think that popes really relied upon *Tu es Petrus*, and pandits upon *imā nārīr avidhavāḥ*, for their preposterous social and pecuniary arrangements: or that historical investigation of Matt. xvi. 18 and *Ṛgveda* X.2.18.7 would either prove or disprove those latter. Referees do not cite, quote, or ostensibly rely on texts because they believe in their truth, or have studied them critically and thus believe themselves bound by them, but rather because they believe the inquirers are, as they claim to be, bound by them; and because a reason should be alleged, if reason indeed must be alleged at all, such as is not susceptible to regress—it must be final. The whole purpose of the reference in the first place is to elicit the verdict of the entire, 'solid' culture on the problem, and that verdict, in a developed old literate society, is capable of being extracted, overtly, from texts.

That which had been internalized and accepted by generations and made working tools by constant application to a variety of crises can be trusted even if referees cannot, and there is an interaction of mutual authentication between the human and the scriptural referees. The texts say, from time to time, what the human referees say they say: and so it should be. There was never a time when texts manipulated men; and it is simple-minded, to say the least, to quarrel with men because they manipulate their scriptures in the slow-moving ferment of time, and so ultimately blend, equally unconsciously and inevitably, their interpretation with their text. To rebel against interpretation is not heresy, it is schism: for the target of the intellectual attack is not the conservative's *exegesis* but the state of society which nourishes him and which he has an ultimate interest in sustaining. Times change, men must change with them, and their shibboleths likewise.[107]

The price of the Hindu society's confidence in Brahmin exegesis of scripture and nominally scripture-based practice was stagnation. Subtle and continuous adjustment to varying needs, flexibility in the matter of regional and even family usages, an intelligent distinction between the immutable ethical rule (which could never be tested by experience) and the fugitive standard to be employed in settling law-cases (which would tend to be much more practical and *ad hoc*)—all these mitigated the principle so as to afford the civilization a kind of stability for centuries. True they failed to develop systematized checks upon their rulers' stupidity and incompetence;[108] but that was a by-product of the want of awareness that popular requirements are the true ultimate authority. This was inevitable, since even by the end of our own millennium no 'public' in any real sense will have emerged. Hence no intellectual alternative to exegesis transpired.

If scripture had persuasive force only because Brahmins continued to expound it, aptly, convincingly, and literally in their lives, what was to happen when the religious beliefs which the scriptures encapsulated lost their hold, when the Brahmins themselves lost confidence in their culture, aping foreign ways and admiring foreign standards, and ceased to embody any definite principles at all? Could the people, by-passing their Brahmins, go, through a kind of Reformation, back to the sources and reinterpret them in an up-to-date style? Some, and S. Radhakrishnan was one, purport to believe that they could. But unless they can find another class of exegete, to whom the chair of infallibility can be conveyed, the plan is unlikely to succeed. This fear is endorsed by the fragments we have with us which amply testify to the methods by which the theory of ancient culture was put into effect until foreign rule was consolidated.

III

Indian Traditional Practice

8. *The ascertainment of rules*

The principle of inerrancy of scripture is rooted in the absence of impartial, efficient enforcement of actual norms. It becomes superfluous once it becomes clear that final decisions in the external forum (as opposed to the internal forum, viz. conscience) can be arrived at and enforced systematically and predictably irrespective of the ethical and religious beliefs of the disputing parties. So long as the implementation of a decision depended on the conscience and social contentment of the contenders it was adequate to refer everyone concerned to a text of general application, the truth of which could not be doubted without the doubter's creating a new society for himself and his kindred. Its verity was a fiction necessary to social stability. Hindus were tolerant in the sense that impugning the Vedas, for example, would not lead to the stake: but they were (as they are still) intolerant on the understanding that those whose dissent can be crystallized in non-Hindu propositions in terms of religion are outside the community. What they tolerate is the co-existence of the incompatible. To return to our theme, when enforcement of laws could at last be envisaged as independent of morals and conscience the fact that beliefs could vary became less significant, doubts as to the authority of particular texts became practicable, and one might even contemplate reform movements which challenged the traditional glosses on them. The next step, the creation of rival scriptures, was only round the corner. Thus a flexible and possibly corrupt administration of law, spiritual or secular, required an inerrant scripture, while an efficient and impartial administration, if not actually embarrassed by it, could certainly do without it. P. B. Gajendragadkar now says openly[109] that the scriptures of Islam, Hinduism, and even Christianity (in particular papal encyclicals) are totally irrelevant to social and political development in a secular society. Our study of the different contents of duty-ascertainment could be divided conveniently between the periods A. D. 600 to 1800, 1800 to 1956, and post-1956. In 1976 the Hindu law was partially reformed, and contact with the scriptures was formally abandoned: this pattern is urged by Gajendragadkar and others as 'obviously' fit to be followed by the other religious communities.

Until approximately 1800 the referees in matters of penance (*prāyaścitta*) and spiritual affairs corresponded so far as we can see to the scheme outlined by Manu. Counterparts to Brahmin sages functioned in Jaina, Lingayat and other 'heterodox' communities. The *guru*-figure emerged in Vaiṣṇava and Śaiva sects, celibate or non-celibate prestige focuses.[110] This voluntary jurisdiction carried on into modern times.[111] It was much objected to by protagonists of the seemingly pre-obscurantist scheme of the *smṛtis*, in whose eyes the single referee was the least worthy guide.[112]

So far as social and legal questions were concerned the British, and their Indian emulators in the Native States, rapidly dropped responsibility for re-admission to the caste and abandoned all except the most trifling supervision over caste discipline and administration. Thus decisive solutions to all questions in which civil rights[113] or property were involved came before the regular (state) courts. On the other hand the jurisdiction of caste *panchayats* was not ended, and its penalty of excommunication remained.[114] Under conditions prevailing in a caste society it was effective until the second half of this century. Independence (1947), the spread of the concept of 'human rights' and 'fundamental rights' protected by the Constitution (1950) and otherwise, weakened traditional *mores* rapidly. Excommunication became, in the public eye, 'caste tyranny'. All authority behind repressive or conservative religious or moral forces was weakened. Many parts of the *śāstric* theory and practice were not only abolished by statute but actually penalized.[115] The virtual confinement of right-definition to the regular courts in matters of crime and property here began to show its price. An integrated and comprehensive system of right and wrong did not exist.

Materials survive for a picture of how disputes over rights and duties were settled before 1800. The first question was whether a doubt would come before an arbitrator or a group. Courts of large size, consisting of a popular element and an official element, are evidenced, and at other periods *panchayats*, which are virtually village courts.[116] In northern India the arrangement of *sabhyas* seems to have become obsolete even by the mid-fifteenth century, since the subject hardly appears in the leading textbooks on procedure.[117] Commercial and other problems arising amongst groups with a high sense of identity seem to have been solved internally in guild tribunals as the *śāstra* recommends. Disputes of an aggravated description were frequently put before officials who, it seems, had an option to decide them by effecting a compromise, by applying some ordinance (e.g. of the Muslim government, that Muslims should not be executed for murder), or by applying some well-known local custom. There are instances where the dispute is to be settled by reference to *dharma*, and the order from the official before whom the case came for disposal reflects this decision, even where one party is a Muslim.[118] The parties agree to accept the award, which, one expects, might, if necessary, be put into effect by the official. Depending on the difficulty of such a case the appropriate reference is chosen. It may be a famous scholar and literateur, whose impartiality can be relied on.[119] It may be a group of pandits learned in *dharmaśāstra* and simultaneously other pandits learned in some other relevant science.[120] It may be a pair of renowned dispute settlers, resident at a place of pilgrimage.[121] It may be pandits learned in the *śāstra* who are repeatedly referred to for legal opinions and are skilled in adjuring witnesses in due form, ascertaining facts, administering ordeals, and setting out the issues and the texts applicable. That the process was recognizably juridicial is evident, and that the *śāstra* was intimately involved in it is clear from the quotations of the Sanskrit texts, sometimes with vernacular translation or paraphrase. That arrangements might be upset due to a reinterpretation of the history of the case and its promoters' motives are clear from one inscription's extremely elaborate reproduction of the 'case' of the promoters, together with supporting scriptural authorities.[122] To inscriptions suggesting that single scholars were appointed as *pariṣads* or *dharma-mantrīs* in the districts we have already referred.[123]

It is clear that the assessor-referees were men of renowned probity. Yet the association of other Brahmin notables with their investigation and judgment in some cases proves that great trust was placed in numbers and in publicity. Yet the arrangement was not palm-tree justice, some sort of compromise. The reliance, overtly, on scripture in a significant proportion of cases shows that the overarching inerrant authority was looked to as the deciding factor. The actual implementation of any decision was a matter of change, and could turn on factors outside the control of the official even irrespective of his indolence or indifference. This had a great bearing on the expectations of poor would-be litigants, whose internal methods of norm-ascertainment must have been the stronger for that.

It is of the greatest importance to note that the *śāstric* texts quoted in the documents we still possess partly agree with our surviving texts as printed. They sometimes quote them in a bizarre order, partly compressing their report of the textual position, and partly ignoring our surviving corpus of rules. They often introduce other material we cannot now locate, and ascribe to ancient authors texts which we can no longer verify, and immediately excite suspicion.[124] Astonishing freedom was taken with what we now believe to have been their *dharma* literature, and a (to us) strange mixture of religious, technical, and *dharma* sources (not to speak of unexpected allusions to the *arthaśāstra*) was used to arrive at support for the argument. Scripture was used with a confidence and a manipulative skill such as was possible only within a fraternity that expected neither supervision nor challenge. Their sources were really their own judgments propped by citations of their own choosing. It was a living technique.

The British period saw an increasingly unreal and inauthentic employment of the limited field of *śāstric* texts available to the judges in the large realm of family and social organization left free for their operation.[125] No explanation has been offered for the want of comment, let alone wrath, on the part of Hindus at the misuse of their scriptures.[126] Prone to complain, in almost every other context, at 'interference' with their religion, they accepted the formal fictional translation of *śāstra* into Anglo-

Hindu law with barely a murmur. By 1947 it had become evident that irrespective of religion, caste, or class a general law of India would be relentlessly applied (making room for a small number of customs only) to citizens as such, and the abandonment of the Anglo-Hindu law for a new version, owing no more than lip-service to the traditional system, rapidly supervened. Schemes for the enlargement of the area of national law (a projected civil code) with a corresponding elimination or shrinkage of the scope of the personal (i. e. religious) laws are well under way and, in spite of notorious difficulties, principally from the side of Muslims, must eventually take effect. When the process is completed the Hindu will look for the definition of his duty first to his parents, then to his closest relations (e. g. the maternal uncle), to spokesmen of his own sub-community, and in acute cases of conflict, to the regular state law, as expressed by the state courts. The *panchayat*, the caste heads and spiritual teachers will impinge increasingly superficially upon him, and it is more than doubtful whether the exhortations of politicians, even those couched in traditional *dharmic* idiom, will move him at all. The very occasional politician who genuinely possesses a charisma, will be found automatically to express himself in recognizably scriptural terms, but to small purpose. Even in the 1970's the caste elders, still called *panchayat*, seemed often called as a mere display, to impress, perhaps, the regular courts that the attitude of a litigant had been ventilated already before a traditional and local public,[127] the claim of which to be considered authoritative was hardly taken seriously.

9. *Finality*

The greatest difficulty in the way of ascertainment of rights and duties is to achieve finality. The recipient of an unfavourable award is reluctant to leave matters there: a better-informed referee might give the wanted answer. If a dispute is settled in favour of *A* and against *B* and *B* refuses to implement it, claiming the decision to be unjust or merely neglecting to comply with it, *A* may seek to re-open the matter by bringing it before a powerful body which can bring pressure to bear on *B*. *B*, under a more regular administration of justice, would approach a higher court by way of appeal on the ground that the existing decree against him was wrong. It is noticeable how, in the nebulous field of 'social justice', the aggressive party, failing to get his way by threats or commotions, seeks to widen the sphere of conflict in the hopes that he may find friends outside the natural forum. Only an optimist would expect a result, so achieved, to endure; but optimists are not so rare.

Since the *dharmáśāśtra* never excluded political considerations from *vyavahāra* (as opposed to *ācāra* and *prāyaścitta*) it is not surprising that disputes were continually re-opened in pre-British times. Decisions were obtained and not acted upon. Higher courts were approached without conclusive result, and larger assemblies approached in order to increase the shame which a non-complying party must incur.[128] Uncertainty as to the appropriate rule of *dharma* was matched by want of confidence in finality. It was and remains to this day characteristic of Indian disputes that they go on for generations and the arrears of cases before the courts and the frequency of appeals are greater than in any other country.[129] The chance of a decision being overturned on appeal is very high.[130] The assemblage of criteria, and alignment of principles, occur with opposite results as the forum shifts from level to level in the judiciary and from place to place geographically. Such a state of affairs may be explained, in part, on the basis that, in the search for right, opportunism reflects a want of faith not in the cold reality of the outcome, which is (logically) certain, but in the referees' fitness to conclude the matter. It is as if there were a hiatus of norm-pronouncement, as might well be the case when the traditional methods have been destroyed without an original growth to take their place. The *dharmaśāstra* did indeed allow appeals,[131] but they were expensive and the ultimate loser was fined, while, in theory at least, a judge who had given a perverse judgment was liable to punishment[132]—two propositions quite foreign to the Anglo-Indian system which has nursed litigation and opportunism. A well-known maxim of English law, that 'Justice must not only be done, but also be *seen* to be done' is perverted in India with the comical, but realistic, 'It is not so important that justice be done, as that it shall *seem* to be done.[133]

10. *Majority-decision: Indian tradition and the modern world*

Finality will never be achieved so long as a division of opinion is possible between referees. Appeal to higher or larger courts implies that a different opinion not only exists hypothetically but can win the day. Famous dissenting judgments which caused bitterness half a century ago are now regarded as classic and truthful. The recent question in India whether the Constitution shall rule the legislatures and the courts, or both may mould and develop it, agitated the country and all its judiciary with alarming intellectual, social, and moral overtones.[134] The great decisions are arrived at by majority. The essence of *dharma*, as we heard, is buried in a cave: who is to recover it? As Manu said, a myriad of fools can never be right; as a Western thinker put it (rather stupidly), 'one man plus God makes a majority'. Appeals, however, to the custom of learned and devout persons are all very well, if these never differ over essentials. Appeals to the practice of ancestors sound attractive if conditions never change and motives are never questioned. Appeals to the *śāstra* are impressive provided the texts (and men's memories of them) agree. They do not.

It is outside our scope to study the means by which discordant texts were harmonized by the experts. Great ingenuity was used to this end and our greater commentaries, such as the *Mitākṣarā*, the principal works of Nīlakaṇṭha-bhaṭṭa and the *Smṛticandrikā* and the *Sarasvatīvilāsa* draw their renown from their very diverse use of the skills of the *mīmāṃsaka*. It suffices to remember that only where two texts were hopelessly irreconcilable did the *śāstrīs* allow that both were right. Then there was an option (a solution open simultaneously to eight theoretical objections). The practising pandits whose decisions we can review did their own harmonizing in a way not open after 1864 to British and British-trained Indian jurists.[135] A late *smṛti* says that discordant texts may be resolved by recourse to the *majority*—one may do what the majority of them advise.[136] This is a principle borrowed by analogy from the practice of sacrificial experts,[137] a far-fetched analogy by no means suitable in our contexts where discussion until consensus is reached was obviously foreseen by all sources.

The western principle (originally Greek) of majority-decision is essentially democratic (as we shall see), has no place in a hierarchical society such as India was and to some extent still remains, and cannot be used to decide what is 'right'. How can a man's duty be determined by counting heads, even wise heads? Majority can only determine what, principle apart, is most convenient in practice. Decision by majority is essentially a pacific way of concluding a difference of opinion about a practical question. Its advantages are that prestige is shared, responsibility is dispersed. The emotional desires for support, and to be admired, balance each other. Votes may be reversed unless finality can be attained, but this risk is worth taking where willingness to be bound by the majority, irrespective of conviction, has taken the place of readiness for schism. Where schism is impossible 'majority' makes little sense. On the other hand it especially suits a non-learned society in which experience is not crystallized in texts such as the older members can be taken not only to have mastered but also tested repeatedly. Where there is no equality of status or learning, decision by majority (whether or not votes are taken secretly or otherwise) makes little sense unless supernatural guidance invariably takes precedence over experience and learning, in which case the latter must be revised (as in the Anglo-American system) to keep pace with each succeeding precedent as it emerges. It is a prerequisite of a majority decision that each minority shall give way in fact and in goodwill rather than face a schism or secession; the prestige-holders must be amenable unless they wish to reappear as leaders of a sect or splinter-group. This, perhaps, explains why, until the nineteenth century, majority decision played no role in the ascertainment of duty or of deciding what it was right and expedient to do in India.

The coming of the British, who could not understand consensus decision (which, except for the verdicts of juries, had disappeared in England with the Middle Ages) made, first, apparent breaches in this picture, and finally (with municipal and legislative councils, and ultimately with the advent of adult suffrage) destroyed it. The transfer from a consensus society, led by 'natural' leaders, to one where the rude multitude were masters is more or less complete and has been studied extensively.[138] It interests us to notice the insidious instances in which faction and strife were encouraged, carelessly and almost unconsciously, in the native scene by Anglo-Indian law. All the decisions of castes,[139] as nowadays of *grām* and *nyāya panchayats*, were supposed to be by majority. The decisions of relations as to whether a widow might adopt were to be taken by majority.[140] There are other examples.[141] This foreign requirement has no doubt often merged into a native achievement of consensus, but the legal principles are there, and they had their influence. That the ultimate decision as to what is right for a man and for the country should be in the hands of a majority even of carefully selected referees seems still as grotesque as it would have seemed before 1800. Whether the results impress can be considered presently. Meanwhile we find it asserted both by slips of the pen[142] and seriously that majority decisions—which deny the authority of a discernible *dharma*—were not unknown to pre-British India. The instances are taken from political history, from Buddhist sources, from *arthaśāstra*, from a passage in the works of Mitra-miśra and from the organization of self-governing local bodies such as Utteramerūr. All have their interest. None disturbs our picture.

That there were republics in ancient India (e. g. the Licchavis) is known.[143] Such *gaṇa* governments probably antedated the coming of Alexander. That decisions of the oligarchical senate were taken, if need be, by majority, is to be inferred from all we have known of them, and from Buddhist evidence which is traceable, as Jayaswal rightly says,[144] to the secular polity of the areas in which the Buddhist *dharma* grew up. Something may conceivably be due to the influence of Greek city-states in modern Afghanistan and Pakistan, the practice of which will have had a prestige-interest for peoples with a republican background even as far north as north-eastern India. After Buddhism ceased to be a force in India no trace of majority decision appears. When examined, the texts of the Vinaya-piṭaka[145] though allowing even (spiritual) legislation by voting, if need be, and explaining the social and moral position of minorities,[146] turn out to indicate as much against majority decision as in its favour. The basic relevant text reads :

> I allow you monks to settle this kind of legal (*dharmic*) question by the decision of the majority (*yebhuyyasikā*).

But this was to occur only in the last resort. It is the fifth of the seven means of settling disputes mentioned in the *Culla-vagga*.[147] When a vote was to be taken voting tickets[148] were not given to unsuitable members (!). That voting tickets were used in ancient India in secular contexts seems inescapable, but the practice is referable to the extinct republican constitutions. The basic method in monasteries was reference to referees,[149] a committee of one (a constant possibility throughout Indian history), or even a number of virtuous and learned monks, whose decision was final. If no other method than majority decision was possible, and a majority could not be obtained in one monastery, the monks had to go to another to get their decision.[150] In a leading case[151] voting tickets are mentioned, but the decision was by reference to a leading personality with special qualifications. In ten (really seven) cases the distribution of tickets (in the extreme cases where a majority must be elicited) was said to be void:[152] (1) Where the question was trifling; (2) where it had been insufficiently ventilated and discussed; (3) where the problem was insufficiently remembered or brought to the memory; (4) where the distributor knows or suspects that a majority of the meeting do not (or would not) speak *dhamma* (i. e. serve as righteous referees); (5) if the result of the vote is bound to be or might be that the order would be divided in schism, the result of majority decision in ill-adapted societies; (6) if a majority would be fraudulently obtained by, e. g., members clandestinely taking more than one voting ticket; (7) where members might change their views in order to side with whichever party might prove to be the majority. The *saṅgha* is a miniature state, all the members of which are theoretically equal: this last qualification is absolutely essential for majority decision. Where voices are of unequal weight there is no point in voting. The matter would be put to the vote repeatedly until the prestige-worthy members had their way. The reservations and qualifications in the Buddhist texts can be taken as evidence of this.

The references to majority in Kauṭilya's *Arthaśāstra* turn out to relate to the king's duty to follow the advice of the majority of his ministers. Policy matters, not themselves questions of duty, may safely be left to a majority of advisers,[153] who must implement them. In Soma-deva-sūri's work it is explained: ministers should be of an odd number to prevent their combining, and so that the ruler may have the benefit of a selection of opinions—if there is no other way of weighing them he may follow the majority.[154] This has nothing to do with *dharma*. The ancient texts recommending *sabhyas* to be of an uneven number did indeed have to do with *dharma*, but it will be remembered[155] that the question was upon what basis a joint opinion (*vyavasthā*) should be tendered to the judge: he could select the minority view if he was aware of it; at any rate some resolution of possibly conflicting opinions was facilitated. Our evidence does not (see below) allow us to suppose that a minority opinion was even formally tendered to him.

A discordant note creeps in with Mitra-miśra.[156] He distinctly authorizes the judge to follow the majority of pandits' opinions even in any obviously *dharma* context. During the early British period the court pandits were usually two in number. Yet numbers of pandits were drummed up to support the cases of litigants, obviously in the hope that the judge would select a well-supported opinion. The explanation for the outlook evidenced both by Mitra-miśra in the seventeenth century and in the early British period seems to be this: if the foreign judge, who had no discretion or ability to adjust *vyavasthās* in a comprehensive cultural survey of the problem, was permitted only to follow a consensus, there was the greatest likelihood that a hierarchy would develop amongst the pandits, and corruption and manipulation would result, and the *śāstra* itself would suffer. A Hindu judge would be a catalyst of consensus, but a Muslim or Christian judge would be at a loss. It is notorious that foreign judges, not conversant with the local culture, are manipulated by 'experts'.[157] Thus Mitra-miśra, himself manipulating the *smṛti* texts which he inherited, sensibly provided that discordant opinions might be tendered to the judge, so that he could make a politic choice. Practical in the hands of a Muslim, who was, at least, an Indian, the notion infuriated the British, for whom certainty (no matter how perverse) seemed essential.[158] No understanding of the process, or its rationale, was ever arrived at during the British period. However, Hindu as well as Muslim judges could employ Mitra-miśra's precept, if they wished, secure in the knowledge that whichever opinion they followed, majority or minority, the result could be *dharma*. One is authorized to follow the majority, not compelled to do so. It would be going a little far to suggest that here we have the beginnings of an infiltration of egalitarian irresponsibility into the ascertainment of *dharma*.

Uttaramerūr takes us back to a much earlier century. Elections, or at least appointments to committees took place and these made decisions.[159] Was voting known? Possibly. But it was equally possible that acclamation was used. We do know that there were qualifications for having a voice, but we do not know how quickly and by what procedure decisions were arrived at. That decisions were made formally by majority is unlikely, but even if it occurred, Uttaramerūr's constitution was an oligarchy of shareholders who were theoretically equal, and there is no suggestion that the moral or other qualifications for membership of the committees was itself taken out of the grasp of *dharma* as interpreted by experts.

All the evidence confirms that mere numbers could never determine any issue in which abstract duty came to be defined. In that definition the wisdom of past generations was brought to bear by specialists whose conscious function was not that of legislation but pronouncement. They did not innovate—they were mouthpieces. The prestige of such a method of ascertaining duty is evidenced even today by the popularity of *dharma* pronounced by traditional orthodox leaders, public recitals of scripture, and allusions to such criteria in nostalgic speeches and articles by public men. That they are not *articulate* in public life, however, is all too evident.

The law enacted by Parliament and the State legislatures has little or no claim to correspond with *dharma*, or with the *shariat* of the Muslim population. Indeed much of it (e. g. birth-control programmes) is flatly opposed to *dharma*. But the forces pressing upon the individual still create a 'duty' which transcends individual-centred prudence. The society is still 'duty-orientated' rather than 'right-orientated'. Why, otherwise, do men enter into arranged marriages in the face of constant romantic encouragement from all media of entertainment? The crisis of duty-discovery in modern India arises from the absence of prestige-figures whose own claim to authority can be based *both* upon a self-validating scripture *and* upon state patronage. Perhaps such figures will be called forth by India's pains, and they will write (like Dayananda Sarasvati) their own scriptures. But they must beware of introducing novelties, however much of the ancient culture they discard. Medhātithi's attitude remains as truthful as it was a millennium ago, *viz.* that only prolonged acceptance by generations of the pious and the good can validate a *smṛti*, and a man of these days, sticking never so close to traditional wisdom and even affecting respectable anonymity, cannot attain authority by his own endeavour.

Notes

[1]*Shorter Oxford English Dictionary*, 3rd edn., 1947, meaning 4.

[2]*Ibid.*, meaning 1.

[3]Useful bibliographies are given with the widely divergent and equally interesting articles here listed: T. V. Smith in E.R.A. Seligman, (ed.), *Encyclopaedia of the Social Sciences* V (1937) *s. v.* 'Duty'; H. Barker in J. Hastings (ed.), *Encyclopaedia of Religion and Ethics* V (1912), *s. v.*; M. Mothersill in P. Edwards (ed.), *Encyclopaedia of Philosophy* II (1967), s. v.; H.L.A. Hart in D. L. Sills (ed.), *International Encyclopaedia of the Social Sciences* IV (1968), *s. v.* (especially strong on legal duties).

[4]*strī-buddher asthiratvāt* (Manu VIII. 77). [The editor feels constrained to register an objection.]

[5]Hemādri, *Caturvarga-cintāmaṇi*, *Prāyaścitta*, IV. 480.

[6]Nārada III. 2. Manu VIII. 18 with Govindarāja. Kane, *History of Dharmaśāstra* (hereafter 'HD'), III, Poona, 1946, p. 274.

[7]Derrett, *Dharmaśāstra and Juridical Literature*, Wiesbaden, 1973, 2 n.l. B. Bhattacharya, 'Hindu Conception of Dharma in the Fourteenth Century', *Ind. Cult.* 6 (1925), pp. 67-70. V. A. Ramaswami Sastri, 'Dharma—its Definition and Authority', *J. Gang. Jha Res. Inst.* 7 (1970), pp. 29-42. U. N. Ghoshal, 'The Relation of the Dharma Concept to the Social and Political Order in Brahmanical Canonical Thought', *J. Bih. Or. Res. S.* 38 (1952), pp. 190-202. D. H. H. Ingalls 'Authority and Law in ancient India', *J. A. O. S. Suppl.* 17 (1954), pp. 34-35; A. B. Creel, '*Dharma* as an Ethical Category relating to Freedom and Responsibility', *Philosophy East & West*, 22/2, 1972, pp. 155-68.

[8]Mahābhārata (hereafter 'MBh'), *Vanaparva*, Bombay edn., 313.117 (crit. edn. III, app. 1, p. 1089). Quoted by Viśvarūpa, prooemium to Yājñavalkya I. 9 (T. S. S., 1922, p. 28). Kane, HD III, 860; V. 1629. The word *mahājana* is a synonym for Brāhmaṇa (especially *agrahāra* Brahmins) in mediaeval inscriptions. In fact the St. Petersburg, Monier-Williams' and Apte's dictionaries offer 'public' 'mass of the people' as the meaning of *mahājana* here. The maxim is referred to as a *nyāya* (maxim) by Medhātithi in his comm. on Manu II.1, but Jha translates the word (I/1, 1920, 161) as 'great men'. *Mahājana* at Caṇḍeśvara, *Kṛtya-ratnākara* (Calcutta, 1925, 30) certainly means 'important people, great ones' (they alone determine which *smṛtis* are authentic [see below]. At Kālidāsa, *Kumāra-sambhava* V.70 the word is beautifully taken in that very sense by R. D. Karmarkar (*Kumārasambhava*,[2] 1951, 86, 281). In O. Böhtlingk, *Indische Sprüche* (St. Petersburg, 1870-3), Spr. 2145 gives the singular in the sense of 'great men'. In MBh. XII. 115, 14 *mahātmane* is significantly read in variants *mahādhane* (rich) and *mahājane*, meaning, unquestionably, 'in the case of an important person' (cf. P. C. Ray, *Mahābhārata* (12) Calcutta, 1890, pp. 369-70) MBh. V. 33, 95 is very significant: *deśācārān samayāñ jāti-dharmān bubhūṣate yas tu parāvara-jñaḥ | sa tatra tatrādhigataḥ sadaiva mahājan-asyādhipatyaṃ karoti||*, 'He who seeks to confirm the customs of countries, (local) agreements, and *dharmas* of castes, being acquainted with traditional lore; he, wherever he goes, perpetually achieves the supreme status of the great man.' Since this verse is precisely in our area, and the verses above and

below it (*vv.* 94, 96) place the meaning beyond doubt (cf. H. Fauche, *Le Mahābhārata* V, Paris, 1866, p. 470) I take this as conclusive, though instances such as Spr. 522 (*ekaḥ pāpāni kurute phalam bhuṅkte mahājanaḥ*) could conceivably be cited in the other sense. *Mahājana* also equals *śiṣṭa* at Anantarāma, *Sahānumaraṇa-viveka* III.9. A more cynical view is that money or power determine what is right: MBh. II.62, pp. 14-15 (crit.); cf. *Rāmāyaṇa* (Bombay edn.), VI. 83, pp. 35-36. *Dharma* (the idea of duty) may respond to circumstances: MBh. XII. 79.32 (crit. edn.) ('...because of the operation of place and time it acquires the character of the country and the era.').

[9]Āp. 1.7.20, 6-8; II.11.29, 14. The remaining duties are to be learnt from women or men of any caste (29,15; cf. *Ibid*, 11).

[10]G. Jha, *Hindu Law in its Sources* I, Allahabad, 1930, p. 37. The theme is very common, especially in the MBh.

[11]Manu IV, 178.

[12]MBh.I.187-188 (crit. edn.), Kane, HD II, pp. 554-6. N. C. Sen-Gupta, *Evolution of Ancient Hindu Law*, London, 1953, p. 79. Drupada claimed that Yudhiṣṭhira's proposal was *loka-veda-viruddham adharmam*, 'sin, repugnant to the general practice and the Veda' (note order of words).

[13]Tait. Sam. VI.6.4, 3; Ait. Br. XII. 11.

[14]See n. 6 above.

[15]Manu VIII. 10; Yājñavalkya II. 2; Nār. III. 5; Bṛhaspati, K. V. R. Aiyangar (ed.), Baroda, 1941, I, 62; (L. S. Joshi, *Dharmakośa* (hereafter 'Dh.k.') 53. Further references at Kane, HD III, 273.

[16]Manu II. 20, VIII. 46, XI. 83-4, XII. 113. Vasiṣṭha I.39-41. MBh. XII. 91.19.

[17]Manu X. 127-8.

[18]Āp. II. 11.29,5.

[19]Kane (ed.), Kātyāyana, pp. 58-9.

[20]Śūdraka, *Mṛcchakaṭika*, Act IX. See G. Jha (ed.), Medhātithi on Manu VIII. 157. H. S. Ursekar, 'An Ancient Murder Trial', (1968) 1 Madras Law Journal, Journal section, 8-16. Kane, HD III, 279-80.

[21]MBh. V. 35, 49; Nārada-smṛti (ed. Jolly), *sabhā-lakṣaṇa* 18 (trans. Jolly, S. B. E. xxxiii, 188a, p. 40.).

[22]Vijñāneśvara, *Mitākṣarā* on Yājñ. 11.2 (Bombay edn., p. 114); Devaṇṇabhaṭṭa, *Smṛticandrikā* II, p. 17.

[23]Manu VIII. 10 with Medh. (one or two will not do).

[24]Below, n. 29.

[25]Ed. Aiyangar, I.59 (Dh. k., 52); cf. I.64.

[26]Mitra-miśra, *Vīramitrodaya*, *Vyavahāra-prakāśa* (1932), 27: not more than seven nor less than three.

[27]But see n. 23 above. Manu VIII. 20 can conceivably be read to permit one assessor to act. *Śāstra-sabhya-virodhe* (i.e. where *śāstras* conflict, *sabhyas* disagree or the latter disagree with the former) the king is entitled to decide for himself: Bṛhaspati, (ed.) Aiyangar, IX, 7 (*lect, var.*)

[28]Yājñavalkya II. 185.

[29]Aparārka (Poona edn., 599) using Gautama XI. 25 (S. B. E.ii, 237; Dh. k. 68) which originally refers to discrepancies between testimonies.

[30]Udyotakarācārya, *Nyāya-vārtikam* (Ben. Skt. Ser., 1916), I.1.14, p. 76.

[31]*Smṛti* references assembled at S. C. Banerji, 'Glossarial index....', *A. Bh. Or. Res. In.* 40 (1959), p. 139. *Lakṣmīdhara, Kṛtyakalpataru, Brahmacāri-kāṇḍa* 35-44 (*parṣal-lakṣaṇam*). A. S. Nataraja Ayyar, *Mīṃāmsā Jurisprudence*, Allahabad, 1952, pp. 63-8. For the *pariṣad* in penance cases see S. C. Banerjee (sic.) 'Prāyaścitta..', *J. G. J. R. I.* 7 (1950), 213 ff. at 255-6.

[32]Vijñāneśvara, *Mitākṣarā* on Yājñ. I.1.

[33]Kane, HD II, 969. K. V. Rangaswami, Aiyangar, *Rajadharma*, Adyar, 1941, pp. 99-100 (referring to Lakṣmīdhara, *K. K. T. Brahmacāri-kāṇḍa*, introd., pp. 39-40 [inaccurate in places]).

[34]Manu XI. 118; *ibid.*, pp. 82-5.

[35]Parāśara VIII. pp. 28-9. Kane, HD II, p. 970.

[36]Gaut. XXVIII. pp. 48-51; Manu XII. 111-12. Kane, HD II, 966ff. Devala, quoted in the *Prāyaścittasāra* (Kane, HD IV, 86) says that the *sabhā* (i.e. *pariṣad*) must speak unanimously (*ekavākyatayā*). Hence the actual number is not so important. On unanimity see Nār. III. 17 (Kane, HD III. pp. 274-5).

[37]Kane, HD II, 968, took Bṛhaspati cited in the *Parāśara-mādhavīya* p. 218, which literally applies to trials, to apply equally to *pariṣads*. Aṅgiras. quoted by Aparārka, p. 23 supports this.

[38]References at Kane, HD, II, p. 968.

[39]Baudhāyana I. 1.13; *Matsya-purāṇa* 143, 27; *Vāyu-purāṇa* 57, 112.

[40]Recognized without hesitation by Medhātithi on Manu II. 6 (trans. Jha, *ubi. cit.*, p. 204).

[41]On the Bṛh. Up. IV. 3.2 (Kane, *ubi cit.*). See Kane, HD pp. 971-4. However, Aparārka on Yājñ. I.9 (p. 23) agrees: *eko' pi pariṣat-kāryakara*, i.e. chairman and 'deputy'.

[42]Vācaspati-miśra was himself called a *pariṣad* (15th cent.). Epigraphia Indica 37 (1968) No. 50 (iii), p. 287 (A.D. 1054) gives particulars of a *dharmamantrī*. D. C. Sircar, 'Dharmādhikaraṇa and dharmādhikārin', *Purāṇa* 6/2 (1964), 445-50.

[43]Kane, HD II, pp. 972-4.

[44]Vijñaneśvara, *Mitāksarā* on Yajn. III. 300 quotes a *smṛti* to the effect that in minor sins a *pariṣad* shall consist of fifty, in others a hundred, but in 'mortal sins' a thousand. He adds that this merely serves to relate the size of the council to the gravity of the sin, since the text quoted cannot be allowed to contradict Manu and others. He is supported by Aṅgiras cited by Aparārka on Yājñ. I (p. 23). It is difficult to know what to make of the undoubted rule that *pariṣads* for the purgation of Kṣatriyas, Vaiśyas, and Śūdras are double, triple, and quadruple those required for Brahmin offenders. (Lakṣmīdhara, *ubi cit.*, p. 41).

[45]See n. 36 above.

[46]As at *Queen* v. *Sri Vidya Sankara*, Ind. Law Rep. (1887) 6 Mad. 382, 384; also Jagadguru Sri Sankaracharya Swamigal in T. R. Venkatarama Sastri and the same, 'Answer to the Questionnaire issued by the Hindu Law Committee', (1941) 1 Madras L. J., Journal section, p. 112-37.

[47]Derrett, cited at n. 7 above.

[48]Gaut. XI. 31; Āp. I. 7.20.9; II. 2.2.5,7; Vas. I.2; Atri-saṃhitā 16. For

the ostensible motives of the *śāstra* see Derrett, *Religion, Law and the State in India*, London, 1968, esp. ch. 4; the same in K. Zweigert, (ed.), *International Encyclopaedia of Comparative Law* II/1, Hamburg, 1974.

[49]See last citation above. The theme is generally handled in MBh. XII. 90-91.

[50]Yājñ. II.21; Kāty. 32; Nār. Introd. I.37. *Mānasollāsa* I. ii.94-5 (ed., Shama Sastry). R. C. Hazra, 'Kauṭilya Studies', *Our Heritage* 11/2, 1963, pp. 59-66.

[51]Gaut. I.1-3 (4).

[52]Baudh. I.1.1, 1-7.

[53]Manu II.1. For *hṛdayen-* see MBh. XII. 130-18.

[54]Manu II.6, following Gaut. I.1-2. See Jha, *op. cit.*, pp. 40-42.

[55]Jha, *ubi cit.*, pp. 37-40; the same, *Manusmṛti*: *Notes III*, Calcutta, 1929 31-34.

[56]Jha, *Notes III* (above), pp. 34-36. Illustration: whether a son's thread ceremony should be performed at the age of 7 or 8 (Vijñāneśvara on Yājñ. 1.7). The Skt. for 'conscience' is *antarapū(pu)ruṣa* (Manu VIII. 85d), which is the equivalent of *svakṣetra-jña* (*ibid.*, 96). Conscience or self-satisfaction is the test of the adequacy of penance according to Manu XI. 233 (234); and bears the quality of Goodness (*sattvaguṇa*): *ibid.* XII.37. See K. V. Rangaswami Aiyangar, *Rājadharma*, Adyar, 1941, pp. 52-3. L. Rocher, *J. A. O. S.* 92/3, 1972, 422 Kumārila, *Vārtika* on Jaimini, I.iii.7.

[57]Manu II.9. Laghu-Viṣṇu-*smṛti* II.17.

[58]Medhātithi on Manu I.9; V. 13. *Nṛsiṃha-prasāda, Saṃskāra*, (unpublished) at Jha, *Notes III* (above), 21. Kane, HD III, 827-9; V, 1259-60. An *interpretation* which has no authority should be ignored: Medhātithi on Manu VIII. 370.

[59]Commentaries summarized by Jha, *ibid.* pp. 18-26.

[60]Manu II.10.

[61]*Ibid.*, 12. Yājñ. I.7 lists Veda, *smṛti*, *sadācāra*, what is agreeable to one's self, *saṃyak-sankalpajah, kamah*, 'desire born of virtuous resolve—these four operate only if not repugnant to the *śāstra*.

[62]Manu II.18.

[63]Brahmāvarta, Madhyadeśa, Āryāvarta: *Madanapārijāta*, 11-12 Jha, *Notes III*, 29, 47-50). Paiṭhīnasi (a late source) takes India as one for the purpose of *dharma*. Viṣṇu LXXIV. 4 takes Āryāvarta to comprehend all regions in which the *varṇa* system operates.

[64]Manu II.20.

[65]Tait. Up. I.11 (*saṃyag-darśinaḥ*) quoted at *Vīramitrodaya, Paribhāṣāprakāśa* 9. Note the text *brāhmanair dharma-mūlatvam* (var. lect. *brāhmaṇo veda-mūlas syāt* implausibly attributed to Bṛhaspati (ed., Aiyangar, Saṃ. 226, p. 263; also Lakṣmīdhara, *op. cit.*, *Brahmacāri-k.*, 262).

[66]Baudh, I.1.1, 5-6; Vas. VI. 43. One who does not accept the Vedas, the *śāstra* or even the sayings of the old (*vṛddha-vākyam*) can never be an authority in matters of *dharma*: Yama at Caṇḍeśvara, *Kṛtya-ratnākara*, 40.

[67]Trans. Jha, *Notes III.*, 29. On this point see MBh. XII. 252 (crit. edn.). It is from *śiṣṭas* that one discovers what verses to recite for a penance

(Bhāruci on Manu XI. 254).

[68]P. V. Kane, *Hindu Customs and Modern Law*, Bombay, 1950.

[69]Dressing in blankets (Kullūka); tying of bracelets (Rāghavānanda, Devaṇṇabhaṭṭa, Mitra-miśra).

[70]Gaut. XI.20-21; Vas. I.5; Kāty. 46. Kullūka on Manu VIII. 41; Bhāruci on Manu VIII. 6; Haradatta on Āp. II.6.15-1. *Saṃskara-mayūkha*, 1. Cf. *Mitākṣarā* on Yājñ. 1.7.

[71]Devaṇṇa-bhaṭṭa, cited and explained at Derrett, RLSI, pp. 209-10. Cf. Haradatta on Gaut. XI. 1, and Medhātithi on Manu VII. 13. Kāty. 38.

[72]Kāty. 41-42. Mitra-miśra, *Vīramitrodaya*, *Vyavahāra-prakāśa*, 89-90. Derrett, RLSI, 162 n.2. Kauṭilya, *Arthaśāstra* II. 7,2 (trans. Kangle, 93).

[73]Quoted at Devaṇṇa-bhaṭṭa, *op. cit.*, p. 58.

[74]Baudh. I. 1.2, 5-8 (*tatra tatra deśa-prāmāṇyam eva syāt*), Bṛh. II.31 Aiyangar, I. 130). Kane, HD III, pp. 857-63.

[75]R. Lingat, *Classical Law of India* (hereafter 'CLI'), pp. 196, 200-2, citing Nīlakaṇṭha and Mitra-miśra.

[76]Manu I. 108. Vas. VI. 1-9 praises *ācarā* extravagantly. Derrett, RLSI, 156 n. 2. Lingat, CLI, pp. 197-8.

[77]Referring to the previous verse in which 'eternal custom' of the four castes is added as a matter taught in the Manusmṛti besides 'the whole of *dharma*' and the good and bad qualities of actions.

[78]Manu VIII.41. Bhāruci explains that laws of public bodies (sāmayika-) relating to the grazing of cattle, protection of water, etc., are involved if they do not (already) have the *śāstra* as their authority. The king must not despise the enactments of public bodies, lest the Rule of the Fish (i.e. of the jungle) prevail. Gaut. XI. 20-1; Āp. II.15.1; Baudh. I.2, 1-8; Vass. I.17; XIX. 7; Bṛh. II. 28 (cf. king's duty to acknowledge and supervise their judicial acts: *ibid.*, 17-19, S. B. E. 33, 348-9); Kāty. 48-50; Śukranīti IV. 5, 89-91.

[79]Manu VIII. 42. Similarly Atri-saṃhitā 25. Bhāruci comments on Manu: 'This commends maintenance of laws made by public bodies'.

[80]Manu VIII. 46. Bhāruci instances eating certain birds as a practice *not* to be encouraged: other customs of the good in one place (not repugnant to the Veda or *smṛti*) may be introduced by royal order in another district. Cf. Gaut. XI. 20; Ap. II. 15.1.

[81]Manu VII. 203. Also Yājñ. I.342-3; Viṣṇu II.42.

[82]Derrett. RLSI, ch. 5.

[83]*Kāla-mādhava* (Calcutta, 1890), pp. 64-5.

[84]Āp. I.1.1, 1-2; 2.7, 31.

[85]N. 77 above.

[86]*Sarvān dharma-śāstroktān sāmayikāṃś ca dharmān vetti* (*Mitākṣarā* on Yājñ. 11-3); *dharma-śāstra-samayācāra-viruddhena mārgena parair ādharṣitaḥ* (*ibid.*, *5*). At Manu VIII. 41 *jānapada* equals *sāmayika* according to Bhāruci (n. 70 above). Note *samayān* in MBh. V. 33, 95, cited above, p. 24 n. 5.

[87]Derrett, RLSI, ch. 7. See also Epigraphia Carnatica IV Gund. 32 (A.D. 1372); South Indian Inscriptions, 9/1 (1939), no. 378. Instances of conventions include South Ind. Ins. 10 (1948), no. 221, 612; Mysore Arch. Rep. 1927, 66.

[88]Bṛhaspati (at Aparārka 794, etc.) quoted by Kane, HD III, 156-7.

[89]Nārada and Kauṭilya : See Dh. K., 12, 69, 91. Derrett RLSI, 148. Kaut. II. 1.39-40 (with Kangle's trans.). H. Scharfe, *Untersuchungen zur Staatsrechtslehre des Kauṭalya,* (sic) Wiesbaden, 1968, p. 226.

[90]At *J. As.* 1962, pp. 489-503; CLI, pp. 255-6. See also L. Rocher, *Orientalia Gandensia,* 1 (1964), 217 ff. 224. Also K. V. Rangaswami Aiyangar, *Introduction to Vyavahārakaṇḍa* of *Kṛtyakalpataru,* Baroda, 1958, pp. 7-9.

[91]Kāty 35-39, 41-44.

[92]Derrett, RLSI, 154-5.

[93]Ed., Aiyangar, I.18-21, IX.7; trans. Jolly, II.18, 24-7.

[94]Kāty. 44-45.

[95]Kāty. 47. No decision made on *either* footing should be reversed.

[96]Manu IV. 176; Yājñ. I. 156; Viṣṇu LXXI. 85.

[97]Derrett, 'Showing a big bull...., *A. Bh. Or. Res. In.* 48-9 (1968), pp. 45-53,

[98]Lingat, CLI, 189-90, 252.

[99]Derrett, *ubi cit.,* n. 7 above, p. 5.

[100]Mahadev Desai, *The Gita according to Gandhi,* Ahmedabad, 1956, pp. 133-4. The word 'treasure' is a reminiscence of Matt. xiii. 62.

[101]*Mediaeval Panorama,* Cambridge, 1949, chh. 32,35. Sir Thomas More took Matt. vii. 15 to refer to the Waldenses (*English Works,* 262, 280, 282, cf. 355) and Matt. xvi. 18 as repelling the royal supremacy. 1 Chr. xvi, 22 was cited for the 'benefit of clergy' (total immunity from secular jurisdiction) (More, *Richard III* : the sanctuary controversy). For a tendentious quotation of the Veda to clinch a practical interpretation see Maskarī on Gau. VII. 25.

[102]Coulton, *ubi cit.,* ch. 49.

[103]Above, p 35 n 64

[104]Such a response was forthcoming when the B. N. Committee (on reform of Hindu Law) interviewed witnesses in the Punjab. *Report of the Hindu Law Committee,* Delhi, 1947, pp. 7-8. India was always more tolerant than Europe, but the same point of view was expressed by Bishop Stephen Gardiner to the bible-translator, J. Rogers (1955) : 'No, thou canst prove nothing by Scripture, the Scripture is dead, it must have a lively expositer'. Rogers : 'No, the Scripture is alive'. Rogers was burnt in the presence of his wife and eleven children. J. Foxe, *Acts and Monuments,* London, 1841, vi. 596. The view that God has abdicated the right of interpretation to the sages and rabbinical decisions are 'binding' on him as well is good Talmudic law (Bab. Tal. *Baba Meṣia* 59b).

[105]Derrett (ed.), *Introduction to Legal Systems,* London, 1968. Some people from India's frontier territories do not, and possibly did not, understand transcendenttal support for justice and right, nor connect religion with morality : C.von Fürer-Haimendorf, *Morals and Merit,* London, 1967, 79, 216.

[106]A close counterpart to reformation bible-text-torturing is provided by a document in the Madras archives : *Petition from the Panchalars from Salem to the Board of Revenue, Madras, 17 Feb. 1840.* They declare that the Vedas and their *śāstras* say that they sprung from the faces of Panchamuga (kha) Brahma. They are artisans and smiths. They alone should be designated Brahmins. They alone were priests to the Hindus. Their *śāstras* show that the Rishis of the Brahmins were born of low-caste people or followed low occupations. Brahmins are a mongrel tribe. Brahmins prejudiced uneducated kings against the

Panchalars. They ill-treat Panchalars still. 'That the foregoing statements relating to our right to the priesthood be duly investigated into and decided.' (A voice direct from the Middle Ages). See n. 120 below.

[107]Jdg. xii. 6. J. Milton, *Samson Agonistes*, pp. 287-9.

[108]Derrett, 'Rulers and ruled in India', *Gouvernés et Gouvernants* I (Rec. Soc. Jean Bodin, XXII), Brussels, 1969, pp. 417-45.

[109]'The Concept of Secularism', *Indian and Foreign Review* 6/12 (1969), pp. 15-16.

[110]Derrett, 'Modes of *Sannyāsīs*. . . .*J.A.O.S.* 94/(1974), pp. 65-72.

[111]See the stories in *Queen* v. *Sri Vidya* (above, p. n. 39) and *Madhavrao* v. *Raghavendrarao* Ind. Law Rep. [1946] Bom. 375. H. M. Sadasivaiah, *Comparative Study of Two Virasaiva Monasteries*. ., Mysore, 1967.

[112]Kane, HD II, 906 ff., 948 ff.

[113]The leading authorities are cited in *Ramchandra* v. *Gavalaksha* (1972) 75 Bombay Law Reporter 668.

[114]Derrett RLSI, index, *s. v.* 'excommunication'. C. von Fürer-Haimendorf, *op. cit.*, index s.v. 'excommunication'.

[115]Notably temple-entry and untouchability. Derrett RLSI, 453ff.

[116]Y. T. Gune, *Judicial System of the Marathas*, Poona, 1953, pp. 39, 49, 66-7.

[117]Vācaspati-Miśra, *Vyavahāra-cintāmaṇi* (Gent, 1956). Kane, HD III, 270ff.

[118]V. K. Rajwade, (ed.), *Marāṭhyaṃcyā Itihāsācīṃ sādhaneṃ* 15, no. 6 (dated equivalent of A.D. 1610), summarized by Gune, *op. cit.*, 151-2. See an article at (1914) 15 Bombay Law Reporter, Journal, 97ff, also Smith and Derrett, J.A.O.S., 75/3, 1975, pp. 417-23.

[119]V. Rāghavan, 'The Vaiśyavaṃśasudhākara...' in *Volume Presented to Sir Denison Ross*, Bombay, 1939, pp. 234-40. Kane, HD III, 252 n.

[120]Derrett, 'Two Inscriptions concerning the Status of Kammālas...' *K. A. Nilakanta Sastri 80th Birthday Felicitation Volume*, London, 1971, 32-55. Lingat, CBI, 273-4. Derrett, *History of Indian Law* (in *Handbuch der Orientalistik*) Leiden, 1973, 23nn. 'Mahazar' at J. R. Gharpure's article at (1905) 7 Bombay Law Reporter, Journal Section, 2ff, at 20-23 (A.D. 1689).

[121]See n. 118 above.

[122]See n. 110 above.

[123]Above, p. 31, n. 40.

[124]All examples referred to in nn. 109-111 above, also n. 101 and Rajwade, *op. cit.*, 18, no. 8 (A.D. 1642), Gune, *op. cit.*, 66 n. 63.

[125]Derrett, RLSI, ch. 9.

[126]L. Rocher, 'Indian Reactions to Anglo-Hindu Law', J.A.S.O., 92/3, 1972, 419-24.

[127]*Rangaswamy* v. *Nagamma* A.I.R. 1973 Mys. 178. Furer-Haimendorf (*cit. sup.*), 164-5 expresses the view that *panchayats* are still greatly esteemed (for their role in modern litigation see Derrett, RLSI, 287nn, 358n, also *Sitanna* v. *Marivada* A.I.R. 1934, P. C. 105, 107) but does he generalize from marginal peoples?

[128]References at Derrett, RLSI, 218 n. 1. Cf. *ibid.*, 219. *Op. cit.*, p. 435 n. 26.

[129]Law Commission of India. *Fourteenth Report* (*Reform of Judicial Administration*), 2 vols, Delhi, 1958. Justice K. S. Hegde at 1972 Kerala Law Times, Journal, 51 (in one High Court there were 85,000 cases pending).

[130]Remarks in speeches by P. B. Gajendragadkar: V. D. Mahajan, *Chief Justice Gajendragadkar*, Delhi, 1966.

[131]Kāty. 81. Yama, cited by Vācaspati-miśra, *Vyavahāra-cintāmaṇi*, 41. The King's jurisdiction fell between appeal and review. Mitra-miśra, *Vīramitrodaya, Vyavahāra-prakāśa*, 337. Kane, HD III, 385-6. Nārada was actually cited and relied on in *Dulari* v. *Vallabdas* I.L.R. (1888) 13 Bom. 126.

[132]See Kane, HD III, pp. 385-56.

[133]Attributed to the late Supreme Court Justice T. L. Venkatarama Iyer by Advocate R. V. Iyer (Tanjore).

[134]H. M. Seervai, 'The Fundamental Rights Case', (1973) 75 Bombay Law Reporter, Journal section, 47-88.

[135]Act 11 of 1864 referred to at Derrett, RLSI, 243, 296, 303n, 317.

[136]Gobhila III. 148-9. Kane, HD III, 870. B. Bhattacharya, *Kalivarjyas*, Calcutta, 1943, 172 n. 2. Manu VIII. 73 (on witnesses) is applied by the commentator Bhāruci to cases where *injunctions* conflict.

[137]Jaimini, *Mīmāṃsā-sūtra* XII. ii, 22 (trans. with Śabara's commentary, G. Jha, iii, Baroda, 1936, p. 2305).

[138]S. Fuchs, *Children of Hari*, Vienna, 1950, pp. 34-7; A. H. Somjee, *Voting-behaviour in an Indian Village* Baroda, 1959; A. C. Mayer, *Cast and Kinship in Central India*, London, 1960, pp. 119-20, pp. 275-8; R. Retzlaff, *Village Government in India*, Bombay, 1962, pp. 24-5; L. I. and S. H. Rudolph, *The Modernity of Tradition*, Chicago, 1967, p. 188. See also E. W. Martin, *The Tyranny of the Majority*, London, 1961. *Pars major vincit meliorem* (Livy XXI. 4 quoted by S. Gardiner, *Letters*, [ed.], J. A. Muller, 1933, 136). Coulton, *op. cit.*, pp. 26-32.

[139]*Narain Das* 2 Select Reports (S. D. A. Bengal), 192 (1815). *Juro Ram Das* v. *Govinda Deb* 12 Cal. Law J. 497, 8 Ind. Cases 124. In 1827 the British judge at Sholapur convened the caste and 'found a large majority of its members' in favour of the claim of a *dāsiputra*, numbers being counted, but respectable persons were found in the minority (related at *Gopal* v. *Hanmant*, 1879, 3 Bom. 273, 284-5). The vote of the majority is given effect to as the law: *Pragji* v. *Govind* I.L.R. (1887) 11 Bom. 533; *Lalji* v. *Walji* (1895) 19 Bom. 507 (the court does not decline to give effect to the expressed wishes of the majority of a caste, which the minority seek to set to naught); *Thiagarayya* v. *Krishnasami* (1892) 15 Mad. 214 (a minority may be a faction and incompetent to challenge the caste's decision).

[140]*Tahsil Naidu* v. *Kulla Naidu* A.I.R. 1970 S. C. 1673; *C. Sankara Viswanadha* v. *C. Ramalakshmamma* A.I.R. 1972 An. P. 270.

[141]In Letter No. 12 of 4 Feb. 1856 the Marquis of Dalhousie speaking of the intended future mode of administration of Oudh, expressed the intention that 'everybody shall count as one, and nobody as more than one'. J. Raj, *The Mutiny and British Land Policy in North India* 1856-1868, London, A.P.H., 1965, 15. The Portuguese were also at fault in their conception of village government: J.H. da Cunha Rivara, *Arch. Port. Or.*, facs. 5, p. 1418 n. (A. D. 1714). For the

Anglo-Indian case-law see above n. 139, also *Venkatachala* v. *Sambasiva* A.I.R. 1927 Mad. 465, 467 ('It is but reasonable that in communal matters the majority should have the final say.').

[142]Kane, HD III, 467 n. 806 (partners).

[143]J. P. Sharma, *Republics in Ancient India* c. *1500 B C-500 B C*, Leiden, Brill, 1968 (see T. Burrow, B.S.O.A.S. 34/2, 1971, 416-17). S. Mukherji, *Republican Trends in Ancient India*, Delhi, 1969, (See W.D. O'Flaherty B.S.O.A.S. 34/1, 1971, 208).

[144]*Hindu Polity*, Bangalore, 1955, pp. 86-97. The question whether early oligarchies actually decided by majority is ventilated by Sharma, *op. cit.*, pp. 198-201. Rhys Davids, *Cambridge History of India*, I (1922), pp. 176-7, relying on material cited below at n. 147, opined that majority decision was not used, arbitration by a council of referees being usual. W. W. Rockhill's notion, based on an unverified (and not contemporary) Tibetan text (*The Life of the Buddha*, London, 1884, 118-19), was that the Śākyas did vote and follow the majority. This is accepted, too eagerly, by A. S. Altekar, *State and Government in Ancient India*, 3rd edn., Patna, 1958, 131-2. Pliny, *Nat. Hist.* VI. 24.90 (Loeb edn., ii, 406) says that in Ceylon a man might be condemned to death by a majority of thirty royal counsellors (*plurium sententia*): what reliance can be placed on this is not clear.

[145]See below, nn. 146-152.

[146]Mahā-vagga II, 16.5 (S. B. E. 13, 1881, 165): four or five may protest, two or three may express their opinion, and one may determine (in his mind): 'I do not think this right'. Gokuldas De, *Democracy in Early Buddhist Saṃgha*, Calcutta, 1955, Bk. 2, ch. 2.

[147]Culla-vagga IV. 9 (S.B.E. 20, 1885); IV. 14.24 (*ibid.*, 54), See Vinaya-piṭaka IV. 207 (I.B. Horner, *Book of the Discipline* III, London, 1942, 153 and n. 6) for further references.

[148]*Chanda*, opinion, will, vote; *śalākā*, pin, ticket. On methods of vote-taking see Culla-vagga IV. 14.26 = Vin. ii 98f. Where opinions are against *dhamma* the majority can be ignored!

[149]Culla-vagga IV. 16.

[150]*Ibid.*, 17-20. The reopening of questions is always an offence: 16, 21, 24.

[151]*Ibid.*, 225.

[152]Culla-vagga IV. 10 = Vin. ii. 85 (Horner, 5, 11i).

[153]An alternative: an expedient project may overrule the majority. *tatra yad bhuyiṣṭāḥ kārya-siddhi-karam vā tat kuryāt* (*Arthaśāstra* I' 15, 29; trans. Kangle, 40). Jayaswal, *op. cit.*, 91 n. 14 points to *Arthaśāstra* II. 9, 16: village elders may decide boundary disputes by majority—but the passage shows that the opinion of the honest or of a referee (or referees), or a middle course, are alternatives to majority decision (*bahavaḥ, śucayo, 'numatā vā*); cf. III. 11, 39).

[154]*Nītivākyāmṛta* X. 68-71 (Bombay, 1923, 127-8). An uneven number leads to the sharpening of individual views, and the self-willed are held in check.

[155]Jayaswal, *op. cit.*, p. 91 n. 14, took Manu VIII. 10 too literally, assuming that majority decision was the rule.

[156] *Vīramitrodaya*, *Vyavahāra-prakāśa*, 27. He applies Jaimini (see p. 50 n. 137 above). So also Kamalākara, *Vivādatāṇḍava*, 123 (Dh. k. 48) relying, oddly, on Yājñ. II. 78 (witnesses' testimonies). Kane, HD III, 275.

[157] The position of the British in India until well into the nineteenth century was exactly foreshadowed by that of Romans administering justice in Greece in the first century: Philostratus, *Life of Appolonius* V. 36.

[158] Preface to F. W. Macnaghten, *Considerations of the Hindoo Law*, Serampur, 1824, vi.

[159] K. A. Nilakanta Sastri, *Studies in Cōla History and Administration*, Madras, 1932. Altekar, *op. cit.*, pp. 230-4. Kane, HD III. 156. Derrett, *ubi cit.*, p. 46 n. 120, at p. 437. F. Gros and R. Nagaswamy, *Uttaramerūr*, Pondichery, 1970.

The Concept of Dharma in *Artha* and *Kāma* Literature

FRIEDRICH WILHELM

Traditional Hindu society is based upon the three aims of life (*trivarga*), the foremost of which generally is *dharma*, which has been defined by Indian and western scholars as legal *and* moral duty.[1] The norms and precepts of *dharma* were expressed in scientific treatises (*dharmasūtras* and *dharmaśāstras*),[2] while the two other aims of life developed their own *śāstras*, too: the concept of *artha* (political and material profit), and the concept of *kāma*, (sensual desire). These two latter concepts answered practical needs of human life. Kings and warriors, but also merchants and courtezans, had to be attached to *artha*, whereas the married householder (*gṛhastha*) had to observe the requirements of *kāma*. However, the fulfilment of *artha* and *kāma* at the right time by the right people is regarded as an act of *dharma* in the *dharma* literature. The norms of *dharma* were not only diversified according to the four *varṇas* (classes) but also to the four *āśramas* (stages of life): the pupil (*brahmacārin*), the married householder (*gṛhastha*), the forest-dweller (*vānaprastha*) and the ascetic (*sannyāsin*). These four stages reconcile the tension between asceticism and the life of the householder. O'Flaherty[3] discusses the ambivalence of Hindu life and Hindu mythology, especially in the cult of Śiva, the strange ambiguity of passion (*kāma*) and asceticism (*tapas*), 'the pendulum (of extremes), whose animating force is the eternal paradox of the myths'.[4]

In one of his articles on India in the *New York Tribune*, Karl Marx[5] describes this ambiguity with literary appeal:

Hindostan is an Italy of Asiatic dimensions.... Yet, in a social

> point of view, Hindostan is not the Italy, but the Ireland of the East. And this strange combination of Italy and of Ireland, of a world of voluptuousness and of a world of woes, is anticipated in the ancient traditions of the religion of Hindostan. That religion is at once a religion of sensualist exuberance, and a religion of self-torturing asceticism, a religion of the Lingam and of the Juggernaut, the religion of the Monk, and of the Bayadere.

Apparently, Marx saw an ambivalence in Indian religion, when he wrote that religion is '*at once*...' but he seems to imply a juxtaposition of the world of voluptuousness and the world of woes.

Hermann Hesse dedicated a poem to Bhartṛhari, the author of the *Śṛṅgāraśataka* and the *Vairāgyaśataka* (besides the *Nītiśataka*) who is said to have become a monk seven times but to have returned again and again to worldly pleasures.

> Like you, forerunner and brother, I too go through life zigzagging between natural ways and spirit, today a wise man, tomorrow a fool, today intimate with god, tomorrow intensely devoted to the flesh. (Transl. A. L. Basham)[6]

We should not overestimate such literary sentiments and falsely generalize that 'zigzagging between natural ways and spirit' has been the characteristic feature of the Indians. Maybe more than elsewhere ambivalence played an important role in Indian religion and society, but there have also been trends which were merely ascetic or merely erotic or advocated a balanced attachment to the three aims of life.

One of the most extensive and possibly oldest discussions of the three aims (with *mokṣa*, release, as the fourth) is found in the Śāntiparvan of the *Mahābhārata* (XII, 161, Critical Edition). Yudhiṣṭhira asks his brothers,

> The course of the world rests upon *dharma*, *artha* and *kāma*. Which of these is the more important, which is the second and which is the last one?[7]

Vidura praises *dharma*, mentions *artha* as second and *kāma* as lowest of these three. Arjuna, however, declares *artha* to be the foremost while Nakula and Sahadeva acknowledge the importance of *artha* but modify it: '*Artha* when connected with *dharma* and *dharma* when combined with *artha* are like honey mixed with *ambrosia*'. In XII. 161 26 they argue that one should first attend to *dharma*, then to *artha* and last to *kāma*. Bhīmasena (XII. 161, 28-38) declares *kāma* the main principle of the *trivarga*, which is not even alleged by the *Kāmasūtra* (see below p. 72):

> One without *kāma* does not strive for *artha*, one without *kāma* does not wish for *dharma*; one without *kāma* is not striving for anything; therefore *kāma* is pre-eminent. (XII. 161, 28)[8]

Bhīmasena's hedonistic statements culminate in the recommendation that the king should enjoy beautiful women who are exhilarated by wine (XII. 161, 36). In the last stanza (XII. 161, 38), however, Bhīmasena argues, in variance with his former precepts, that *dharma*, *artha* and *kāma* are to be practised in the same way. We shall see that the Kauṭalīya *Arthaśāstra* mitigates its preference for *artha* by a comparable argumentation.

The Dharmarāja (i.e. Yudhiṣṭhira) reflects upon the words of his brothers, regarding them as false (*avitathā*). Yet in his speech (XII. 161, 41 ff.) he acknowledges all his brothers as *niścitadharmaśāstrāḥ* and as *viditapramāṇāḥ*. Yudhiṣṭhira preaches the fourth aim, *mokṣa* (release), which presupposes non-attachment to *artha, dharma* and *kāma* (XII. 161, 42), and he is approved by his brothers.

The debate reminds one of certain discussions in the Kauṭalīya *Arthaśāstra*,[9] where authentic views are presented in a fictitious style as the statements of legendary teachers. In the Kauṭalīya *Arthaśāstra*, too, the last place in the debate is the best. Like Kauṭalya there, Yudhiṣṭhira here winds up by giving his conclusive opinion. The discussion with Yudhiṣṭhira belongs to the Āpaddharmaparvan within the Śāntiparvan, and the sermon of release psychologically fits the frame of mind of the heroes after the great battle. Nevertheless we have to interpret the arguments of Arjuna in favour of *artha* and those of Bhīmasena in favour of *kāma* as authentic ones which were actually expressed by Indians in ancient times, especially by Kṣatriyas.

The introductory salutation of the *Kāmasūtra* is to *dharma*, *artha* and *kāma* (*dharmārthakāmebhyo namaḥ*), in the traditional sequence. The later Kokkaka starts his treatise with a stanza to Kāmadeva, and the *Arthaśāstra* bows to Śukra and Bṛhaspati.

Mahābhārata XII. 59 refers to a legendary treatise by Brahma himself on the *trivarga* and *mokṣa*, containing 100,000 chapters, which is said to have been reduced to 10,000 by Śaṅkara, to 5,000 by Indra, to 3,000 by Bṛhaspati, and to 1,000 by the Yogācārya Kāvya. The *Kāmasūtra* (I. 1) supports this legend to some extent, alleging that Prajāpati conceived 100,000 chapters on the *trivarga*; afterwards, the *dharma* portion of it was separately treated by Manu Svayambhūva, the *artha* portion by Bṛhaspati, and the *kāma* portion by Nandin (servant of Śiva). Only the last portion is explained at greater length: it was further reduced, divided into seven chapters treated by seven authorities and finally abridged by Vātsyāyana. There is no proof that a *trivarga* treatise ever did exist. It is more probable that manuals on the three aims of life were separately elaborated.

It goes without saying that all *dharma* treatises consider *dharma* as the fundamental aim of life, and even the norms of royal politics are treated in this literature as '*dharma* of the king' (*rājadharma*).

The *kāma* literature does not dispute the pre-eminence of *dharma*, but the most elaborate of the *artha* works, the Kauṭalīya *Arthaśāstra*, says clearly in 1, 7,6-7 (ed. Kangle):

> *artha eva pradhāna iti Kauṭilyaḥ; arthamūlau hi dharmakāmāv iti*
> Artha alone is the main thing, says Kauṭilya (alias Kauṭalya), for *dharma* and *kāma* have their roots in *artha*.

This statement is one of the few self-quotations of Kauṭalya in the *Arthaśāstra* which lacks a preceding quotation of another teacher. Obviously *iti Kauṭilya* is to emphasize the importance of the verdict. Preceding this statement we find the view that the king should attach himself to *kāma* without doing harm to *dharma* and *artha* and that over-attachment to one of the three aims hurts the other two (1, 7, 3-5). In later *artha* treatises (which prefer the denomination *nīti*) there is a tendency to reinstitute the priority of *dharma*. Thus we read in Kāmandakīya *Nītisāra* I. 51:

> *dharmād artho 'rthataḥ kāmaḥ kāmāt sukhaphalodayaḥ|ātmānaṃ*

hanti tau hatva yuktyā yo na niṣevate

From *dharma* proceeds *artha*, from *artha kāma* and from *kāma* comes the fruit of happiness. He destroys himself who does not reasonably attend to (these three) having destroyed these two (other aims).

The commentary (Jayamaṅgala) of Śaṅkarārya gives the explanation that by over-attachment to one of these three aims the other two are destroyed.

In the *Nītivākyāmṛta* of Somadeva the first chapter deals with *dharma*, the second with *artha* and the third with *kāma*. In III, 14 it is stated: *dharmārthakāmānām yugapatsamavāye pūrvaḥ garīyan.* (When *dharma*, *artha*, and *kama* coincide simultaneously, the one which precedes is weightier than the one which follows [trans. ed.]. In O. Botto's translation: 'Nell incontro simultaneo fra Legge morale e religiosa, ricchezza, amore, quello che precede è constantemente di maggior peso che il successivo'.[10] The next sentence, however, reveals the prerogative of *artha* under special circumstances (III, 15): 'Ove il tempopoi non consenta (di tener dietro a tutti e tre) è la riccezza (che predomina).'[11]

The *Bṛhaspati Sūtra* (=*Bārhaspatya Arthaśāstra*), (*ed.*) F. W. Thomas, writes in II, 5:

sarvathā laukāyatikam eva śāstram arthasādhanakāle; II, 6: kāpālikam eva kāmasādhane; II, 7: ārhataṃ dharme.

Universally the Lokāyata system of doctrine is alone to be followed at the time of acquiring gain; Only the Kāpālika as regards attainment of pleasure; The Ārhata in regard to right (transl. F.W. Thomas).

The statement in II, 5 is in line with the materialistic reputation of Bṛhaspati elsewhere. However, since Bṛhaspati II, 8-35 attacks the Laukāyatikas, the Kāpālikas etc. as detestable heretics, F.W. Thomas suspects II, 8-35 to be a later interpolation.[12] As the *Bṛhaspati Sūtra* is a late text we may argue that II, 8-35 are due to Brahmin revision and that II, 5-7 preserve the older traditional opinion of Bṛhaspati.

We notice that among the *artha* treatises only the Kauṭalīya *Arthaśāstra* 1, 7.6 f. emphasizes the general priority of *artha*. Nevertheless the same text enumerates in 1,3 the special duties of the four classes (*varṇas*) and of the four stages of life (*āśramas*) in conformity with the *dharma* literature. The *Arthaśāstra* supports the tradition of *dharma* if it stabilizes the security and welfare of the state. Before we discuss the deviations from *dharma* in the *Arthaśāstra*, we will examine the position of *dharma* and the other two aims of life in the *kāma* literature. In the *Kāmasūtra* of Vātsyāyana the presentation of the three aims of life (*trivarga*) is intertwined with that of the stages of life (which are not identical with the four *āśramas*) in the *trivarga* discussion of I,2.

Man should divide the 100 years of his life into three periods. In his childhood he should acquire knowledge etc. (which is part of *artha*, according to the definition of the *Kāmasūtra*), in his youth he should be attached to *kāma* and in old age to *dharma* and *mokṣa*.[13] Or he may attend them according to circumstances, which is explained by the commentary (Jayamaṅgala) as indicating that he may pursue in his childhood besides *artha* also *dharma*, in his youth besides *kāma* also *dharma* and *artha*, and in his old age also *artha* and *kāma*. The commentary discusses in full the nine possible combinations of the three aims of life: 1. *dharma* with *artha*, 2. *dharma* with *kāma*, 3, *artha* with *dharma*, 4. *artha* with *kāma*, 5. *kāma* with *dharma*, 6. *kāma* with *artha*, 7. *dharma* with *artha* and *kāma*, 8. *artha* with *dharma* and *kāma*, and 9. *kāma* with *dharma* and *artha*. *Dharma* is combined with *artha*, if one who wishes offspring goes to his legal but unloved wife at the proper time; *dharma* is combined with *kāma*, if one who wishes offspring goes to his legal and beloved wife at the proper time. In this way all nine cases are exemplified. The mutual dependence of the three aims is also relevant in case of over-attachment to any one of them. The *trivarga* discussion ends with the *śloka*:

> One should perform that action which fosters the three aims, or two or one of them, but not such an action which hurts one for the sake of the other two.

The commentary explains that by extraordinary liberality *dharma* hurts *artha* and *kāma*, and by excessive penance one injures *kāma* and hurts *artha* because of the decay of the body. Similarly the results of over-attachment to *kāma* and *artha* are specified.

In cases of collision between the three aims (*dharma*, *artha* and *kāma*) the *Kāmasūtra* represents the standpoint of the *dharma* literature in declaring the preceding to be more important, but it makes the restriction that *artha* ranks first for kings and prostitutes.[14] The *Kāmasūtra* avoids direct opposition to Brahmin traditionalism and does not teach the pre-eminence of *kāma* on principle, as Bhīmasena does in the *Mahābhārata*. The *Kāmasūtra* even gives warning examples of kings and gods who were disgraced on account of their over-indulgence in *kāma*. Yet the greater part of the *Kāmasūtra* teaches such a variety of plays and pleasures, and the daily routine of the *nāgaraka*-playboy contains so many snobbish and vain distractions, that obviously the *Kāmasūtra* is less in conformity with *dharma* than it claims to be. *Kāmasūtra* I.2, 7-8 gives a short definition of *dharma* (as well as of *artha* and *kāma*):

> *Dharma* is (1) the prescription by *śāstra* to do certain things, such as the performance of sacrifices, which are not (in general) done, because they do not belong to this world and produce no visible effect; and (2) the prohibition by *śāstra* to do certain things, such as eating meat, which are done because they belong to this world and have visible effects. *Dharma* should be learnt from the *śruti* and from experts on *dharma*.[15]

This definition pinpoints the two decisive aspects of *dharma*: prescription and prohibition. Obviously Vātsyayana stresses the necessity of *śāstra*, as he later on argues to justify his treatment of *kāma* in the form of a manual.

The discussion on the three aims of life is far more extensive in the *Kāmasūtra* of Vātsyayana than in the Kauṭalīya *Arthaśāstra*. Later *artha* works still reflect on this subject, but later *kāma* books such as the *Ratirāhasya* or *Anaṅgaraṅga* which are partly dependent on the *Kāmasūtra* do not discuss the relationship between *dharma* and *kāma*. We may suppose that writers and readers of these later treatises were no longer interested in a dogmatic dispute on *kāma* and *dharma*. Topics of the *dharma* literature are mentioned only occasionally in the *Kāmasūtra*, e.g. the acquiring of a wife and the forms and ceremonies of marriage in the third book. Later *kāma* treatises shorten such explorations or leave them aside. They restrict themselves more to the description of sexual love, but often retain a superstitious belief in spells and recipes.

The *Kāmasūtra* does not define *kāma*, as is done in the *Artha-*

śāstra, *Tantrākhyāyika* and other texts. *Arthaśāstra* 8.3 discusses the vices (*vyasana*) which spring either from anger (*kopa*) or from *kāma*. The three vices from anger are harshness of speech, violation of property, and cruelty of punishment (*vākpāruṣyam arthadūṣaṇaṃ daṇḍapāruṣyam*) and the four vices from *kāma* are hunting, gambling, women and drink (*mṛgayā dyūtaṃ striyaḥ pānam*). There is no mention of drugs, which we would have to subsume under *pānam*, if they were regarded as a vice at all. *Soma*, the famous intoxicant of the *Ṛgveda*, has been identified with the fly-agaric mushroom by R. G. Wasson, and this is still the most probable equation. I. Gershevitch argues convincingly that this fly-agaric was no longer used by the Vedic Indians but had been used by their prehistoric ancestors in the Middle East.[16] The effects of drugs have now begun to be scientifically examined, and it is extremely unlikely that the fly-agaric had any influence on the composition of the Vedic hymns. Neither do we believe that any other drug was responsible for the philosophical creativity of the ancient Indians. *Arthaśāstra* 2.25 discusses the function of the Surādhyakṣa (supervisor of alcohol), who regulates the trade and production of spirituous liquors. Several of the ingredients ennumerated here may well be regarded as drugs. The *Kāmasūtra*, which in 1.3 describes drinking bouts of playboys and prostitutes, reveals a similar permissiveness with regard to alcohol. However, the *dharma* books condemn it strictly; for example, Viṣṇusmṛti 35.1 states:

> *Brahmahatyā surāpanaṃ brāhmaṇasuvarṇaharaṇaṃ gurudāragamanam iti mahāpātakāni.*
>
> Killing a Brahmin, drinking alcohol, stealing the gold of a Brahmin and sexual intercourse with the wife of a teacher are high crimes.

The *dharma* abhorrence of alcohol which is not shared by the *kāma* and *artha* treatises should not be regarded as widely accepted. In Halhed's *A Code of Gentoo Laws* (London, 1776), many whimsical regulations of the old *dharma* books are faithfully preserved (e.g. those regarding defloration), but the long dissertations on alcohol are generously reduced to one single case: 'If a Brahmin is guilty of drinking Wine, he shall be branded in the Fore-head'. (p. 321)

The third book of the *Arthaśāstra* is called *dharmasthīya*, (Concerning Judges) and treats law in its proper sense. Whereas in the *dharma* books a list of 18 titles with 'Recovery of debts' (*ṛṇādāna*) as the first has been elaborated,[17] the *Arthaśāstra* places a long dissertation on marriage (*vivāhasamyuktam*) and related problems in the beginning (after the 'Filing of law-suits'). The order in the *Arthaśāstra* is reasoned, as marriage is regarded as the presupposition for legal transactions (3,2,1 : *vivāhapūrvo vyavahāraḥ*), and the married householder is qualified to act and to transact. In 1,3,9 the householder is enumerated as the first of the four stages of life. According to *Kāmasūtra* I, 4,1 one has to become a householder to lead the playboy life of the elegant citizen.

In the *Arthaśāstra* the interest of the state in the *yogakṣema* (welfare and security) of the subjects leads to a greater protection not only of the women, but also of slaves, hired workers etc., than in the law books. Moreover, the importance of the caste system and the privileges of the Brahmins are less emphasized. The absence of ordeals (which are a favourite subject of many of the law books) means a progress towards circumstantial evidence. In the fourth book of the *Arthaśāstra*, *kaṇṭakaśodhana* (Removal of Thorns) which also deals with the criminal law, investigations through interrogation and through torture are treated. Exempted from torture are not only Brahmins, but also any person 'whose offence is trifling, or who is a minor or aged or sick or intoxicated or insane or overcome by hunger, thirst or travel' etc. (Trans. Kangle of 4,8,14). Circumstantial evidence is advocated in 4,8,9 : 'In the case of one about whom suspicion has arisen, he should produce tools, counsellors, accomplices, (stolen) articles and agents' (Transl. Kangle). Psychologically outstanding for the period of the *Arthaśāstra* is the precept that in the absence of corroboration of the evidence 'he should hold a person, though prattling, as not a thief'. (4,8,11). *Arthaśāstra* 4,8,12 refers to Āṇi-Māṇḍavya 'declaring himself to be a thief though not a thief, because of the fear of the pain of torture'. We should acknowledge the *Arthaśāstra* version[18] as one of the earliest objections against torture, and praise Kauṭilya for his humane restrictions of torture. Yet, if one believes in the progress of jurisprudence, torture means a step forward, as it breaks with the belief in divine manifestations of guilt and admits only evidence and confession. Still it is an awful step forward, which marks an important chapter in the history of sadism. Sadism is less in evidence in ordeals. The *dharma* books ignore torture, though they must have known that it was applied, whereas Kauṭilya does not refer to ordeals, the favourite subject of the *dharma* books. However, in 7.17.4-5, Kauṭilya recommends oaths and declarations of truth (plight of faith) to affirm pacts—besides hostages and surety. He refutes teachers who only advocate the last two (7.17.3) Obviously, Kauṭilya himself did not believe in the force of oaths, as he does not hesitate to break a contract if necessary, but he finds oaths useful because the other king might sometimes feel bound by them.

The treatment of civil and criminal law in the third and fourth books of the *Arthaśāstra* did not add to the bad reputation of this treatise, nor did the forms of corporal punishment which are in conformity with the *jus talionis* of ancient civilizations.

The ill-fame of this book is not primarily a result of its 'philosophy of success'[19] (which is taught with great elaborateness) but is due to the scandalous offensiveness of numerous detailed precepts. Such frankness is not characteristic of the *rājadharma* chapters of the law books, though we find it sometimes in didactic chapters of the *Mahābhārata*,[20] and it is omitted from the later *artha* books which come closer to the line of *dharma*. I refer to *Arthaśāstra* precepts such as:

> But against those treasonable principal officers, who cause harm to the kingdom, (and) who, being favourites or being united, cannot be suppressed openly, he should employ 'silent punishment finding pleasure in (doing his) duty' (*dharmarucir upāṁśudaṇḍam prayuñjīta*). 5,1,4
>
> Or, when he has gone to a fair or on a pleasure-trip, the (king) should invite treasonable officers to see him. These, entering together with assassins with concealed weapons, shall allow a search of their persons....Then the assassins, seized by the doorkeepers, should say, "We are engaged by the treasonable officers". After proclaiming that, they should kill the treasonable men. 5,1, 23-26 (Kangle).
>
> Or, agents appearing as holy men, after showing danger from an evil spirit in a tree demanding the tax of a human being, should ward it off for the citizens and the country people for money. 5,2, 41.
>
> Or, an agent appearing as a trader should trade with plenty

> of goods and assistants. When he has amassed wealth by entrusted deposits and loans against the value of goods, he should get him robbed at night. 5, 2, 46-47.
>
> Or, an agent working as a servant of the treasonable person should throw in a false coin in the money received as wages and point that out. 5, 2, 66.
>
> Or, an agent appearing as a holy man, living on the border of the country, should induce the king to have a sight of the enemy. When he agrees, he should make an effigy and invoke the enemy, and should kill (the king of the other state) in a secluded spot. 13, 2, 18-19.[21]

Such perfidious tricks advocated in laconic prose, the great variety of spies and *agents provocateurs*, the misuse of religious ceremonies, oracles and temples, the silent punishment (*upāṃśudaṇḍa*) without trial cannot be taken as a mere phantasmagoria, after the experiences of history, though we do not know whether the political and legal norms of the Kauṭalīya *Arthaśāstra* were applied in any Indian state.

Even the *Kāmasūtra* of Vātsyāyana contains considerations which reveal the influence of the *Arthaśāstra*:

> With the help of this woman, I shall gain access to the king's enemy who is sheltering with her, and slay him, as the king has commended me to do. I, 5, 17 (Trans. S.C. Upadhyaya).

Such statements recur in the *Ratirāhasya* in a mitigated form:

> This woman's husband is the friend of my enemy who wishes to kill me. By uniting with her, I may be able to break their alliance. XIII, 9.[22]

However, the *Kāmasūtra* has been decried not for such *artha* deviations from *dharma* but for its precise descriptions of sexual love, including the *auparisṭaka* fellatio (II, 9) which is criticized by the holy texts and omitted in later *kāma* books. Even the *Kāmasūtra* looks down upon it, though it describes it with all details. (The passage may refer to homosexual practices in ancient India, about which very little is known. Nowhere is cunnilingus mentioned).

Obviously the *Kāmasūtra* has not always been freely accessible. The text editions have the remarks *nitāntagopanīyam* (i.e. to be strictly preserved) and 'for private circulation only', and translations like that of S. C. Upadhyaya were allowed only for restricted circulation. The German translation by R. Schmidt (1897) rendered the presumably scandalous passages into Latin, and another unexpurgated German translation led to a lawsuit in Germany as late as in 1964. There has never been a trial on a translation of the *Arthaśāstra*, though the verdict of obscenity[23] seems today more appropriate to certain passages of this book.

In some ways, the line of Hindu *dharma* has been enforced by the British Raj. The norms of international law are diametrically opposed to many teachings of the *Arthaśāstra*, as are the moral standards of Christian puritanism to the hedonistic precepts and recipes of the *Kāmasūtra*. The modern world has become more sensitive to the misuse of *artha* than to anomalies of *kāma*. The India of today recollects the heritage of her past and does not exclude the *kāma* literature or the sculptures of Khajuraho, nor her political tradition,[24] and we too should appreciate the *kāma* and *artha* texts—even if they deviate sometimes from the standard of Indian and western *dharma*—as sophisticated elaborations of the two vital aims of human life.

Notes

1For the definition see Robert Lingat, *Les Sources du droit dans le système traditional de l'Inde*, Paris, 1967, pp. 18ff. (translated by J. Duncan M. Derrett, *The Classical Law of India*, Berkeley, 1973); J. Duncan M. Derrett, *Dharmaśāstra and Juridical Literature*, Wiesbaden, 1973, pp. 2 ff.

2See the standard work P. V. Kane, *History of Dharmaśāstra* (Vols. 1-5), Poona, 1953-1973.

3*Asceticism and Eroticism in the Mythology of Śiva*, London, 1973.

4*Ibid.*, p. 318.

5Issue of 25 June, 1853. Marx may have been influenced by Hegel's 'Philosophie der Weltgeschichte', which emphasizes the wild exuberance of fantasy, the adoration of the living generative power, as well as the quality of asceticism. Whereas for Herder, 'The Hindus are the sweetest tribe of mankind' (der sanftmütigste Stamm der Menschen), Hegel is mainly insulating: 'Cunning and slyness is the main character of the Indians. . . . Especially immoral are the Brahmins. They only eat and sleep, say the English ... If engaged in public life they are greedy, deceitful, voluptuous. An honest man, so says an Englishman, is not known to me'. Or: 'The Indians are so impudent in their speech that it puts even English sailors to the blush'. Marx did take over a number of Hegel's prejudices, but not these. Marx quotes Prince Soltykov that the 'Indian is more refined and abler than the Italian', and adds that even his submissiveness is balanced by a certain calm distinction and that his undaunted courage amazed the British officers. All ethno-psychological generalizations are questionable, but if they are insulting generalizations they are revealing for the character of those who propagate them.

[6]'Wie du, Vorfahr und Bruder, geh auch ich im Zickzack zwischen Trieb und Geist durchs Leben, heut Weiser, morgen Narr, heut inniglich Dem Gotte, morgen heiss dem Fleisch ergeben...'

See Friedrich Wilhelm and H. G. Rawlinson, 'India and the Modern West', in A. L. Basham (ed.), *A Cultural History of India*, Oxford (in the press).

[7]Mbh. XII, 161, 2: *dharme cārthe ca kāme lokavṛttiḥ samāhitā/teṣāṃ garīyān katamo madhyamaḥ ko laghuśca kaḥ//*

[8]*nākāmaḥ kāmayaty arthaṃ nākāmo dharmam-icchati/*
nākāmaḥ kāmayāno 'sti tasmāt kāmo viśiṣyate//

[9]Friedrich Wilhelm, *Politische Polemiken im Staats-lehrbuch des Kauṭalya*, Wiesbaden 1960.

[10]*Il Nītivākyāmṛta di Somadeva Sūri*, Torino, 1962, p. 41.

[11]*Ibid.*

[12]F. W. Thomas, *Brihaspati Sutra*, Lahore, 1921, p. 9 of the translation, p. 8-35.

[13]*Kāmasūtra II*, 1-4: *śatāyur vai puruṣo vibhajya kālam anyonyānubaddhaṃ parasparasyānupaghātakaṃ trivargaṃ seveta. bālye vidyāgrahanādīn arthān; kāmaṃ ca vauvane; sthāvire dharmaṃ mokṣaṃ ca.*

[14]*Kāmasūtra* 1, 2, 14-15: *eṣāṃ samavāye pūrvaḥ pūrvo garīyān. arthaś ca rājñaḥ, tanmūlatvāllokayatrayaḥ, veśyaśceti trivargapratipattiḥ.*

[15]*Kāmasūtra* 1,2,7-8: *alaukikatvād adṛṣṭārthatvād apravṛttānāṃ yajñādīnām śāstrāt pravartanam, laukikatvād dṛṣṭārthavācca pravṛttebhyaśca māṃsabhakṣaṇādibhyaḥ śāstrād eva nivāraṇaṃ dharmaḥ. taṃ śruter dharmajñasamavāyācca pratipadyeta.* 1, 2, 9 defines *artha* as: *vidyābhūmihiraṇyapaśu-dhānyabhāṇḍopaskaramitrādīnām arjanam arjitasya vivardhanam arthaḥ.* '*Artha* is the acquisition of knowledge, land, gold, cattle, food-grains, utensils, friends etc., and the increase of the acquired'.

[16]'An Iranianist's View of the Soma Controversy', in *Mémorial Jean de Menasce*, Louvain, 1974, pp. 45-75. F. Staal, in *Exploring Mysticism*, Penguin, 1975, pp. 148 ff., discusses the parallels between mystical and drug-induced states and points out that generally 'the religious use of drugs has not met with the approval of the religious establishments' (p. 156).

[17]E.g. Manu 8.4-7, Nārada 1.16-19.

[18]In *Mahābhārata* 1.101, Āṇi-Māṇḍavya observes the vow of silence, even when accused of theft. He is impaled, since he does not defend himself.

[19]This term is used in Heinrich Zimmer, *Philosophie und Religion Indiens*, Zurich, 1961, pp. 89 ff: 'Die Philosophie des Erfolges'.

[20]E. g. in the Kaṇika-nīti in *Mahābhārata* 1.140; Wilhelm, *op. cit.*, pp. 56-62.

[21]The quotations are from Kangle's translation, 1963.

[22]See Friedrich Wilhelm, 'Die Beziehungen zwischen *Kāmasūtra und Artha-śāstra*', in ZDMG 116, 2, 1966, p. 302.

[23]An early instance of the use of this word in a political context is found in Thomas Mann's B. B. C. speech of 27 June 1943 : '. . .die obszöne Ansprache eines Nazi-Bonzen. . . .' [Ed. : When Professor Wilhelm presented this paper in London, this reference led to a lively discussion of the relationship between Indian political thinkers and modern German political thinkers. At my request, Professor Wilhelm supplied further information on this subject, which I found so interesting that I include it here despite its marginal relevance to the central topic :]. In their attitudes towards Nazi Germany, Nehru was far more clear-headed than Gandhi, who in his journal, *Harijan* (26 November 1938), had compared the situation of the Jews in Germany to that of the Indians in South Africa. Finding 'an exact parallel', he advocated the methods of Satyagraha. Martin Buber (in *Briefe an Gandhi*, Zurich, 1939, letter of 24 February 1939), strongly protested :'. . . . Yet do you know or don't you know, Mahatma, what a concentration camp is and what happens there, what the tortures of the con-centration camp are and what its methods of slow and quick killing are?' Nehru on the other hand, wrote 'The Nazi Triumph in Germany' (in *Glimpses of World History*, letters to his daughter, written in prison) as early as 31 July, 1933 : 'The programme of the Nazis was not a clear or a positive one. It was intensely nationalistic, and laid stress on the greatness of Germany and the Germans, and for the rest it was a hotchpotch of various hatreds. . . .Behind all this lay an extraordinary philosophy of violence. Not only was violence praised and encouraged, but it was considered the highest duty of man'. There were other Indian politicians like Subhas Chandra Bose who gave in to the temptations of *artha* and regarded Nazi Germany as a natural ally against British rule, though Hitler had written in *Mein Kampf*: 'England will only lose India, if either its administration becomes a victim of racial decomposition or if it is overcome by the sword of a powerful enemy. . . . Despite all, as a Teuton I prefer to see India under English rule than under another'. Nietzsche did not look down upon the Indians as a whole, but he despised the lower castes, insulting the Śūdras by calling them 'Dienstbotenrasse' (race of servants) and the Caṇḍālas as 'Auswurfstoffe' (riff-raff). He found admirable 'the absolute separation of this riff-raff of society, and the tendency to destroy them', and he enthusiastically praised the law-book of Manu for the privileged position assigned to the warriors and philosophers.

[24]See Johannes H. Voigt, 'Nationalist Interpretations of *Arthaśāstra* in Indian Historical Writing', in *St. Antony's Papers*, No. 18, *South Asian Affairs*, no. 2, Oxford, 1966, pp. 46-66.

Veda and Dharma

J. C. HEESTERMAN

The whole of *dharma*, we are told over and over again, rests on the Vedas.[1] The respect for the Vedas and the acknowledgement of its ultimate authority are therefore quite logically given as the decisive criteria for Hindu orthodoxy. All this is clear and consistent. But it is really? In fact the forceful statement that all *dharma* rests on or even is contained in the Vedas hides a curious paradox.

To begin with, the Vedas were and are largely unknown. When the *dharma* appeals to the authority of the Vedas, it more often than not refers to an unknown entity. The fact is that the high prestige of the Vedas is paralleled by an equally high disregard for its contents. Or, as Louis Renou has said, the respect accorded to Vedas is only a *coup de chapeau donné en passant à une idole dont on entend ne plus s'encombrer par la suite.*[2] This statement seems too caustic in so far as the relationship of Hinduism to the Vedas has considerably troubled Hindu thought. If the recent rumpus about the performance of the complicated *Soma* ritual in a small corner of Kerala—a rumpus that degenerated into the first-ever Vedic 'media event'—is any indication, it continues to trouble the mind even in this modern time and age.

But the problem is no less curious for it. On the one hand there is the unique phenomenon of some small Brahmin communities who by means of incredible mnemotechnic efforts have faithfully, word by word, preserved the Vedas and as the Government Sanskrit Commission found to its surprise and elation, as late as 1958, [3] even the complicated Vedic *śrauta* ritual, which until recently was supposed to be a dead letter already at the time of the *Mīmāṃsā* commentators.[4] On the other hand the Veda, for all the effort that went with its preservation, did not have a productive follow-up. There are only resonances and archaisms, but no concern with its contents. Even the *Karma-mīmāṃsā* uses the Vedas only as a practicing ground for its method, which is then applied to something else, the *smṛti*. One might perhaps say that its rigorous, unchanged preservation has cut the Veda off from its living surroundings. The exclusive concern with mnemotechnics and the intricacies of recitation and chanting has apparently left no room for a productive concern with its contents. Even though the theory of the meaninglessness of the Vedic formulas is rejected, the fact that such a theory could be discussed is significant.

More importantly, however, even a perfect knowledge and understanding of the Vedas would hardly be of any help in deciding questions of *dharma*. For strictly speaking, the Vedas contain no positive injunctions that could be used directly as rules of conduct. In the *Brāhmaṇas*, to be sure, one may find references to usages and rules of conduct, but such references have to be gleaned from passages that are devalued as *arthavāda* and therefore devoid of interest from the viewpoint of the ritual injunction. So the connection between the Vedas and *dharma* is at best a tenuous one, if it exists at all.

So, it would seem, the Vedas are simply there, gloriously preserved, as an impressive prehistoric megalith, a *monumentum aere perennius*, a boon for antiquarians but singularly devoid of relevance to the living concerns of the *dharma*. This then is the paradox: the Vedas are the ultimate *fons et origo* of the *dharma* to which, however, they are in no way related. Now we may, of course, explain away this paradox by saying that the word 'Veda' in connection with the *dharma* does not refer exclusively to the Vedic texts, but aims at the *summa* of all true knowledge, whether contained in the Vedic texts or not. Indeed, Hindu thought seems to have favoured this line of reasoning. But it is not all that smooth and easy. *Grosso modo* we can discern two distinct views.

On the one hand we find the strict and narrow definition: 'Veda' is exclusively *mantra* and *brāhmaṇa* formulas and description of the ritual.[5] In this definition the focus is exclusively on the solemn sacrificial ritual. The same text leaves no doubt in this point, for it goes on to say:

Mantra and *brāhmaṇa* form the guidelines for the sacrifice;

the *brāhmaṇa* gives the rules for the sacrificial acts, the remaining part of the *brāhmaṇa* is explication (*arthavāda*); everything else is *mantra*.[6]

This shows how exclusively the sacrificial ritual is put in the centre. Even the hallowed *mantras*, qualified, or rather unqualified, as a simple 'everything else' are somewhat pushed into the background. This statement, representing the general view of the ritual *paribhāṣās*, the predecessors of the *Mīmāṃsā*, is a forceful plea for the view of the Vedas as a strictly organized and fixed corpus of texts with an equally strict purpose, the sacrificial ritual.

Next to this well-defined corpus, the *śruti*, we find a considerable and not strictly bounded mass of texts going under the name of *smṛti*. Here lies the connection with the other, unbounded usage of the term 'Veda'. Since all tradition, whatever its content and origin, in order to be valid has to claim Vedic authority, it is practically unavoidable to hold that it is contained explicitly or implicitly in the Vedas. Thus *Mānava Dharmaśāstra* says that all that is taught by its mythical author Manu is completely contained in the Vedas, for, the same passage adds, Manu was omniscient. Here Manu's omniscience is invoked to bridge the gap between 'Veda' and *dharma*. For omniscience means in the first place perfect knowledge of the Vedas. The rules and usages propounded by Manu must then by implication be the same as those of the Vedic sages, to whom Manu himself moreover belonged. In this way the *smṛti* becomes all but co-terminous with the Vedas. But the same pious ploy obviously could and did open the door to unlimited expansion of the Vedas.

It would be wrong to dismiss this expansion as insignificant hyperbole or a pious hoax. For one thing, it is not devoid of a certain justification. The point is that the Vedas, as in so many other respects where we are frantically looking for decisive statements, are ambiguous as to their source and origin. The catchword is vision—the supranormal vision of the *ṛṣi*, *vipra* or *kavi*, who attains his vision through his own efforts, especially through *tapas*. But we equally find that he received it from the gods. Moreover the gods themselves can be called seers. Both gods and men have to exert themselves mutually to achieve the vision of transcendent truth. It would then seem that the seer's vision is, in the words of Gonda, the result of

> a cyclical process or a circular course. The godhead from whom the vision is expected is at the same time invited to accept it graciously.[7]

But by the same token the source of the Vedas remains hidden, so to say, in the middle space between gods and men. Given this apparently intended and, one might add, quite meaningful ambiguity the road towards the revelatory vision remains in principle open. In this perspective the Vedas are indeed unbounded, not limited to a particular time, place or seer. This then means that, as a matter of principle, new ideas, doctrines, usages and 'visions' cannot be barred from claiming Vedic or Veda-like authority, as indeed has been happening all the time.

But apart from its justification or otherwise, the expanded use of the term 'Veda' would seem to be the expression of a problem, namely the problem of the paradoxical relationship between the exclusively sacrificial *śruti* on the one hand and on the other the *dharma* that has to take all aspects of life, and not only the ritual one, into account. Far from glossing over this problem, Indian thinkers were actutely aware of it. It is the very divergence of their answers, none of which is completely satisfactory, that bears out their serious and abiding concern with the problem. Thus some, following the *Mīmāṃsā* teacher Śabara, maintained that the *smṛti* rules were from times immemorial honoured by the Vedic sages themselves and therefore should be taken *prima facie* as resting on the Vedas. The decisive test then is only whether a particular *smṛti* rule is opposed to the *śruti*: In the few cases where such a question might crop up it was obviously not too hard a nut to crack for a well-trained Mīmāṃsaka, who would be inclined to argue that in fact there was no conflict. Others on the contrary, such as the followers of Kumārila, would hold that all *smṛti* is contained in the *śruti*, while appearance to the contrary can only be due to either the loss of the relevant *śruti* text or to our feeble-mindedness which bars us from the perfect knowledge of the Vedas that the *smṛti* authors possessed. This then means that the *smṛti* is co-extensive with the Vedas so that in case of conflict one would be free to choose.[8] In both cases—Śabara's or that of Kumārila—the outcome would, of course, be the same, namely the ultimate Vedic validity of any *smṛti*.

But why then all this complicated effort? Why should the *smṛti* be dependent on the *śruti* that has no direct relevance for the *smṛti's* concerns, instead of standing on its own—as in fact it does? The answer is a simple one: the inescapable need for ultimate authority. In order to fulfil its task of giving guidelines for society it has to take into account the exigencies of normal life as well as the various, often conflicting customs and usages of many and varied communities, ranging from tribals to sophisticated urbanites and from socially active men to solitary hermits. The *dharma* cannot simply limit itself to the rules of solemn sacrifice as the *śruti* with its sovereign disregard for reality can do. The *dharma* has to function in the middle of the rough and tumble of society. But for the same reason the *dharma* cannot do without a source of authority that transcends man and his society and provides an unchangeable reference point. This transcendent function seems to be cut out for the Vedas, in the strict sense, the *śruti*, exactly because it is unconcerned with and untouched by the vagaries of human life and society. Perhaps this is the reason for the Veda's international exclusivism and separation from the world that surrounds it. In order to be truly transcendent the Vedas had to be safeguarded against the eroding effect of the shifts and changes of religious and social life by breaking off from reality.

Though we may understand in this way the meaning of the paradoxical relationship between the Vedas and *dharma* it only sharpens the edge of the problem. For either one adheres to the transcendent authority of the Vedic word in the strict sense which, because of its intentional limitation, does not pronounce on *dharma*, or one relies on the transcendent 'vision' of a human authority—sage or guru—for which, however, there is then no criterion to judge the validity of the claim to absolute authority. The solution of this tangle remains therefore suspended in mid-air, between either the absolute and therefore ultimately arbitrary authority of the guru—a well-known phenomenon—or the equally absolute *śruti* word which, however, cannot deliver the ultimate decision. The *via media* is then to posit the thorough knowledge of the *śruti* as the objective criterion for trustworthiness, as for instance in the case of Manu's omniscience, or more generally of the *śiṣya* whose *ācāra*, behaviour, is then an authoritative source of *dharma* because of his intimate knowledge of the Vedas.[9] This is irrespective of the relevance, or rather lack of it, for the case in hand.

Now all this does not yet explain why of all things the dysfunctional apparatus of *mantra* and *brāhmaṇa* should have been selected as the source of transcended authority for the *dharma* with all the problems that it involved. The question is the more puzzling since the Vedas' transcendence seems to be intentionally contrived. The Vedas themselves hardly give support to the doctrine of their being not man-made, eternal and infallible, while the demotion of everything that could be directly useful for *dharma* to *arthavāda* strikes one for its sheer contrariness. Moreover there is the embattled point of animal sacrifice that has been a stumbling block practically from the beginning[10] and still is able to create nation-wide commotion. The simple need for a transcendent reference point, obvious though it is, does not by itself render a sufficient explanation for the pivotal place accorded to the Vedas. Nor can we ascribe this phenomenon to some unquestioning antiquarian inertia. The Vedas must therefore have some intrinsic value that gave them their ironcast authority and justified the efforts for their unique preservation.

It seems obvious to think here of sacrifice as the decisive value that gives the Vedas their authority over man and universe. Sacrifice as the ultimate law of the universe is not only a readily understandable idea, but it might even cancel the gap between the Vedas and *dharma*. For both would be united in having sacrifice as their central concern, as the primary *dharma*. The *dharma* would then in effect be a sacrificial order. Indeed the *dharma* texts do not oppose themselves to such a view. Thus, for instance, there is the well-known notion of the origin of the social order of the *varṇas* from the sacrifice of the cosmic *puruṣa*. Since the primary duty of the king is the maintenance of the *varṇa* order, it is quite consistent that his activity is equated with a lifelong sacrifice.[11] It would be easy, though tedious, to quote the evidence for the important place given to sacrifice in *dharma*. However, it would be equally easy to overstate the case for sacrifice as the pivotal duty. In fact there is a strange ambiguity about the duty to sacrifice. Insofar as the *śrauta* sacrifice is concerned—and that is, of course, the important one for the connection between *śruti* and *dharma*—the authorities are divided.

Technically the question hinges on the duty to establish the three *śrauta* fires, and some authorities do indeed make the *ādhāna* of the three fires obligatory,[12] but then failing to do so is only an *upapātaka*.[13] Other authorities, however, consider the *ādhāna* as optional.[14] In that case there obviously cannot be a binding duty to perform any *śrauta* sacrifice. Moreover, if the *ādhāna* is made obligatory, it is only so for the Brahmin. This leaves out the king, admittedly the guardian of *dharma*, however much his royal activity may be metaphorically extolled as a life-long sacrifice. What is worse, the king is singled out as the one for whom the Brahmin should not officiate as *purohita* or *ṛtvij*.[15] So the king is actually barred from being a Yajamāna in a *śrauta* sacrifice. How he is then to have his *rājasūya* or even simple *abhiṣeka* is left to his own inventiveness or power of persuasion. And this notwithstanding the fact that the *kṣatra*, the royal power, is said to be based on the *brahma*, while the Brahmin in practice depends on the material support of the king. The two parties obviously need each other but they are not supposed to meet. In fact we come up against the same paradox we already encountered in the relationship between the Vedas and *dharma*. Now we may, of course, suppose that all is well as long as the Brahmin performs the sacrifice on his own for the well-being of the whole community. This idea is indeed fairly popular and widespread. Thus, for instance, it is said that the sun would not rise if the *agnihotra* were not performed every morning.[16] But on the other hand the *agnihotra* appears to be solely concerned with the individual interest of the single sacrificer, as when the same text states that the sacrificer,

> who knows that release from death in the *agnihotra*, is freed from death again and again.[17]

Generally speaking the *śruti* only promises the benefits from sacrifice to the single sacrificer without giving any thought to the common weal. The notion of *sacra publica* seems to be alien to the sacrificial *śruti*. Even in such rituals as the *aśvamedha* or the *rājasūya* no concern for the general well-being is evinced, while the representatives of the community such as the 'jewel-bearers', who for once are admitted to the ritual, are limited to the role of rather passive supernumeraries.

If we turn to *gṛhya* ritual the situation seems somewhat different. Here at least the duty to establish the sacrificial *gṛhya* fire is binding on the Brahmin householder and consequently the duty to perform the regular offerings in this fire—at least for the Brahmin. But the *gṛhya* sacrifice is again solely concerned with the individual householder. More surprising, however, is the fact that the notion of sacrifice itself no longer appears to be of pivotal importance. For the *Āśvalāyana-Gṛhyasūtra* starts out by quoting a number of *Ṛgveda* passages in order to show that real sacrifice may be replaced by knowledge of the Vedas and the simple act of adoration (*namas*). So wherever we look for confirmation of the central place of sacrifice, we end up with ambiguities and paradoxes.[18]

Apparently something has happened to the idea of sacrifice—a shift in meaning of which the opening statement of the *Āśvalāyana Gṛhyasūtra* is indicative. This possibly is the crux of the matter and it may therefore be worthwhile to investigate this further. We must begin with the nature of sacrifice. When taken seriously sacrifice is, quite bluntly, an act of controlled death and destruction. This act purports to force access to the other world, the transcendent. The gap, the vacuum created by the sacrifice has to be filled by the other side with the opposite of death and destruction, that is the goods of life, in the most tangible sense of food and survival. Or in simple terms one must sacrifice a cow in order to obtain cows. It is definitely not an ethereal business for the delicate metaphysical-minded, but essentially a rather gruesome exercise in controlled catastrophe. An exercise in which, moreover, one is never quite sure of the outcome, for it involves two parties who ever and again have to renew their cruel compact. The Vedic texts offer ample illustrations of this theme. Think, for instance, of King Hariścandra in the Śunaḥśepa story, who obtains a son but only on condition that he will sacrifice that same son.

The two partners in the sacrificial drama, as we can still discern them in the *śrauta* texts,[19] are, briefly, the party of life and the party of death. The one group or their leader, the Yajamāna, offers the sacrifice; the other group is formed by the guests and recipients of the sacrificial food and gifts. At the start the host is in possession of the goods of life; at the end the positions are reversed. But the guest and recipient has to pay the price of taking upon himself the onus of the death and destruction involved in the sacrificial largesse. For, though it is the host who offers the 'goods of life', it is the guest who is required to give the order for the killing and the preparing of the sacrificial food, as can be seen in the rules for the solemn guest reception, the Arghya.[20]

One may wonder where in this set-up the gods are. The answer is that the two parties enact the roles of gods and anti-gods, of *devas* and *asuras*. It does not seem fortuitous that still in Purāṇic mythology, the *asuras* are often in the role of munificent sacrificial patrons, as in the case of the *vāmana avatāra* where Viṣṇu, the champion of the gods, enters as a Brahmin guest and cheats his *asura* host out of his realm and possessions. Nor is it just an embellishment that the Brahmin officiants at the moment when they receive their often astronomically liberal gifts are equated to gods. In the same way we may try to understand an otherwise obscure and discarded rule, which has it that the sacrificial fires—or at least one of them—should be taken from the home of a rich man who surprisingly has to be 'like an *asura*' (*asura iva*).[21]

Let me try to illustrate this original agonistically risky and dangerous character of the sacrifice at the hand of a well-known ritual, in many respects the epitome of Vedic sacrifice, namely the *agnihotra*. At first sight it is a straighforward and innocuous affair without any gruesome associations. Two libations of milk are made both at sunset and at dawn and the rest of the milk is consumed by the Brahmin priest. Though the sacrificial substance is primarily milk, ghee, rice, *Soma* and even meat, in short all forms of food and drink are equally acceptable. Thus the *agnihotra* ritual clearly turns on the feeding of a Brahmin guest. And thus a Kṣatriya, for whom, as the texts explain, a Brahmin should not perform the *agnihotra*, simply sends food to a Brahmin in lieu of having the ritual performed.[22] So far it is a peaceful and charitable institution. But, curiously, in the context of this nice and quiet *agnihotra* we find an expiatory rite for a somewhat surprising mishap during the performance of the ritual. This untoward occurrence is that a cart or even a war- or racing-chariot passes between the fires.[23] One wonders how such an accident could come about at all. Do we have to suppose that wanton aggression was rampant to such an extent that it was quite normal to pass expressly with cart or chariot through some pious man's small sacrificial plot? I think that the answer can be easily found in the importance that the chariot has in the ritual texts. Not only are there the well-known cases of ritualized chariot races and chariot raids, but the texts generally abound in references to warlike raiding and transhuming expeditions. And the field of ceremonial but none the less real clashes seems to have been by preference the sacrificial area, just as in the case of the *Mahābhārata* war's locale, Kurukṣetra, which is at the same time called 'the gods' place of sacrifice'. It is then not so enigmatic that one Aruṇa Aupaveśi declared that by offering the *agnihotra* every evening and every morning he hurled a *vajra* against his enemy.[24] Against this background we may equally understand that the rice meal offered to the Brahmins at any simple and unbloody sacrifice, the *anvāhārya* dish, is not motivated by charitable considerations but, as the texts explain, by the need to mend all that is 'cruel and injured' in the sacrifice.[25] In the same vein the *mantras* say that the sacrificer overcomes death by means of offering the *anvāhārya* to the Brahmins. For it is the Brahmin guests who have to pay for their food by taking over the burden of sacrificial death and destruction.

This is perhaps not so surprising after all. The real surprise is in the *agnihotra's* further career in the later Vedic texts. I refer to what is known as the *prāṇāgnihotra*, the offering in the life breaths, the *prāṇas*. That is, quite simply, taking a meal preceded and accompanied by cleansing acts and consecratory *mantras* derived in part from the *agnihotra* ritual. The *prāṇāgnihotra* then, as was made clear by Dr. Bodewitz who collected the relevant materials, is a regular part of the Brahmin's ordinary daily *bhojana*.[26] Now the main point of this conclusion is that, like the original *agnihotra*, it simply pertains to *bhojana*. But there is one essential difference. Instead of offering a meal which then has dark consequences for the recipient, the *prāṇāgnihotra* means eating by oneself, independent of others, with no darkly hidden strings attached.

It may be worthwhile to look also at the origin of the *prāṇāgnihotra*. This can be found in the meal eaten by the *dīkṣita* who prepares himself for performing a *Soma* sacrifice. The milk that he takes as his food is considered an offering in his *prāṇas* and is then equated with the normal *agnihotra*, which the *dīkṣita* should not perform.[27] The point is that the *dīkṣita* is not yet a munificent patron. On the contrary, during his *dīkṣā* phase he must, by means fair or foul, collect the riches or rather the booty, the *sani*, that he will distribute at the sacrifice. Even the omniscient Manu still allows him to go on a raiding expedition for this purpose. He can therefore at best be a guest at the tumultuous contests at other men's sacrifices, forcing his way in if need be, by driving his chariot through the rich man's sacrificial area enclosed by the fires and taking by force what is not willingly given. In the *prāṇāgnihotra,* however, both opposite phases—that of the *dīkṣita* and that of the munificent sacrificial patron—have been fused into one. The Brahmin householder is both *dīkṣita* and Yajamāna, both his own patron and his own priest, his own host and his own guest. He performs the sacrifice in and through himself and by the same token has emancipated himself from the oppressive bonds that tie him to his partners. Even if he be in actual practice dependent on others for his subsistence, this fact has no threatening consequences any more. Insofar as there are still ties they have been emptied of religious value. Opting out of society he strikes out on his own and creates in himself his own ideally ordered ritual universe.

At this point it is clear that something important has indeed happened to the sacrifice. The burden of violence and death has been effectively removed from the ritual. Or, since death and violence in reality cannot be completely eliminated, they have been relegated to the social world, outside the *śrauta* ritual.[28] For it is there that we find till the present day numerous instances of real sacrifices in so-called village festivals, which pass practically unnoticed. It is, however, significant that the immolation of a goat in the *śrauta* ritual (although the actual killing takes place outside the place of sacrifice) was always the most important bone of contention. And the national rumpus, mentioned in the beginning of this paper, over the performance of the *Soma* ritual again centered on the killing of goats, which then had to be replaced by *piṣṭapaśus.* What was left after the elimination of real sacrifice is mere ritual, which then can only develop ever greater precision regulated by ever stricter rules.

So it is not the idea of sacrifice that is the central value of the *śruti,* deeply moving as it may be, but the strict ritualism that was left after the elimination of sacrifice proper. This actually dry and perfectionist ritualism may seem to be an irreparable loss. But it should be valued, rather, as a decisive breakthrough. Instead of the ever renewed contest with its attending violence and uncertain outcome, a different and completely opposite ideal was posited, namely that man can create his own ideally ordered universe beyond death and destruction. The *brahman* from which the *Brāhmaṇa* texts derive their name is no longer *l'énigme essentiel du védisme ancien* but the clear-cut, or, if one prefers, cut and dried identification of microcosmic, macrocosmic and ritual elements which form the intellectual basis of a rationalized objective ritual cosmology. Success and failure, gain and loss, life and death are no longer dependent on the unpredictable outcome of the contest, but only on the precision of ritual detail. Death in this rationalized system has been replaced by the ritual mistake. And the Brahmin priest instead of having to carry the burden of death and destruction simply repairs the mistake by technical ritual means and, what is more, can still have his food and *dakṣiṇās* without any dire consequences.

The difference between the ancient Vedic enigma, expressed in unresolved paradoxes, and the positive cosmology, based on hard-headed identifications, is clear. Whereas the first, though bound by conventions, cannot be fixed and learned, but has to be ever renewed, the latter is perfectly fixed and meant to be taught and learned by rote. It is a positive, transferable knowledge that promises to him 'who knows thus' mastery over a perfectly ordered universe, undisturbed by death. The unexpected consequence is that it is more important that it is learned and mastered in all its hypertrophic perfectionism, than that it be actually performed. In this way we can understand that the *Āśvalāyana Gṛhyasūtra*, as we saw, declares the knowledge of the Vedas and the simple act of worship equivalent to the execution of the ritual, while the *Viṣṇusmṛti* declares in the same vein that the recitation of the Vedas vastly outweighs the performance of both *śrauta* and *gṛhya* sacrifices.[30]

This, I think, is the foundation of the Vedas' transcendent prestige: not sacrifice but the knowledge that overcomes death. The knowledge offered by the Vedas is therefore in the true sense transcendent. But here the Vedas stop dead in their tracks. They cannot have a follow-up; they can only be learned and transmitted. They can only exhaust themselves in even greater precision and systematization of ritual rules or, alternatively, develop the identificatory technique to its logical end, the ultimate identification of *ātman* and *brahman* where the whole cosmos implodes into one spaceless point.

But what then about the *dharma*? We might surmise that the Vedas and *dharma* have their common ground in the notion of a ritually ordered universe that excludes all risks. Again, *dharma* is in many respects sympathetic to this idea, but again the argument is fatally flawed. When the *dharma* tries to impose a strict ritual order as in its central doctrine regarding the rigorous separation of the *varṇas*, excluding all relationships between them, it ends up in a practical impossibility. For it is hard to see how any society can function on the basis of rigorous separation. The concept of separate *svadharmas* for each *varṇa* is hardly fit to remedy this. The point is, of course, that society simply does not submit to a strict ritual ordering. And it is a mark of the sincerity with which the *dharma* authorities grapple with the realities of society that in the final analysis they admit that local custom, communal *svadharma*, must prevail, even if it be directly in conflict with the explicit prescripts of the *dharma*.[31]

So the Vedas remain isolated in their transcendent grandeur. Whereas the original sacrifice was meant to link the human and the transcendent worlds, the Vedas as we know them from the ritual *Saṃhitās* and *Brāhmaṇas* exclude the social dimension. The Yajamāna is alone, without social partners, and by reciting and performing the ritual in mind only (*manasā*) he can even eliminate the need for expert assistance. The *śrauta* ritual's physical locale is outside the community, for which it has no consequences, and at the end of the ritual the enclosure is destroyed and the implements thrown into the water. Even for the Yajamāna himself nothing has changed. At the end of the ritual he has to say: 'Here I am just who I am' (*idam ahaṃ ya evāsmi so 'ham*) and unchanged he goes back to his daily world. The Vedas then are intentionally divorced from human reality. They are transcendence itself.

Far from resolving the paradox of the *dharma's* foundation in the Vedas our investigation has shown the gap that separates them to be not only intractable, but a matter of principle. Now this paradox may seem a satisfying conclusion to us, but for the Hindu this is obviously not acceptable. He cannot get away with just *un coup de chapeau*. The crux of the matter is that the Vedas hold the key to ultimate legitimation. Therefore, even if the Vedas are in no way related to the ways of human life and society, one is still forced to come to terms with them. This is especially true of the premier representative of society and guardian of the *dharma*, the king. Even if he is not qualified to perform the ritual himself—though the *Arthaśāstra* requires him at least to have studied the Vedas[32] while the Brahmin is warned in strong terms against serving him in this as well as in other respects—he can endow Brahmins with *brahmadeyas* so that they at least can keep up the study and transmission of the Vedas and perform the ritual. While for the Brahmin the mental recitation of the Vedic texts may be sufficient or even preferable, it is clear that the king has a vested interest in their actually performing the ritual undet his protection and endowment as a visible sign of his legitimacy, even if he is excluded from the ritual's performance. It would seem that this is the primary motivation of numerous *brahmadeyas*, and it may well be that the actual force that kept up the Vedic tradition over the ages was in fact not so much the Brahmin's unworldly piety as the king's need for legitimation.

But what about modern India? Obviously the modern secular state needs and has other sources of legitimation. Should the demise of the old-style Rājā not signal the disappearance of the Vedic tradition? Curiously, the opposite seems to be the case, and this not only in the circles of the Ārya Samāj with its back-to-the-Vedas ideology. Even *śrauta* performances, though understandably few and far between, are more numerous than previously expected, when the German Sanskritist Martin Haug was supposed to have been the last to have witnessed a *śrauta* ritual. The reason is that modernity and especially the modern nation brings in its wake the problem of national identity. As long as one lives mostly in a context of personal face-to-face relations, one does not have much trouble identifying oneself and the others. Thus Hindus did not need 'Hinduism'—significantly this term first came up in the West—for their sense of identity. Their universe was sufficiently circumscribed by the little community and its ramifications.

Modern society and its political manifestation of the nation base themselves not on personal relationships, however important they may be in actual practice, but on the concept of the unrelated individual. Or, in pragmatic terms, man has increasingly to function outside the confinement of his personal universe. But how is he to recognize his otherwise unknown brethren, identify himself and generally mark the boundaries of his universe? Here the need for universally recognized badges of cultural identity becomes a pressing problem. Identity in this sense is not of the parochial type but should on the contrary transcend the parochial confinement. Though at first it may be somewhat surprising, the Veda, as the transcendent reference point that in principle it has always been, is cut out for filling this modern need. It is by now well-known that what has vaguely been called Sanskritization found new uses and stimulti under modernization and that in fact Sanskritization and modernization go hand in hand. But the core of Sanskritization is essentially the attempt to approach the ideal of the Brahmin and his privileged attribute, the Veda.

This trend is in no small degree favoured by the preserving activity of philological scholarship and the divulging effect of the printing press, recently joined by the tape-recorder and the camera. All this cannot but have an impact on the nature of Vedic tradition. For it is no longer the exclusive affair of small Brahmin communities, each jealously guarding its own variety of the tradition. The new interest supported by philology and the props of the modern media can only blur these local and communal peculiarities, but this equally means that the universality of the Vedas is strenghtened in a new way. The recent performances of *śrauta* rituals may well signify something else than an antiquarian oddity or the swan-song of a parochial tradition. They may be a modern phenomenon. Of course, the paradox of the Vedas—their having ultimate authority over a world to which they are in no way related—is by no means resolved under modern circumstances. It has only grown more intractable. Nor do the Vedas stand unchallenged, but then they always were controversial. However, the public interest as well as the controversy they are able to arouse even in our time, do validate the Vedas as a true *monumentum aere perennius*.

Notes

[1]The present paper takes up and develops some themes from another paper, 'Die Autorität des Veda', in G. Oberhammer, (ed.), *Offenbarung*, Vienna, 1974, pp. 29-40.

[2]'A raising of the hat given in passing to an idol with which you do not wish to involve yourself any more'. L. Renou, *Le Destin du Veda dans l'Inde*, E. V. P. VI, p. 2.

[3]Report of the Sanskrit Commission, Government of India Press, Delhi, 1958.

[4]R. Lingat, *Les Sources du Droit traditionnel de l'Inde'*, Paris, 1967, p. 170.

[5]*Āpastamba* SS. 24-1.31.

[6]*Ibid.*, 24.1.32-34

[7]Cf. J. Gonda, *The Vision of the Vedic Poet*, The Hague, 1963, p. 66.

[8]Lingat, *op. cit.*, p. 28.

[9]*Ibid.*, p. 201.

[10]Cf. L. Alsdorf, *Beiträge zur Geschichte Vegetarismus und Rinderverehrung in Indien*, Wiesbaden, 1962.

[11]Cf. *Mānava DhS.* 5.93; 8.306.

[12]Cf. *Vāsiṣṭha DhS.* 11.45.

[13]*Viṣṇu Smṛti*, 37.28.

[14]Cf. P. V. Kane, *History of Dharmaśāstra*, II, p. 677.

[15]*Mānava DhS.* 3.64; 153; 4.85-86.

[16]*Śatapatha Br.* 2.3.1.5.

[17]*Ibid.*, 2.3.3.9.

[18]*Aśvalāyana* GS. 1.1. 3-4.

[19]Cf. 'Brahmin, Ritual and Renouncer', *WZKSO*. 8, 1964, pp. 1-31.

[20]Cf. review of Alsdorf, *op. cit.*, in *Indo-Ir. Journ.*, 9, 1966, p. 148.

[21]Cf. Kāṭhaka S. 8.12 : 96.7; *Āpastamba SS.* 5.14.1.

[22]Cf. P. E. Dumont, *L'Agnihotra*, Baltimore, 1939, pp. 38, 87, 136.

[23]*Maitrāyaṇī* S. 1.8.9 : 130.9 : *Taittirīya Br.* 1.4.4.10; *Śatapatha Br.* 12.4.1.1-2; *Jaiminīya Br.* 1.51.

[24]*Taittirīya Br.* 2.1.5.11.

[25]*Taittirīyā S.* 1.7.3.1.

[26]H. W. Bodewitz, *Jaiminīya Brāhmaṇa* 1.1-65 with a study of Agnihotra and Prāṇāgnihotra, p. 318.

[27]Cf. *Maitrāyaṇī S.* 3.6.10 : 74.7-8; *Kāṭhaka* S. 23.7 : 82.21.

[28]Someone other than the *ṛtvij* kills the animal, *outside* the place of sacrifice. Thus, it is said, '*Grāme dīkṣite, araṇye yajate*' ('one is consecrated in the village, but the sacrifice takes place in the wilderness').

[29]L. Renou, 'La Notion de Bráhman', *Journ. As.*, 1949, pp. 37 ff.

[30]*Viṣṇu Smṛti* 55.20.21.

[31]Cf. R. Lingat, 'Time and the Dharma', *Contrib. to Indian Sociology* 6, 1962, pp. 12 ff.

[32]*Kauṭilīya Arthaśāstra* 1.2.

The Clash Between Relative and Absolute Duty: The Dharma of Demons

WENDY DONIGER O'FLAHERTY

The Hindus recognize two different levels of duty: relative (*svadharma*, one's own particular duty) and absolute (*sanātana*, eternal), also called *sāmānya* (equal, the same for everyone) or *sādhāraṇa* (common, general). *Svadharma* is very complex; *sanātana dharma* is rather like the ten commandments—easily memorized, not so easily followed. The term *dharma* usually designates the specific duty of a class (*varṇa*) or stage of life (*āśrama*).[1] Some authorities distinguish five kinds of *dharma*: the *dharma* of class, of stage of life, of class and stage of life together, the *dharma* dependent upon a particular cause (such as an expiation), and the *dharma* in herent in the possession of certain qualities.[2] Others add a sixth type of *dharma*: *sādhāraṇa dharma*, the *dharma* for everyone, even outcaste Caṇḍālas, such as the duty to speak the truth and refrain from injuring living beings.[3] The *Arthaśāstra* states that all men must cultivate non-injury, truth, purity, goodwill, mercy, and patience.[4] Later texts somewhat modify this list: the ten-limbed *dharma* for all classes is non-injury, truth, purity, not stealing, charity, forebearance, self-restraint, tranquility, generosity, and asceticism.[5]

According to the lawbooks, there should be no conflict between the two levels: all of us must perform our common, absolute duty, as well as the particular requirements of our social class and stage of life. But the specific and the general come into conflict in cases where one's specific duty involves injury and thus violates the injunction of non-injury. The duty to kill is an ancient Hindu duty derived from the ancient code of the Vedic warriors (the Kṣatriya class), while the duty *not* to kill enters Hinduism at the time of the rise of Buddhism and Vedānta. The conflict between them appears often in the *Mahābhārata*, notably in the dilemma of Yudhiṣṭhira (who is often called a crypto-Buddhist by his more hawk-like companions), in the sin of Indra (who slaughters the Brahmin demon),[6] and in the famous conversation between Arjuna and Kṛṣṇa in the *Bhagavad Gītā*. Theological texts such as the *Gītā* offer sophisticated and not altogether satisfactory answers to the problem; but as it is the primary task of mythology to resolve irreconcilable conflicts,[7] it is in Hindu myths that the most dramatic examples of the conflict may be found.

The contradiction first arose in the post-Vedic age, when *svadharma* became rigidly codified in the lawbooks while *sanātana dharma* became defined in a non-sacrificial context. The Hindus themselves often noted the contradiction between the strictures of the two codes but were unable to resolve the contradiction within the lawbooks; in post-Vedic myths, the contradiction was almost always resolved simply by having *svadharma* overrule *sanātana dharma*; and later, in the age of *bhakti* (loving devotion to a loving god), both *svadharma* and *sanātana dharma* were overruled by *bhakti*.

The contradictions in the formal moral system are particularly sharp in the case of demons, whose class and stage of life may be clear (there are Brahmin demons, ascetic demons, householder demons, demon kings) but who are said to have a basic, characteristic demonic *dharma* of their own. In the cases cited, the Brahmin demon and ascetic demon are paradoxical (because of the elements of sacrificial generosity and non-violence implicti in the Brahmin class and ascetic stage of life) while the householder demon and demon king are not paradoxical. Further confusion is encountered because of the uncertainty in the force of the adjective 'demonic' (*āsura*) : is it descriptive or prescriptive? The adjective is applied to several types of marriage; of the eight forms of marriage, three are demonic: marriage by purchase (*āsura*), marriage by capture (*rākṣasa*), and marriage by trickery (*paiśāca*).[8] Similarly, one of the three types of conquest is demonic—conquest in which rape and pillage take place.[9] In these contexts, the adjective is almost certainly descriptive rather than prescriptive; but, as we shall see, the duty of demons to do the things thought to be typical of them—killing men and opposing the gods—is often taken in a prescriptive sense. The doctrine of *svadharma* assumes a limited but not totally negligible element of free will: though one's role in life is inherited, one can choose to do it well, to do it badly, or not to do it at all. In the view of the lawbooks, this third possibility is frowned upon; in the view of Vedāntic and *bhakti* texts it is often welcomed: man has a preordained fate, but he can deny his fate.

In early myths, the authors of the texts usually feel that *svadharma* should prevail when any conflict arises, and demons are expected to behave demonically; but in many of the later texts, 'good' demons are often allowed to abandon their *svadharma*, their own demonic *dharma*. This shift may be a result of the change in the nature of religion in India and the subsequent change in the relationship between gods and men. In Vedic times, when the gods were thought to live upon sacrificial offerings provided by devout men, the gods helped men to be virtuous and were expected to protect them from the demons who constantly attempted to kill men and to steal from the gods the sacrificial offerings which were their only sustenance—in effect, the life of the gods. But this straightforward alignment of forces—gods and men together against demons—changed when sacrificial power came to be replaced by ascetic and meditative power in the post-Vedic period, and men and demons threatened the gods with ascetic virtue; at this stage, jealous gods often treated good men as their enemies, while ascetic demons were more dangerous to gods than were 'demonic' demons.

Asceticism introduces ambiguities in the post-Vedic alignment of loyalties because, while Vedic gods want men to be good (sacrificial), post-Vedic gods do not want men to be good (ascetic). The sacrifice helps the gods, creating a situation of mutual dependence; asceticism hurts the gods, producing a challenge from men which breaches the basic Vedic relationship of man's dependence on the gods or demonic inferiority to the gods. Asceticism negates the distinction between the categories of gods, demons, and men, producing a problem which can be resolved in either of two ways: one can negate the negation (destroy the ascetic power of the man or demon) or negate the categories (make the ascetic man or demon into a god). The first solution is usually accepted by post-Vedic mythology; the second occurs in *bhakti* mythology.

For *bhaki* resolves the conflict between gods and good men or demons by reintroducing the Vedic concept of man's dependence upon the gods; thus devoted (*bhakta*) men and devoted demons are protected by the gods, who encourage virtue in men—and (unlike the Vedic corpus) in demons too. In the Vedic age, gods and men are complementary, while demons are antagonistic to both; in the post-Vedic (Epic-Purāṇic) age, men and demons are complementary to one another in that they are both often antagonistic to the gods; and in the *bhakti* age, men and good demons are complementary to each other and to the gods, who oppose only evil demons. These three stages somewhat approximate the three paths described in the *Bhagavaḍ Gītā* : the sacrificial stage (*karma*), the yogic or meditational stage (*jñāna*), and the devotional stage (*bhakti*). The oppositions between the three groups of forces (gods, demons, and men) remain remarkably rigid in each stage, regardless of the apparent 'virtue' or 'sin', the *dharma* or *adharma*, of any of the individuals involved in the myths. Indeed, attitudes appropriate to earlier alignments often persist in later myths where the moral qualities of the characters make these attitudes totally illogical.

The priests of the demons form a transitional bridge between each of these stages, mediating between the two 'opposed' categories, whatever their temporary moral standing might be. The basic Vedic function of the priest—to mediate between gods and men—is thus easily extended so that the post-Vedic priest comes to mediate between gods and demons as well. Not knowing the actual parentage (god or demon) of some of the most important priests accentuates the ambiguity; there are priests who are demons, priests who merely sacrifice for demonic demons, or priests who sacrifice for 'good' demons. The priest's role is ambivalent, but there is no question of his primary loyalty: his priestly aspect predominates; his membership in the union takes precedence over his ties to the old-boy network of gods or demons.

In Vedic times, the demon priests follow their *svadharma* as priests rather than demons and thus avoid any conflict with *sanātana dharma* : they perform the sacrifice, and it does not matter whether they sacrifice for gods or for demons; for these two groups, in Vedic texts, pursue the same goal—sacrificial power—though the groups are, by definition, opposed. Thus the priest helps either side to complete a sacrifice, and the treachery of the demon priest who defects to the gods does not affect the character of the priest himself. At the second stage, when it becomes necessary for good demons to be corrupted by evil gods, the treacherous priest of the gods mediates by corrupting the virtuous demons. Finally, in the *bhakti* myths, the demon priest acts either as priest (advising the demon devotee to worship the god) or demon (advising the demon devotee to try to destroy the god).

The complex permutations of the myths of 'dutiful' demons clearly demonstrate the impossibility of resolving the underlying conflict between traditional *svadharma* (according to which the duty of a demon is to interfere with the sacrifice and to kill gods) and *sanātana dharma* (according to which the duty of a demon is to sacrifice to the gods and refrain from killing anyone). Both of these duties may be traced back to very ancient texts, separately. Demons and gods are, by definition, antagonists; the demons try to get the sacrifice for themselves in the earlier texts, but by doing this they are behaving exactly like gods; the two sides are in conflict because the demons are the same as the gods, not because they are morally or spiritually opposed to or even different from the gods. Thus demons must at first ensure that the sacrifice exists (i.e., they must adhere to *sanātana dharma*) but then they must ensure that it comes to them instead of to the gods (*svadharma* for demons, in conflict with *sanātana dharma*). This paradox is heightened by two developments at the time of the Upaniṣads and Buddhism: the demons have developed more specifically injurious characteristics (they rape and pillage and include in their ranks Rākṣasas and Yakṣas who drink blood), and *sanātana dharma*, on the other hand, has developed more specifically non-injurious characteristics (the duty to sacrifice animals is partially replaced by the duty not to kill animals, the duty to tell the truth and to be restrained). By this time, the conflict between the *svadharma* and *sanātana dharma* of the demons is inescapable.

The solution offered by the *Bhagavad Gītā* has proven the basis for the spiritual perceptions of Hindus over several thousand years and cannot be tossed off lightly here; but one of the answers, and the one most pertinent to the subsequent mythology, is the *bhakti* answer: devotion to Kṛṣṇa makes it possible for Arjuna to fulfil both *svadharma* and *sanatana dharma*. When applied to demons, this simple solution was not quite so simple, for indeed the *Gītā* glosses over and over-simplifies several problems. Two examples of conveniently explicit myths dealing with the conflict will illuminate some stumbling points:

> There was a Yakṣa [a fairly benevolent sort of demon] named Harikeśa, devoted to Brahmins and to *dharma*. From his very birth he was a devotee of Śiva. His father said, "I think you cannot be my son, or else you are indeed ill-begotten. For this is not the behaviour for families of Yakṣas. You are by your nature (*svabhāvāt*) cruel-minded, flesh-eating, destructive. Do not behave in this evil way (i.e. the way that you are behaving, worshipping Brahmins and Śiva); the behaviour ordained by the creator should not be abandoned; householders should not perform actions appropriate to the hermitage. Abandon this human nature with its complicated scale of rites; you must have been born from a mortal man, to be set on this wrong path. Among mortals, the appropriate ritual duty arises according to caste (*jāti*); and I too have ordained your duty in the proper way". But Harikeśa went to Benares and performed asceticism until Śiva accepted him as a great yogi, one of his own hosts.[10]

Thus the traditional doctrine of *svadharma* as explained by Harikeśa's father is rejected by the 'good' demon, who prefers to worship Śiva and who is praised for doing so; *bhakti* has become the new *sanātana dharma*, but this time one in which the particular is overruled by the general. More elaborate, but similar in essence, is the tale of Sukeśin:

> There was a great Rākṣasa (night-wanderer, a particularly malevolent sort of demon) named Sukeśin, who received from Śiva the boon that he could not be conquered or slain. He lived according to *dharma*, and one day he saw a hermitage full of sages who taught him about *dharma*, at his request. They began by describing the particular *dharmas* of gods (to perform sacrifice, know the Vedas, etc.), demons (Daityas : fighting, politics, aggression, devotion to Śiva), Yakaṣa (study of the Vedas, worship of Śiva, egoism, aggression), Rākṣasas (raping other men's wives, coveting others' wealth, worshipping

> Śiva) and Piśācas (flesh-eating, lack of discrimination ignorance, impurity, untruth). Then they went on to explain *dharma* in general at great length, including the ten-fold *dharma* for all classes (non-injury, etc.). They concluded: "No one should abandon the *dharma* ordained for his own class and stage of life; he would anger the sun god. Let no one abandon his *svadharma*, nor turn against his own family, for the sun would become angry with him".[11]

The sages' instruction is contradictory: they address Sukeśin as a Rākṣasa and warn him not to abandon his own *dharma* (raping, stealing), but then they tell him about *sanātana dharma*, which involves self-restraint (not easily compatible with rape) and generosity (not easily compatible with stealing). The one ray of light in this dark conflict is the statement that it is part of the *svadharma* of Rākṣasas to worship Śiva. Sukeśin seizes upon this and begins to proselytize his people:

> Sukeśin invited all the demons in his city to an assembly and taught them the primary and ancient *dharma*—non-injury, truth, etc. (i.e., *sanātana dharma*). All the demons began to practise this *dharma*, and due to their brilliant lustre the sun, moon, and stars were paralyzed; night was like day; the night-blooming lotuses did not bloom, thinking that it was still day; owls came out and crows killed them. People thought that the city of the demons was the moon, and that it had overcome the sun. Then the glorious sun thought that the entire universe had been swallowed up by the Rākṣasas, and he learned that they were all devoted to *dharma*, worshipping gods and Brahhims. Therefore the sun, who destroys Rākṣasas, began to think about their annihilation. Finally he realized the weak point [*chidrā*] of the Rākṣasas: they had fallen from their *svadharma*, a lapse which destroyed all their (*sanātana*) *dharma*. Then, overpowered by anger, the sun cast upon the city of Rākṣasas rays that destroy enemies. The city dropped from the sky like a planet that has exhausted its merit.
>
> When Sukeśin saw the city falling he said, "Honour to Śiva", and all the devotees of Śiva began to cry, and when Śiva learned that the Sun had hurled down the city of the demons he cast his glance at the sun, and the sun fell from the sky like

a stone. The gods propitiated Śiva and put the Sun back in his chariot, and they took Sukeśin to dwell in heaven.[12]

The enmity of the sun—predicted by the sages—is based upon a complex of factors, various reactions to the virtuous demon: as a god, the sun is naturally a destroyer of demons and automatically seeks to annihilate any who rise too high; this jealousy is enhanced by his offended *amour propre* when the demon outshines the sun. But a more laudable motive may be seen in the fact that the demon, by being virtuous, is destroying not only his own *dharma* and the *dharma* of his own family (the factor which the sun uses as his excuse to destroy Sukeśin) but the *dharma* of the whole world—owls and stars and lotuses are disturbed by the sudden imbalance in the social order. For cosmic order is maintained by the proper performance of all *svadharmas*.

This is the traditional view: for a demon, evil is its own reward; a demon who tries to be 'good' is violating his *svadharma*, paving the road for his own ruin as well disrupting the cosmic order. Another example of this view may be seen in the myth of the churning of the ocean: when the gods and demons grasp the serpent who serves as the churning rope, the demons are given the tail; they complain that they should not have this 'inauspicious' part of the animal, since they are given to reciting and hearing the Vedas and they are pre-eminent by birth and deeds. Viṣṇu smiles and agrees to their request—whereupon the demons grasp the serpent's head and are overcome by the smoke and flames which issue forth from his mouth.[13] Thus they are ill-served by their Vedic virtues.

A more explicit example of the *svadharma* view may be seen in the myth of Bali, who is viewed here as a good demon.

The demon Bali, ruling in the Kali age (the final, present age of diminished virtue), protected the universe with great virtue. When Kali (incarnate) saw this he sought refuge with Brahmā, for his own nature was being obstructed. Brahmā said, "Bali has destroyed the nature of the whole universe, not merely your nature." Then Kali went to a forest, and the Golden Age (the age of truth, the first of the four ages) took place; asceticism, non-injury, truth, and sacrifice pervaded the world. No one was starving or poor or miserable. Mankind remained devoted to *dharma*. But Bali had usurped Indra's throne, and so, in order to protect the gods, Viṣṇu conquered Bali and made him rule in hell.[14]

Once again, the 'disruption of natural order' appears in close conjunction with the more immediate reason for destroying the good demon—the simple jealousy of Indra, who in this text is said to be particularly sinful and hence particularly vulnerable: Bali was able to usurp Indra's throne because Indra had committed a terrible sin in destroying the embryo in the womb of Diti, mother of demons.[15] The gods—though evil—must be in heaven; the demons, though virtuous, in hell.

But this *svadharma* doctrine is overthrown in the Sukeśin myth by the doctrine of *bhakti*. Śiva punishes the sun and reinstates the good demon by taking him out of the social fabric altogether, transposing him from a lower level to a higher one, removing him to Śiva's heaven, where his virtue will no longer interfere with stars and owls. Thus *bhakti* does not so much contradict *svadharma* as move the problem into another realm where the conflict no longer arises.

Thus Hindus distinguish two categories of duty: *svadharma* and *sanātana dharma*, relative and absolute. This distinction does not pertain to the Vedic age but arises after the advent of Buddhism and Upaniṣadic thought. The contradictions between the two sets of categories were due to the change in the value structure first at the *sanātana dharma* level (when the importance of sacrifice declined and greater emphasis was placed upon asceticism and meditation) and then at the *svadharma* level (when social roles were more rigidly codified). Further changes in the structure of Hindu value systems took place when the stress on *bhakti* eliminated the contradiction by superceding both sets of duty structures.

The good demon is an ambiguous being, whose ambiguity lies in his relation with the gods: he is a non-god and at the same time he shares attributes of the gods. He is P and not-P, a real contradiction. He is by (ideal) definition inferior to the gods, just as the ascetic man is by (ideal) definition dependent upon the gods; but in actuality he is equal or superior to the gods. These two ambiguities could be removed either by de-naturing the good demon or ascetic man (transforming him into a god) or by destroying his 'godly' attributes—killing him, corrupting him, or removing his power. The first of these methods is rare in the case of demons (it does occur in the myth of Prahlāda) but common in the case of men; the second is, however, by far more prevalent in both instances, particularly in pre-*bhaki* texts.

The ambivalence of the priest in the myths is two-fold: the 'bad' priest of the gods and the 'good' priest of the demons. The first instance is relatively simple: where the victory of the gods is the absolute (to be achieved at any cost), the use of any means to defeat the demons appears to be justified. Moreover, the priest may change his patrons and his loyalties through motives neither of *svadharma* nor of *sanātana dharma*, but rather through simple self-interest—greed and opportunism. The demon priest is more complex and comes in a variety of types. The demon priest serving a demonic demon upholds the *svadharma* of demons and the *svadharma* of priests but comes into conflict with *sanātana dharma*. The demon priest who serves a good demon creates no conflict unless he chooses to oppose the good demon, to exhort him in his demonic duties; then he upholds *svadharma* but violates *sanātana dharma*, like the complying priest of the demonic demon.[16]

The role of the demon priest in forming a transitional category between the opposed categories of *svadharma* and *sanātana dharma* changes in each of the three periods. In the Vedic period, the priests mediate by shifting from one patron to the other without contradicting their own priestly nature. In the post-Vedic period, the priests mediate by providing the means to eliminate the ambiguous good demons—by corrupting them, making them consistently demonic. In the *bhakti* period, the priests as mediators sponsor consistency by bringing good demons under the hegemony of the gods. In all cases, the structure of relations between the gods and the demons is preserved; inconsistency (the self-contradictory category of the demon priest) makes possible consistency (the perpetual separation of the ideal categories); mediation preserves distinction.[17]

Notes

[1]Manu 1.2; Yājñavalkya 1.1; cf. P. V. Kane, *History of Dharmaśāstra*, 2nd ed., 1968, vol. I, p. 4.

[2]Medhātithi on Manu 1.2.

[3]*Mitākṣarā* on Yājñavalkya 1.1. Cf. also Vasiṣṭha 4.4, Yājñavalkya 1. 122, Gautama 8.23-24 and 10.52, Manu 10.63, and *Matsya Purāṇa* 52.8-10.

[4]*Arthaśāstra* 1.3.13. (ed.) R. S. Shastry.

[5]*Vāmana Purāṇa* 14.1. (All-India Kashiraj edition).

[6]Cf. Georges Dumézil, *Heur et malheur du guerrier*, Paris, 1969, and *The Destiny of the Warrior* (trans.), Alf Hiltebeital, Chicago, 1970.

[7]See Claude Lévi-Strauss, 'The Structural Study of Myth', in Thomas A. Sebeok (ed.) *Myth : A Symposium*, Bloomington, Indiana, 1958; and my *Asceticism and Eroticism in the Mythology of Śiva*, London, 1973, pp. 33-40.

[8]*Arthaśāstra* 3.2.2.

[9]*Arthaśāstra* 12.1.3.

[10]*Matsya Purāṇa* 180.5 ff. (Ānandāśrama Sanskrit Series edition).

[11]*Vāmana Purāṇa* 11-15. (All-India Kashiraj edition).

[12]*Vamana Purāṇa* 15-16.

[13]*Bhāgavata Purāṇa* 8.7.1 ff.

[14]*Vāmana Purāṇa* 49-51.

[15]*Vāmana Purāṇa* 49-50.

[16]I am indebted to Alex Gunasekara for bringing several of these conclusions into order when I could not see my own way through the chaos of the myths.

[17]An expanded version of this paper forms one chapter of my study of Hindu theodicy, *The Origins of Evil in Hindu Mythology*, University of California 1976.

The Duty of a Buddhist according to the Pali Scriptures

RICHARD F. GOMBRICH

My subject is duty in Buddhism; it is not the word *dharma* in Buddhism. The Ven. Dr Rahula, quoted above by Dr Kunst, has drawn attention to the fourteen meanings of *dharma* listed in the *Abhidhānappadīpikā,* and none of them is 'duty'. This is not to say that I disagree at all with the discussions of the term *dharma* by Dr Kunst and by Dr Weightman and Dr Pandey. But, as Dr Taylor tells us, the classical view differentiated between *varṇāśramadharma* and *sādhāraṇadharma*, between the duty attached to one's station in life and one's duty as a sentient being. The former, of course, is the major subdivision of *svadharma*; Dr O'Flaherty's paper on the *svadharma* of demons reminds us that the two are not synonymous. However, the terms *varṇāśrama-dharma* and *svadharma* are absent in Buddhism, and that for an obvious reason. Buddhism is *prima facie* the religion of a renouncer, a man who has left society and its norms behind him.[1] A Buddhist layman, who has not yet left society behind him, may have duties deriving from his station in life, whether he be king or outcaste, but these are not his duties *qua* Buddhist. As a Buddhist he is on his own, seeking salvation; and it is rather forced to call that a 'duty'.

When I turned my mind to the topic of 'duty in Buddhism' the one phrase which kept echoing through my thoughts was *kataṃ karaṇīyaṃ,* 'what had to be done is done'. This is part of the stereotyped description of an attainment of Enlightenment; it occurs again and again in the Canon. Once a person has been converted to Buddhism he wishes to attain *nirvāṇa*; in Buddhist terminology, he enters on the Noble Eightfold Path by acquiring 'right views' (*sammā diṭṭhi*), which lead him directly to 'right resolve' (*sammā saṃkappa*), and that resolve is to follow the path to its end. But that is hardly a *duty*, for it is self-imposed; it is a duty to no one but oneself. One might object that to speak of duty to oneself is not happy in the Buddhist context; but in the language of daily speech Buddhists did of course talk of 'self'. In the *Attavagga* of the *Dhammapada* it says: [2]

> One should not subordinate one's own good (*atta-d-atthaṃ*) even to the great good of another; having understood one's own good one should be intent on the true good (*sadattha*).

Therefore I would summarily answer the question of what is a Buddhist's duty *qua* Buddhist—of what is the *svadharma* of a Buddhist, one might say—by replying that it is only to seek *nirvāṇa*; then the decision whether we should call that a duty is arbitrary; but the fact that the phrase '*svadharma* of a Buddhist' is my jocular coinage indicates to me that we should not.

The lack of a Buddhist *svadharma*, to remain for a moment with these Sanskrit categories, leaves us with the *sādhāraṇa dharma*, the duties common to all, but, as Dr Taylor well puts it, this was never more than a preceptual tradition. *Sādhāraṇa dharma* is banal. It is generally expressed in platitudinous maxims: be kind, tell the truth. The primary Buddhist formulation of this universal morality, the five 'precepts' or rather undertakings of the laity, is expressed negatively: don't kill, don't steal, don't have wrong sex, don't lie, and don't drink, because that leads to the other four things. No details. To call these rules platitudinous is not to call them flabby; such blanket commands and prohibitions are terrifying in their generality, for it is hardly possible to keep them. Ethically they are admirable. But their generality makes them intellectually uninteresting: they provide little material for discussion. If I were just to say that Buddhists are not supposed to kill or steal or lie or sleep around, one might object that I had not differentiated them from anyone else; and yet there is not that much more to tell.

Not that much more; but there is something. Without erasing the rather negative picture of my subject which I have drawn, I can add some details by mentioning the comparatively few things which Buddhists are positively told to do, as a more specific corollary to what they are to avoid.

There are within Buddhism four social statuses: monk, nun, laywoman and layman. For our purposes we can reduce these to two; using the unmarked gender, I shall refer to monks and laymen.

The Buddhist laity retained their status obligations as members of the wider sociey, except that the obligations otherwise due to Brahmins were transferred to Buddhist monks; Brahmins who converted to Buddhism were of course, from the Buddhist point of view, on a par with other lay householders, and inferior in status to any monk. To denote lay people of respectable status the doublet *brāhmaṇa-gahapatiyo*, 'Brahmins and householders', is often used, but it does not mean that Brahmins were not themselves householders; it is rather a summary expression to denote the propertied classes. Members of these classes are often referred to individually as *kulaputta*, literally 'son of a family' but more accurately 'man of respectable family'. These remarks on social stratification are extremely relevant to Buddhist ethics, for the Buddhist ethos has a distinct flavour of what one might loosely call 'middle class values'—very different, for example, from the Sermon on the Mount. No Buddhist layman was asked to emulate the lilies of the field; disregard for property was all very well for monks, but their material wants would be met by those who remained in society. Thrift is a virtue often commended. Though Buddhist ethics are not couched in terms of *svadharma*, or of the doctrine of *varṇa*, they undoubtedly reflect the values of a particular class.

The most celebrated text on Buddhist lay ethics is the *Sigālovāda* (Advice to Sigāla) *Sutta*;[3] it is the only long sermon devoted to the subject. Its form is interesting, and typical of the Buddha's explicit reformism; he substitutes for a traditional ritual an ethical practice. Nominally he claims to be reinterpreting the ritual, but in fact he is abolishing it. He meets a householder called Sigāla, who is worshipping the six directions: the four cardinal points, nadir and zenith. Questioned, Sigāla says he promised his dying father always to worship the six directions. That is not how to do it, says the Buddha. He proceeds to give a lot of general moral advice, and ends up[4] by identifying the east as parents, the south as teachers, the west as wife and children, the north as friends and companions, the nadir as slaves and servants (*kammakara*) and the zenith as religious wanderers (*samaṇa*) and Brahmins. The nadir and zenith plot Sigāla's social position.

The general moral advice which precedes this identification is heavily weighted towards thrift and prudence. Six outlets for wealth are to be avoided:[5] drinking, being on the streets too late, visiting fairs, gambling, keeping bad company, and laziness. On all these the Buddha expatiates. There follows a lot of advice on choosing the right friends; though it is extremely sound, it may strike us as slightly priggish. Qualities to be desired in a friend include that he should restrain you from wrong and exhort you to right, that he should 'tell you what you have not heard before', and that he should show the way to heaven. In another text,[6] however, the Buddha says that only compassion should make one follow, serve or honour a person inferior to oneself in morality, concentration or wisdom. This may serve to remind us that in India self-righteousness is rarely considered a grave defect.

Most of the duties enjoined on relatives and associates require no comment here, excellent though they are, because they are unsurprising. It is worth nothing that one of the five duties of a husband towards his wife is to provide her with adornment. The wife, for her part, is no lady of leisure, but must look after what the husband earns, and be skilful and hard-working. The duties towards servants are also noteworthy: to assign work according to their strength; to provide food and wages; to look after them when they are ill; to give them a share of rare delicacies; and to give them holidays. The servants are to reciprocate by rising before their master, retiring after him, taking only what he gives them, doing good work, and speaking well of him. The very last duties to be listed are perhaps not the least important: the householder is to be friendly to religious wanderers and Brahmins in thought, word and deed, to keep open house for them, and to provide their temporal wants (*āmisa*).

A similar spirit pervades all moral advice to laity. In a text addressed to women[7] they are recommended to be skilful and industrious at their husband's indoor work, whether it be wool or cotton; to manage the servants; to do what pleases the husband; and to guard his earnings. In these four ways a woman will 'win this world'; the next world is to be won by trust in the Buddha, by keeping the five precepts, by giving alms, and by understanding the Buddhist way to liberation. This distinction between the virtues which 'win' this world and those which win the next clearly conveys to us the relatively humble place assigned to these social duties.

Moreover, the call to these humbler virtues is made explicitly in terms of self-interest. It is true that in a certain refined sense all Buddhist ethics invoke self-interest, as they serve the ultimate end of one's own spiritual liberation. The ethic is an ethic of intention; the pure thoughts purify the mind, and so bring it nearer to attaining *nirvāṇa*. This however is quite a different order of self-interest from the prudential ethic invoked in the Buddha's sermon to the householders of Pāṭaligāma (later to become Asoka's capital, Pāṭaliputra) shortly before his death.[8] Here the Buddha preaches that immorality entails five disadvantages: poverty, a bad reputation, social diffidence, anxiety on one's deathbed, and a bad rebirth. As a corollary, morality brings five benefits, from wealth in this life to a good rebirth in the next.

Five again are the things to be gained from wealth.[9] This wealth is characterized as 'acquired by strenuous effort, amassed by the strength of one's arm, gained by sweat, righteous (*dhammika*), righteously acquired'. With it a man can properly care for his dependents; care for his friends; guard against such catastrophies as kings and thieves; give their due tithe to kin, guests, the dead members of the family, the king and the gods; and make to religious wanderers and Brahmins offerings which will lead him to heaven. If his wealth then diminishes, a man has no regrets, because he has used it well; he is equally free from regret if it increases. In another text, however,[10] the Buddha reassuringly says that the wealth of a man who uses it thus may be expected to increase, not diminish.

The kind of moral advice purveyed in the *Sigālovāda Sutta*[11] is echoed in Asoka's edicts: Asoka enjoins children to obey their parents, masters to behave well towards their servants. These are examples of *dhamma*, a term which Asoka uses in the Buddhist way. Whether or not Asoka was as thoroughly and exclusively imbued with Buddhist teachings as later Buddhist texts claim, there is no doubt that everything in his edicts conforms to the spirit of Buddhist ethics found in the Canon, and in particular to a concept of royal duty radically different from the *kṣatriya svadharma* of the *dharmaśāstras* and the *Bhagavad-Gītā*. This difference can be expressed, as I have suggested, as the absence of the very idea of *svadharma*; a king has the same duties as anyone else, except that his greater power naturally gives him greater responsibilities. Fascinating as they are, Asoka's edicts unfortunately do not give us enough information to decide whether he followed the advice which the Buddha gave in the *Kūṭadanta Sutta*. That text, like the *Sigālovāda Sutta*, is a sermon given in the form of a reinterpretation of a traditional ritual. The Brahmin Kūṭadanta (Crooked-teeth) has heard a rumour that the Buddha knows how to perform a great sacrifice; he himself does not, and wishes to learn. He so far demeans himself as to go and ask the Buddha, a non-Brahmin, to instruct him. The Buddha tells him a fable of how a great king was instructed by his chaplain in the performance of a great sacrifice. The chaplain told the king that there was much lawlessness and civil disorder in his kingdom; property was insecure. The king should deal with this not by taxation, nor by attempting to suppress it by force, but by improving the lot of the people directly.

> The king should supply seed and feed to those who are working at agriculture and animal husbandry; he should supply capital to those who are working at commerce; he should organize food and wages for those working in his own service. Then those people will be keen on their job, and will not harass the countryside. The king will acquire a great pile. The country will be secure, free from public enemies. People will be happy, and dancing their children in their laps they will live, I think, with open doors.[12]

The king took this advice, and only after taking these measures performed a sacrifice in the traditional sense—though in his sacrifice of course no animals were killed. At the end of the story the Buddha admitted, when challenged, that he himself had been the chaplain.

It does not in any way detract from the beauty of this famous passage to point out that it is above all, or at least in the first instance, the interests of the propertied classes which are being advocated. The first thing the chaplain deprecates is the raising of extra taxes; he then goes on to recommend (and the Buddha adds that there occurred) the supply of capital to businessmen, a measure more radical than any monarch can actually have undertaken on a wide scale. But one would love to know what Asoka made of it.

In some verses in the *Sigālovāda Sutta*[13] the Buddha recommends that half of one's wealth should be used for one's business, a quarter consumed, and a quarter saved against an emergency. That suggests to me a high rate of reinvestment. If one wonders where religious donations and offerings are to come from, the commentator Buddhaghosa answers[14] that they are part of consumption; a very fair view, if we remember that such donations (*ceteris paribus*) buy a seat in heaven.

Pasenadi, King of Kosala, is said[15] to have asked the Buddha one day whether there was one thing (*dhamma*) which could accomplish both ends, those of this world and the next. Yes, said the Buddha: diligence (*appamāda*). Just as the elephant's foot is the chief and paragon of all feet, so (we may understand) diligence is chief and paragon of all moral qualities. Diligence can win you longevity, health, beauty, heaven, birth in a good family, and pleasures (*rati*). The modern salutation 'Take care' would have met with the Buddha's approval. The Buddha's own words are so explict that it hardly needs repeating that this diligence, which in psychological terminology is called *sati*, 'awareness', and was probably the Buddha's distinctive contribution to yogic soteriology, is in economic terms realized as the virtue of thrift.

Again, there is nothing pejorative about pointing out that for the symbiosis of laity and religious mendicants (*bhikhku*) it was essential for the layman to be generous; but in order to be generous he had first to be thrifty. The distinctively Buddhist social relationship I have designated as that between monk and layman; within this relationship the layman is in fact known as 'donor' (*dāyaka*), a status which in Buddhist countries is ascribed even before it is achieved. A good *dāyaka* has to be dependable; and he in turn is likely to take kindly to a doctrine which stresses a careful, Apollonian attitude to life and its problems.

But social relations are reciprocal. What now of the monk's side of the bargain ? It is reported[16] that soon after the Buddha had begun preaching his message, at the point when the world contained sixty-one enlightened beings (*arhat*) (including himself), he said to the others,

> Go, monks, travel for the welfare and happiness of many people, out of compassion for the world, for the benefit, welfare and happiness of gods and men. Let no two go the same way.

In asking his disciples to spread his message to the public, he was acting in consonance with his own decision, a little earlier, not to remain in solitude, quietly enjoying the bliss of his own Enlightenment, but to give himself the trouble of announcing his discovery to the world—an activity which was to dominate the remaining forty-five years of his life. Though it is never so expressed, the principal duty of a monk—his own search for salvation apart—is to maintain this tradition, and to preserve the *Dhamma* for those who have ears to hear it.

The two claims on a monk—his own quest for Enlightenment and his spreading of the Buddha's word—are not always easy to reconcile. The conflict between them came to a head in a famous episode in Buddhist history. Late in the first century B.C., in the reign of King Vaṭṭangāmaṇī, Ceylon suffered from invasion and a terrible famine. Many monks died; others emigrated to India. Those remaining feared that the Canon, which still depended on oral tradition, would be lost. Their concern led to a meeting near the town of Mātalē at which the Pali Canon and its commentaries were for the first time committed to writing. The same crisis produced the controversy whether religious learning was more important than the practice which led directly to Enlightenment. Obviously both are desirable; they appeared as alternatives only at a time of crisis. On this occasion the monks decided that the basis of Buddhism (*sāsana*) is learning. Though this decision certainly appears discordant with the Buddha's own views, it was perhaps a lucky one for us. What in fact emerged as a result was division of labour : a tradition, still today of great importance in Theravāda Buddhism, that a monk can choose either of two roles: book duty (*ganthadhura*) or meditation duty (*vipassanādhura*).[17] (The word I have translated as 'duty' literally means 'yoke'.) The corollary of choosing book duty is likely to be living in a village; the corollary of choosing the contemplative life is likely to be living in isolation in the jungle. I should stress that the two roles do not involve *exclusive* emphasis : the village monk is supposed to meditate, and the forest monk to be learned. But the roles are just that: prescriptions for action in social circumstances. The 'book-monk' is to consider it his *duty* to preserve (and promulgate) knowledge of Buddhism; the meditator recognizes no such claim upon him. But these two roles are, in theory at least, freely chosen, and may be abandoned or exchanged, just as a Buddhist monk is in theory free at any time to revert to the status of layman. (The constraints on this freedom are the societal pressures which may operate in individual circumstances, and thus do not concern us here.)

The duty of the monk towards the laity may, then, be summed up as the duty to preach to them and to instruct them in Buddhism. Monasteries have of course been the traditional schools of Buddhist countries, and the instruction they imparted went well beyond what was necessary for the preservation of the scriptures. The involvement of monks in ritual, demanded by the laity—an involvement very limited compared to that of a Christian priest, but nevertheless onerous—occurs as an extension of preaching: sermons at funerals, commemorative ceremonies for the dead, the recitation of sacred texts to avert misfortune. Most of these rituals are occasions for the formal and demonstrative presentation of food (and sometimes of permissible possessions) to monks by the laity, so that they dramatically illustrate the reciprocity between the Buddhist roles of monk and layman.[18]

Finally, there is one other kind of Buddhist duty which deserves mention. The Buddha's followers were distinctive not in renouncing the world and becoming medicants, but in forming an organized community, the Sangha. Insofar as they were a social community, they had roles and obligations towards each other. Monastic duties were called *vatta* in Pali, and there is not a great deal about them in the Canon. That section of the Canon devoted to the externals of a monk's life, the *Vinaya Piṭaka,* has two main parts, of which one consists entirely of an exposition of the rules governing the life of the individual,[19] rules which are but an elaboration of his basic renunciations and abstinences. The other main part deals with the life of the community, but even here many of the formulations are negative or in terms of things permitted, rather than in terms of positive injunctions. Monks are exhorted to look after each other when they are sick. Most of their duties towards each other, however, are summed up in one chapter[20] and the fourteen heads of this chapter came to be known as the fourteen major duties (*duddasa mahā vatcani*).

Despite the term 'major' (or 'great'), the duties are laid out in the detailed and sometimes even trivial practical terms which are typical of the whole *Vinaya Piṭaka*. The fourteen headings are: the duties of a monk arriving at a new monastery; of a resident monk (towards arrivals); of a monk leaving a monastery; behaviour in a refectory; on an alms round; of a forest-dwelling monk; of (cleaning) lodgings; of using a bathroom; of washing after defecating; of using a privy; of sharing a cell with one's preceptor; of a preceptor towards the junior who shares his cell; of a teacher towards his pupil; and of a pupil towards his teacher. A teacher (*ācariya*) is but a surrogate preceptor (*upajjhāya*), and the relation of each towards his pupil is identical, so the last two sets of duties are a verbatim repetition of the previous two. Many of the other ordinances, notably the precise instructions on cleaning out a cell, are also repeated under different heads. To give the flavour of this material, I quote one paragraph from the seventeen which describe a monk's duties towards his preceptor (with whom he shares a cell); it begins when the two are entering a village, which would normally be to beg for food.[21]

> He should not interrupt the preceptor when he is speaking. (But) if the preceptor is bordering on an offence, then, speaking himself, he should warn him. When he is returning, he should make ready a seat, having come back first; he should set out water for washing the feet, a foot-stool, a footstand; having gone to meet him, he should receive his bowl and robe, he should give back the inner clothing(given) in return, he should receive his inner clothing. If a robe is damp with perspiration, he should dry it for a short time in the sun's warmth, but a robe should not be laid aside in the warmth. He should fold up the robe. When folding up the robe, having made the corners turn back four finger-breadths, he should fold up the robe, thinking "Mind there is no crease in the middle". The waistband should be placed in a fold (of the robe). If there is almsfood and the preceptor wishes to eat, having given him water, almsfood should be placed near (him).

Other duties mentioned in the commentaries include sweeping the monastic premises and whitewashing the stupa. But I need not expatiate further on details of the monastic life, on which there is good secondary literature.[22]

The kinds of Buddhist duty discussed in this paper may now be summarized: *a*) The true duty of a Buddhist is to progress spiritually towards Enlightenment; *b*) monks and laymen have certain reciprocal duties: (i) The laity must materially support the monks. In harmony with this purpose, they are exhorted to thrift. (ii) Monks are to preserve the doctrine and preach to the laity; *c*) From the existence of a monastic community arise certain duties, minutely prescribed, of monks towards each other.

If in this paper I have taken the subject all the way down from the lofty generalities and philosophical speculations of *Dharma* to the details of how to fold up a monk's robe, is not only (I hope) malice or incompetence on my part. It reflects the nature of my subject. One can never stress enough that Buddhism, for Buddhists, is *practical*: there is a goal, and all you need is to get there. The 'big questions' which interest most people are the very questions the Buddha refused to answer. Take care of yourself, he said, have enough to eat, be sensible; eschew metaphysics. Then one day you will find that what has to be done is done (*kataṃ karaṇīyaṃ*). Taking the words in a more modest sense, I end my paper on the same note. *Kataṃ karaṇīyaṃ.*

Notes

Abbreviations

AN—Anguttara Nikāya

DA—Dīgha nikāya Atthakathā

DN—Dīgha Nikāya. Small roman numerals are the serial numbers of the *suttas*, large roman the volume numbers.

SN—Saṃyutta Nikāya

[1]Compare Lingat on the *dharmasūtra* tradition: 'Pour le saṃnyāsiṇ on devra admettre qu'il n'y a plus de règle de dharma'. On the other hand, Lingat shows that in the orthodox tradition a *śūdra* was not supposed to become a *saṃnyāsin*. *Les Sources du Droit dans le Systéme Traditionnel de I'Inde*, Paris, 1967, p. 67.

[2]*Dhammapada* 166

[3]*DN* xxxi.

[4]Op. cit., §27=*DN* III, pp. 188-189.

[5]§7, p. 182

[6]*AN*. I. 125

[7]*AN*. IV. 269-271.

[8]*DN* II. 85.

[9]*AN* III. 45-6

[10]*AN* III. 75-8.

[11]*DN*. v.

[12]*DN* I. 135

[13]*DN*. III. 188

[14]*DA*. III. 177

[15]*SN*. I.86-7

[16]*Mahāragga* p. 21

[17]On this question, see especially Walpola Rahula, *History of Buddhism in Ceylon*, Colombo, 1956, pp. 158-161.

[18]For an excellent anthropological study of these complementary roles today see Jane Bunnag, *Buddhist Monk, Buddhist Layman*, Cambridge, 1973.

[19]These rules are known collectively as the *pāṭimokkha.*

[20]*Cullavagga* VIII. I am grateful to the Ven. W. Rahula for this reference and to Mr. Michael Carrithers for first drawing my attention to the fourteen major duties.

[21]*Cullavagga* VIII. 11.4 (Trans) I. B. Horner, *The Book of the Discipline*, vol. V, London, 1952, p. 312.

[22]E.g. Rahula, *op. cit.*; E. W. Adikaram, *Early History of Buddhism in Ceylon*, Colombo, 1946; the books of Sukumar Dutt.

Rājakāriya or the Duty to the King in the Kandyan Kingdom of Sri Lanka

ALEX GUNASEKARA

Introduction

This paper focuses attention on one aspect of the relation between the subject and the king in Kande Uda Rata, better known to the West as the Kingdom of Kandy or the Kandyan Kingdom. It discusses the duty of the subject to the King. This short essay is divided into four sections :

I. The Sinhala notions of duty.
II. The duty of the subject to the King.
III. The social bases of duty.
IV. The presuppositions and conditions of the duty of the subject to the King.

In a study of this nature, based as it is on documents, not all answers to the investigators' questions can readily be found. The researcher is limited by the data available—a dilemma an anthropologist, a good one, is not faced with. My informants are dead. Some of the ideas and explanations that they may have provided cannot be retrieved. This would be true of any historical study. But there is another difficulty. There were no jurists or works on law written by the people of the time. Indigenous legal exegesis is absent. The extent to which the judicial authorities or any others consulted Sanskrit works on law one does not know for sure. The comment made by the Kandyan monk, who in reply to the Dutch governor said that the *dharmaśāstras* were consulted by the King, may be true but there is no evidence to support it. None of the judicial decrees (*sittu*) refers to any compilation of law, not even to the *dharmaśāstras*. They need not, since the judicial authorities, in giving their judgements, were guided by custom and morality. In case of doubt they resorted to what we would call ordeals. Therefore from the point of view of legal practices, the Kandyan system was traditional in the Weberian sense.

I. The Sinhala notions of duty

(*a*) *The approach to the study of duty:* In the first instance in treating a subject such as the theme of this paper one is faced with the problem of translation. This is the expression of the ideas of one language through the concepts of another. This process entails the examination and selection of semantic fields of the terminology of each language. Here one has to take into account not only the respective terminologies but also the categories of thought.

Secondly a study of this nature consists of the identification of those acts relating to expressions of the notions of duty.

From then on, the student's attention diverges into either of two directions depending on his interests. On the one hand he could examine the acts as propositional acts, which leads him to an examination of the logical contents of those acts. In doing so the student is engaged in examining the logical implications of the statements made by the people under study. On the other hand, the student could examine the presuppositions of the notions of duty.

There appear to be two categories of presuppositions of duty. The first is that of the normative presuppositions. The second is that of the structural presuppositions. The normative presuppositions are part of the total ideology of a people, while the structural presuppositions refer to social structure. The relation between ideology and social structure is problematic.

This paper is not concerned with the intricacies of the logic of thought. It consists of an attempt to grasp the normative and structural presuppositions of the Kandyan Sinhala notions of duty.

(*b*) *Towards a definition of duty*: When one refers to duty in English one has to be sure of what one means by it before one can look for analogous notions in another society. In English the term duty tends to be used synonymously with obligation. In a strictly juristic context in English duty could be distinguished from obligation.[1] It is proposed that for the purposes of this paper the wider connotation will be used. The other meanings of duty in English will be ignored for the present.

Duty in the sense of obligation expresses the notion that someone should, ought or must do something.[2] These terms 'should', 'ought' and 'must' have connotations other than action that one is obliged to do. For a study of duty only the imperative connotations of these terms are relevant. One needs to note the difference between being obliged to do something and having an obligation to do something. In these days of hijackings this distinction hardly needs to be discussed, not that the relation between duty and physical coercion is irrelevant.

Where someone should, ought or must do something in an imperative sense one can speak of the existence of a rule. Duty then consists of a rule. All rules do not imply duties; Von Wright[3] makes this point very clear. Duties are implied or expressed by rules regulating relations between persons or groups. These rules therefore are regulative rules prescribing what action should or should not be done. Again not all regulative rules prescribe duties because regulative rules range from mere prescriptions of action to rules imposing a high degree of constraint on the actor or actors. Analytically the concept of a sanction being associated with a regulative rule helps one to distinguish those rules which imply duties from those which do not.

(*c*) *Sinhala conceptions of duty:* When the Kandyan Sinhalas, as much as any other Sinhalas, expressed the notion that something should, ought or must be done they used the term *yutu*,[4] as in *yā yutuyi*[5] 'should go' or *no kiya yutu*[6] 'should not speak'. Imperative forms were naturally used to express commands: *karapan* 'do' (singular) *karapallā* 'do' (plural).[7]

Any action that should be done was *kartavya* and what should not be done was *akartavya*. These are literary forms. The *katikavata* issued in the time of *Rājādhirājasiṇha* refers to *akartavya kriyāvan*[8]—prohibited acts. *Kāriya* was a more popular term which expressed the idea of what should be done. It is derived from the Sanskrit *kārya*, that which should be done. In the Gadaladeniya slab inscription the local ruler refers to such actions quite clearly:

> ...(we) will summon the militia of the country and go with it on our service and will carry out the work referred to in accordance with the mighty command (*ē kiyana kāriya*).[9]

Though the identity of the King to whom this promise was made is not clear, the terms are significant. Codrington[10] translates the word *kāriya* by 'business'. I will argue later that the people's conception of business in such a context included the notion of duty. Even in this instance the defeated rebels agree to do any work according to the commands of the King. What is noteworthy is the complexity of the term *kāruja*. On the one hand it has a descriptive connotation and on the other a prescriptive connotation. The word used to express this complex notion is derived from a term expressing prescription. The modern *kaṭayuṭu* conveys the same ambiguity.

The rules that prescribed the duties in the Kingdom consisted of those arising from *siritā* (custom), *susiritā* (good conduct as opposed to *dusiritā*, evil conduct, also referred to as *kupāḍam*), *sila* (precepts of Buddhism), *dharma* (righteous conduct), and *āgnā*, *panata*, and *vyavasthā* (three terms for the commands of the King).

Susiritā and *dusiritā* consisted of conventional definitions of good and bad ways of behaving. *Kupāḍama* is from the Tamil which in turn is borrowed from the Sanskrit *ku patha*, the low way, evil path.

In the Kingdom neither custom nor the commands of the King were codified. The rules prescribing action were part of the oral tradition of the country. The King's specific commands were issued from time to time and conveyed to the country by the officials and their underlings.

Dhamma is a fundamental Buddhist concept used by the Sinhala people through the ages. In its broadest sense it signifies righteous action. This was based on Buddhist ideas of good and evil action. The prescriptions of *dhamma* applied to King and subject alike. The King in addition was expected to follow the ten kingly virtues, *dasarajadhamma*. The Kandyan text *Mandarampuvata* describes approvingly a King's reign with the words:

> The inhabitants of the country abandoned bad conduct (*dusiritā*) and practised good conduct (*susiri*). They offered the four

> requisites to the order of monks with devotion. They paid homage to (their) parents, teachers and elders of their families. They constantly gained their livelihood righteously (*dāhāmin*) according to the commands of the King (*raja ana iesina*).[11]

In this idealized account of the actions of the inhabitants in the time of Vimaladharmasuriya II one notes the actions that they were expected to do. The Buddhist rules of good conduct are touched upon. The idea that the inhabitants secured their livelihood in accordance with *dharma* and at the same time complied with the injunctions of the King expresses the Buddhist ideal. This view implies righteous subjects and an equally righteous King. But there is no hint here of whether any of the occupations violated the Buddhist ideals of *dharma*. This conception of *dharma* is prescriptive. In the *Mandarampuvata* story of the reaction of the ministers to King Narendra's violation of custom they are made to say:

> It is not a *dharma* that a person of low caste should be considered to be high caste. It is not consistent with the Solar Dynasty that the King should harass his subjects.[12]

Here *dharma* refers to the rules of caste which the king is accused of violating. The ministers are portrayed as admonishing the King for violating the norms of custom.

II. The duty of the subject to the King

(*a*) *Rājakāriya*: Before one could discuss in abstract terms the duty of the subject to the King, it would be preferable to look for specific duties of the subject and the way in which they were conceived by the people. It is only after this is done that one could attempt to infer whether the different categories of duty could be brought within a general category of the duty of the the subject. It will be shown in what follows that separate categories of persons had specific duties. But these duties were conceived of by the people as the duty to the King. Nevertheless these did not encompass all the duties of the subject to the King.

In the Kandyan Kingdom *rājakāriya* meant several things. The fundamental notion among these was the duty to the King.

Again this is the abstract way in which we translate this term into English. In Sinhala, *kāriya* meant both work done and work which ought to be done—hence duty. The same term has a descriptive and prescriptive aspect. *Rājakāriya* was the King's work in the sense of work done for the King rather than by the King. It was not just any work done for the King but work one was obliged to do for the King. To speak of *rājakāriya* in the Kingdom was to speak of anything done for the King as a duty. What was done as *rājakāriya* by the king's subjects ranged from personal services to contributions in kind. When the inhabitants spoke of doing *rājakāriya* they referred to the specific action that they performed for the King as in *kada rājakāriya*. The notion of duty, the abstract notion, was also expressed by the same word as in (i) 'the *rājakāriya* belonging to me ... ", (ii) the correct *rājakāriya*.[13] No distinction was made in terminology between the performance of an action as a duty and the duty to do such action. This, after all, is the way language is ordinarily used. *Rājakāriya* was action regulated by specific rules. These rules were part of the body of legal rules of the Kingdom. The rules of *rājakāriya* presuppose other rules which regulate the actions of the King and subject. These in turn presuppose the rules on which the whole social order was based. These latter rules defined the roles of the King and the subjects, and they comprised the ideological structure of Kandyan society. They may be distinguished from the regulative rules and be designated the constitutive rules. These define how the world came into being and how the institution of Kingship arose.

In the grants of the King it is not usual to find any reference to *rājakāriya*. It is customary for the King to express the fact that the grantee was granted the estate described in the charter so that he and his progeny for generations to come could enjoy the estate 'in the heritable manner'. In exceptional circumstances where the grantee and his descendants were exempted from any of the levies to the King, this was recorded. Where such a privilege was of a temporary nature, no mention of it was made in the charter. The grant to laymen, under normal conditions, implied that some form of *rājakāriya* was provided by the holder of the estate to the King.

The charter of Kirti Sri Rajasinha (of Saka Era 1698/A.C. 1776) however is one of those exceptions.[14] It records the assigning of an estate in the village of Dombagammana in the Province of Sabaragamuva once held by Dombagammana Danapala Mudaliyā to his *munubura* (grandson) Vellakkattu Mudaliyā. The charter states that this estate was enjoyed by the former while performing *vada rājakāriya* with goodwill and loyalty. The charter refers to the estate as that of the village of Dombagammana, though the paddy land of the estate of the grantee was only four *amunu*. It was evidently a *nindagama*, an estate held on superior tenure. Here the King does refer to *rājakāriya* that was due from the estate and performed to the satisfaction of the King.

Another term that is relevant to this discussion of *rājakāriya* is *nile*. *Nile* usually means office but the term is also used to denote a landholding as 'X's *nile*', i.e. X's landholding. It is possible that the latter term is derived from the Tamil for 'land.' But since obligations were attached to land, performance of *rājakāriya* on the basis of holding land was analogous to the performance of an office (which was also *rājakāriya*), where remuneration was in the form of a landholding. It appears that the ambiguity of the homonyms was based on the ambiguity of the relation of the subject to the King through land.

The connection between legal claims, claims upheld by the courts of the Kingdom, and *rājakāriya* is clearly stated in a text of a decree issued by the governor of a province. The decree states that the assignee is to enjoy the land while performing *rājakāriya*. Though this statement in the decree reads as a matter of fact and that is how the judicial authorities and the people expressed the notion, as a matter of fact, there is an underlying rule. In analytical terms one would refer to it as a normative rule. It was so well understood that there was no need to enunciate the rule. One notices that the word *yutu*, 'should', is not used in the decree. It was obvious to the people that if the *rājakāriya* was not performed *bhukti*, enjoyment, could not be legally maintained. Of course there were other rules about resumption of estates.

This paper is concerned with the evidence for the ideas and and actions concerning the duty of the subject to the King. The term *rājakāriya* does not occur in the early grants of Senasammata Vikramabahu or in the accounts of that time in the *Rajavaliya*. Yet there is a word which expresses an analogous idea. This is the term *mehe* (*meheya*) which means service. It is found in the

Alutnuyara Slab Inscriptions[15] indited in the time of Senasammata Vikramabahu, in the *Rajavaliya*[16] and in the poem written in the time of the Kandyan Kingdom—the *Mandarampuvala*.[17] The latter text also uses the term *mehevara* which connotes the same thing. The word *mehe* has a long history and was used both for compulsory service, as in *vahal mehe*, the service of a slave, and for a voluntary service. There is nothing specific about the term that links it with the King unless the context of a statement brings in the meaning of service to the King. Reference has already been made to the notion of a *meheya* of a slave. *Meheya* can be from anyone who offers services and the nominal form which connotes someone who performs service is *mehekaru*, servitor, servant. The latter term has a clear connotation of subordination. Service to the King was performed by the subjects in the time of Senasammata Vikramabahu though it was not called *rājakāriya* but *mehe*. Sometime before the emergence of the independent kingdom of Kande Uda Rata, a local ruler by the name of Jotiya Situ, evidently the same as the signatory to the Madvala Inscription in the early part of the fifteenth century, is reported in the Kotte Rajavaliya as not having furnished the King with taxes and tribute and not supplying men for service (*mehevara*). In the same idiom King Sri Sangabo Sri Jayavira Prakramabahu, identified by Codrington as Dharma Parakarama Bahu IX of Kotte (circa A.C. 1513), refers to the militia who are summoned for the King's service (the King is speaking here, so he says 'for our service' *ape sevākakamata*)[18] and states that the obligation, *ē kāriya*, should be done to the best of their ability. This service is not called *rājakāriya* but just *sevākakam* and *kāriya*. That there was a notion or a practice of service to the King is clear. In this inscription the service of the soldiers is called *sevākakama* and in the *Mandarampuvata*, military service is referred to as *heva mehe*; again the term *rājakāriya* is not used in this context. This is certainly not due to reasons of metre. The words *mehe* and *meheya* occur several times in this text while the word *rājakāriya* occurs only once, and this towards the end of the work. It is very likely that the term *rājakāriya* came into popular use later in the history of the Kingdom. The earlier term for obligatory service to the King was *mehe* and this continued to be used in the Kingdom. *Mehe* is the synonym of *kāriya* and is interchangeable with *mehevara* in the sense of service. However, the term *rājakāriya* in its primary sense makes clear the notion of obligation to the King which neither *mehe* nor *mehevara* makes explicit without the appropriate context.

A noteworthy feature of Kandyan ideology of obligatory service is the transfer of the idiom of service to the King into a metaphor to express the obligatory service on account of holding land or using land. Service to the King and service to the King under the administration of the officers of the King are literally *rājakāriya*. The transfer of the idiom into a metaphor occurs when the obligatory service arising from the use of land is provided for service in the estates held on privileged tenure, *nindagam*. The services of dependent tenants in the estates of religious establishments were also known as *rājakāriya*. Of course, in the latter instances the service subsequently provided to the holders and controllers of these privileged estates would in principle have been provided for the King. If any estate reverted to the King the dependent tenants would continue to perform *rājakāriya*.

The legal use of land or the claim to legal enjoyment of land brought in a legal obligation to provide *rājakāriya* to the appropriate receiver of *rājakāriya*. The fact that the King took this for granted was shown by his omission of any reference to this condition except where some unusual incident made him mention the fact. The question then arises whether the people, the subjects of the King, conceived of *rājakāriya* as an obligation that was formulated as a rule, and if so, how they expressed the notion. On the one hand we can for the purpose of argument postulate, following Weber, that Kandyan society being tradition-oriented, the rules of custom prevailed, and that the inhabitants followed the practice of *rājakāriya* as a matter of habit. Indeed one could adduce in favour of this view the fact that the King himself did not refer to the conditions under which lands were held or granted. The premise on which this paper commenced its exposition of obligation was that an obligation was something that people had to do and that this notion was embodied in a rule. Further, that a breach of an obligation was liable to make the person who breaks the rule subject to some reaction against this. In any case, a breach of a rule was naturally considered wrong; one might go a step further and argue that wherever a question of wrong action was raised, a question of a rule of action and the breach of it was involved.

The terms *niyama* as an adjective and *niyamaya* as a noun are crucial to an understanding of the people's notions of their obligation to the King. This is not to say that there are no other relevant terms but they too come within the range of the connotation of these terms. *Niyama karanava* is to order, to command, to prescribe, and *niyamaya* is an order, command, rule. A *niyamaya* can come from someone wielding power such as the King. But for the commands of the King other terms were in use, some of them of long standing.

If the inhabitants referred to *niyama kala rājakāriya*, then they were speaking of the obligatory service that was commanded to be performed. The notion of command was expressed by the terms *āgnāva* and *panata*, both conveying this denotation as does *niyamaya.* A term which was more current in the early part of the Kingdom was *vyavasthava* and its variant *vavasthava*. The *Mandarampuvata* uses both terms, *vyavastha* and *niyama karanava*, to express the notion of royal command as in

> *kalē vyavasthā niyamayen*
> he did by his command[19]

Any instruction given by the King was by way of command. The implication of a command to a subject was that it was the obligation of the latter to obey it. Even a grant of land to a subject was phrased in terms of a command of the King. In the latter part of the history of the Kingdom the term often used in land grants expressing the fact of the King's command was the term *panivuda panata*, *panivuda* and *panata* having the same meaning.

I have brought two separate ideas into this discussion: the first is that the obligations of the people under discussion were conditional, that there was a contractual element in them, and the second that they were seen as commands of the King. These two notions might at first sight appear antithetical. Then again I have suggested a third idea, that the obligation of the subjects arising from the use of land might be guided by custom. In the discussion already presented it was suggested that the subjects of the King were obliged to obey the commands of the King, being subject to his power. The question that one immediately formulates, given these three conditions, is how were they conceived by the people? Take the first. This is the analyst's own formulation, but could it have escaped the attention of the people? The text *Ket Habevinisa* shows how the inhabitants thought of the relation of the King to the land. The King was *bhupati*, the lord of the earth:

> Those who are the Masters of the earth are called *Bhupati*. . .[20]

From the point of view of the King, all the paddy lands of the Kingdom were divided into units for purposes of *rājakāriya*. Any person claiming paddy was liable to be required to furnish *rājakāriya*. As I described earlier, in the current ideology of the people, that is the dominant ideology in the time which was upheld by the King and his government (*rajaya*), the subjects were required to provide *rājakāriya*. Periodically the officers of the King would carry out cadastral surveys for purposes of *rājakāriya*. The legal relation of the subject to the land and the politico-legal relation of the King to the land, and therefore to the subject who made legal claims to it, established a relationship which had a structure of exchange. The assignment of *rājakāriya* was an act of the King; it could be assigned by his officers on his behalf. Therefore *rājakāriya* was conceived by the inhabitants as originating from the command of the King. The allocation of the services to the different landholdings was also, directly or vicariously, an act of the King. Where services were freshly allocated the caste status of the landholder had to be taken into account by the King and his officers. Then vacant land could also be allocated by the King or on his behalf, so far as the formal rules of allocation were concerned, to a subject of the King according to the appropriateness of the service required from the land allocated to the caste status of the allocatee. It is here that custom came into force directly. The legal norms of service, as one would express it analytically, needed to conform to the norms of caste. Norms of caste were essentially matters of custom. The King was expected to uphold them.

(*b*) *Loyalty to the King*: *Rājakāriya* clearly was duty imposed on some of the subjects by virtue of their holding claims over land. Others, though not holding titles, were required to do *rājakāriya* for using land. If we speak of the politico-economic basis of this duty there were duties which were entirely of political origin. The latter were duties which fell on all the subjects of the King. Loyalty (*paksa piramana*)[21] and faithfulness (*hondai viśvasa*)[22] were duties that fell on the subjects of the King. Outstanding instances of loyalty and self-sacrifice were rewarded by the King. These were only for exceptional circumstancess The rule becomes very much in evidence when it is broken. A man could be accused of being a rebel (*parali*)*a*)especially if he was suspected of plotting against the King. The punishment for being a traitor was death and confiscation of property. The Metale *mahadusane* Kadim Pota [23] gives us a legendary account of the King's reaction to the insubordination of the Mudaliyas of Metale. Their lands—and elephants—were confiscated and they were put to death, 'pushed', *tallukalā*. It was the duty of the subjects also to be obedient (*kikaru*) and subordinate (*yafahat pahat*). The very concept of king, *rāja*, implies authority; loyalty and subordination are the complementary attributes of the King-subject relation.

III. *The social bases of duty*

The model of caste relations is implied in the concepts of the prevalent ideology, a model which is repeatedly found in the manuscript material attributable to the eighteenth and nineteenth centuries, and in the *Mandarampuvata*. Earlier I noted the terms *mehe, mehevara, mehekaru* meaning service in the first two instances and provider of service, servant, in the last. The idea of *kula*, castes which were the servants and who provided services to the superior castes, *maha sal kula*, is found in the *Mandarampuvata*.[24] The ideology depicts the *govikula* as having claims to hold the high office of ministers of the King (*mahamatikam*); the servant castes, *mehekuladanan*, serve them and, what is more relevant to my exposition, it is the King who assigns land and services of the servant castes to the high caste officers of his administration. These officers in turn are described as attending on the King with their retinue including the servant castes (*mehekula danan saha privara vena vena*).[25]

But this model relates to the subordinates of the King. For a model which pictures the ideal relations of the service of the subject to the King one has to turn to the language and the myths of the people. There is no articulated exposition of a theory of kingship in Kande Udarata. The people's conception has therefore to be pieced together.

It may sound a little too demanding if one were to ask what conception the King himself had of kingship. The Kings did express their notions of the office in their statements in edicts, epistles, and grants that they issued. They made public declarations of their exalted nature, and when reaffirming their claims they asserted their royal ancestry. They did more. They used myths and symbols, known to the people, by which they asserted the legitimacy of their claims and the validity of their power. These were drawn both from myth and history.

The articulate and polyglot King, Rajasinha II, went further. He justified his being addressed as *deviyo*, which in its primary sense means a god—an expression which the Dutch found uncom fortable to use.[26] The King explained that it was the convention-for his subjects to address him by this epithet. His expostulation would have sounded acceptable to his subjects. After all, did not the Buddha declare that of the three kinds of *deva*, the King was *sammuti deva*—a god by convention. A similar conception is evident in a letter of Rajasinha's half-brother, Vijayapala.[27]

The Kings of Kande Udarata also claimed to be descended from Mahasammata, the primaeval King of the Buddhist tradition. Again they claimed to be descended from the Solar line of descent (*surya vamsaya*), the lineage of Mahasammata.[28]

The ritual of transforming a claimant to kingship (*raja kama*) into a King transforms the person of the claimant. He assumes a new name. This is done at the shrine of the gods. He girds the Sword of State, *magul kaduva*, and ascends the throne, *sinhasanarudha venava*.[29] From there on the King is subject to ritual rules of behaviour and, similarly, the subjects are required to observe corresponding ritual rules which separate the King from the rest of the people.

In the prevalent ideology the King belongs to the royal caste, therefore the royal family. He has assumed the office of King which by tradition has been the privilege of a person of royal descent. In the ritual of assuming the office, the country *rata* is consulted and accepted. This acceptance is recognized by the *radalavaru* of the King's court. He is the valid claimant to the office, having been selected by the preceding King or by the will of the gods and the consent of the people and the ministers.

The King was entitled to *yasa* and *isuru*, fame and wealth. He was entitled to exercise power, *balaya*. The King was the lord of men, *narapati*, lord of the earth, *bhupati*, the master of Sri Lanka, *Sri Lankesvara.*[30] He was the protector of the people (*janaya*).

In the myths of the people the first King, Mahasammata, provides an archetype of kingship. The Sinhalas, being Buddhists, have no Creater, but the Buddhist tradition does have a myth of the periodic creation in every *kalpa*, aeon. Mahasammata was a King elected by common consent at the beginning of the Bhadra Kalpa. The succession of kings continues from him in the solar dynasty. In the same line were born the great kings of yore, including Manu.

Just as human beings had kings, so had animals. To have kings was part of the order of things. The theory of *karma* explained how some are high and others low, some powerful and rich and others subordinate and poor. It was *dharma* that there should be a difference between those of high caste and those who are low, *hina*.

A feature of the dominant ideology was that of the caste hierarchy. Earlier I referred to the model of giver and receiver of services and the relationship of master and servant (*mehekaru*) between them. This is the first theme in the classification of castes on a hierarchical basis of service, services which are hereditary. The second is the notion of purity, *pirisindu.*[31] This notion is expressed several times in the *Mandarampuvata* in referring to the royal caste, *rajakula.*[32] The opposite category of this binary division of purity/pollution in Sinhala is *kilutu*. The *Rajavaliya* refers to the myth where a member of a royal caste finding that he could not give away his sisters in marriage, says, 'This is a *kiluta*, blot, on our royal caste. . .'.[33] The third is the rule implied in this myth of not contracting marriage outside the limits of caste. When the *bandaravaliya*, the royal lineage, became mixed (*musu*, from the Sanskrit *miśrita*) its claim to the office was destroyed on the grounds that the King should have a consort from an unmixed royal family and thereby make the royal lineage pure (*pivitura*).[34] The same value is affirmed in the myth from the *Rajavaliya* already referred to where the prince says that he would rather lose his life than destroy his caste.

Still, within the prevalent ideology, how did the caste rules fit in with the obligations to the King? In Kande Udarata, rules of caste were primarily a matter of custom and the services from different castes to the King were channelled through the use of land. Conflicts of caste specializations could occur if land from which a particular service was attached was claimed or held by a person whose caste status was inconsistent with the obligatory service. Such problems did arise, sometimes in more subtle ways. In hypothetical terms a conflict of obligation could arise when a landholder was required to perform services by the King or his officers which conflicted with the landholder's caste status, or when any subject of the King came into possession of land to which services incompatible with his or her status were attached. In either case it was the landholder who was personally affronted or embarassed. In either case the solution was to abandon the land, the landholder thus being absolved from the awkward task.

The first hypothetical conflict brings on the question of the norms of kingship. The King was the guardian of the social order, the protector of the country, the people (*jatiya*) and the Buddha *samaya*—we would say Buddhism. The literate inhabitants expected the King to follow the Laws of Manu and the *Dharma* of the Kings of Lanka and indeed the *dasarajadharma*, the ten duties of a King. These ten duties of a King are derived from the tradition embodied in the Pali text. They were upheld as the norms that a King of the Sinhala people should follow. The Kings of Kande Udarata were enjoined to follow these duties at their consecration ceremony. Kings were assessed by the people in their own evaluation of the performance as to whether they followed these ten duties. It was also the tradition among the Sinhala people to consider whether a King was *dharmista* (*damitu*),[35] righteous, or not.

Not withstanding this notion, the King was expected by the subjects to rule with a sense of fairness. The expectation of the subjects of the King is clearly stated in a text which refers to the King approvingly, but to the analyst shows the norms by which the King was judged:

> . . .(the King) who delivers judgements avoids falling into the four wrong ways (*satara agati famanaya*) having adopted an attitude of impartiality towards all. . .[36]

These were also Buddhist values and it is not surprising that the writer of this text was a Buddhist monk. There are two questions that arise from the recognition of the fact of the use of norms derived from the Buddhist tradition, which is a literate tradition or to put it differently, is the tradition of the literate. The first is the extent to which Buddhist values and norms were incorporated in the dominant ideology. The second question is to what extent these notions were accepted by the people. Both are equally difficult to answer with the material at hand.

IV. *The presuppositions and conditions of the duty of the subject to the King*

There are two aspects of the obligations of the subject to the King. The first is that of the domination of the King over the subject. This involves an exercise of power ultimately based on the use of the instruments of coercion. The second is the legitimation of the authority of the King and the validity of the rules imposing obligation on the subject.

From a normative standpoint the King's power was derived from his consecration. His office was legitimized by tradition. When one discusses kingship as an office one is discussing what was known as *maharajakama*. Jotiya Sitano and subsequent rulers who were treated as subordinates of the King of Kotte did carry out royal functions, but they could only assume the status of a *maharaja* by usurpation, judged from the point of view of the King of Kotte. The assumption of the powers and the symbols of kinship in such instances was related to the balance of power within the country. Yet kinship itself was identified by the rules of tradition. The validation of the power of the King is a complex matter partly depending on the meaning attached to the term validation. If with Weber one means by validation the acceptance of the power of the King by the subjects, then acceptance has also to be defined in order to avoid a tautology. It is perhaps apposite that this question be raised since a parallel question is confronted by anyone discussing what law is. And this certainly relates to the main theme of this paper—the definition of the duty of the subject to the King.

In the ideology of the Sinhala people of Kande Udarata, kingship was an office that existed from the time of Mahasammata. The Sinhala people (*jatiya*—birth, caste, people) have had Kings from the days of the first Sinhala King Vijaya. They were aware of the procedure by which the King was consecrated. In their eyes the King was expected to follow the norms (*dam*, *dharma*) of the kings of the past and indeed the norms of good kings known as the Ten Duties of a King—a matter I have already discussed. They accepted kingship as a traditional office that had existed from the past. In their way of thinking, kingship was an office they accepted. There was no counter-ideology current among them.

The King did not rule by himself. He was a part of the whole apparatus of government—a state apparatus. The people's notion of the reign (*rājya*; *rājya karanava*=to reign) of the King included a conception of an assembly or a retinue of royal ministers, *mati amativaru*. The image of the King that is publicized in the formal documents of the King was that he was like Sakra, the King of the Gods who lives in heaven.

The groups formed by the dominant caste collectively go to form a ruling class and the dominant caste at the same time. The *radalavaru* of the court were the representatives of this class—the ruling élite of the ruling class. They not only constituted a class from the point of view of the political structure of the Kingdom but had a consciousness of belonging to a class that claimed the right to appointment to the highest offices in the King's administration. They could define themselves with reference to the King. From the point of view of the peasants the ruling class through its representatives, the ruling élite, confronted them with their authority and represented to them the King's power.

The *radalavaru* of the Court lived in the city, it is true, but they were not an urban class. Yet they were removed from the lives of peasantry, in that they had to reside in the capital. They were linked to the peasantry in two ways: first through their official duties as part of the King's administration and secondly as holders of their personal estates.

The estates held by the ruling class were in no way comparable to the feudal estates of barons in medieval Europe, though Leach, in generalizing from the exceptional case of the *vanniyas*, seems to imply they were. The Governors of the Provinces (*disava*), the Chiefs of Districts (*raterala*) were, as I have shown earlier, appointed to these offices by the King. So were the Chiefs of all the administrative units of the King's government. Their only claim to these offices was their being members of the ruling class. It was the appointment to office that gave them greater authority over the other subjects of the King and greater wealth as well as prestige.

Next to the ruling class were the bigger landlords, bigger by the standards of the country. They were by no means comparable to medieval barons, but somewhat comparable to the gentry of medieval England. They were local notables. Some of their estates were, in tenurial structure, analogous to the estates held on superior tenure by the members of the ruling class. The rest of the population consisted of peasants, some rich, some poor. Many of these held lands directly from the King and the rest engaged in cultivating lands in the estates of the King, the ruling class, the gentry or the estates held by religious establishments.

The surplus of the direct producers that was appropriated by the landed and ruling classes was primarily in the form of surplus labour, though, in addition, they also appropriated the surplus of the produce. The appropriators of the surplus of the greatest number of direct producers was the King. In ideological terms the surplus labour was *rājakāriya* and the duty of the direct producers. In more precise legal form, *rājakāriya* was due to the King for the use of the means of production by the direct producer. Where the direct producer claimed legal title his *bhukti* depended on *rājakāriya*—enjoyment on obligation of labour service. The same relationship of the transfer of the surplus to the ruling class, the gentry and the holders of the religious estates was *rājakāriya*—which now meant obligatory labour service on which the use of the land depended. This is legal dependent tenure analogous to feudal forms of property claims in medieval England.

Though in legal terms the King was the controller of land in the kingdom, yet the position of the ruling class as part of the state apparatus gave them effective control over the peasants and gentry. The ruling class stood in the relation of patrons to the latter. The procedure of not letting a member of the ruling class govern a region in which he was born was an attempt on the part of the King to minimize the possibility of a chief wielding his influence through both kinship and ties of patronage.

There was no class consciousness among the peasantry but they were conscious of the ties of kinship and of caste. As far as their relations through the land was concerned, their ties with the

King and the ruling class were both economic and political at the same time. The relations of production were both relations of appropriation of the surplus and the domination by the controller of lands over the direct producers. It is quite consistent with this view of the relations between the ruling class and the rest to find the ruling class referred to as seeking domination (*adipati kama*).

Though both the ruling class and the King were in a relation of exploitation vis à vis the rest of the population, one party could make the other appear more oppressive than themselves. It is remarkable how both the King and a member of the ruling class used the same expression to refer to the subjects of the King in describing the oppression by the other. The expression they used was 'these poor people'.

Where the ruling class was seeking to oppose the King it is not difficult to imagine that they could appear to defend the 'poor people' against an 'unrighteous' King. Where the King is denied his legitimacy for failing to conform to custom and to the canons of good government—the norms of the Kings of the past—the duty to him by the subject could be withdrawn. What the subjects thought in such a situation one has no way of finding out. One does not find evidence of spontaneous peasant movements against the King where the King is denied loyalty or the obligations due to him from his subjects. When the people rose up in revolt against Senasammata Vikaramabahu the King entered into a compact with the rebels. In granting amnesty to them the King set up an inscription declaring his purpose, and the former rebels symbolically indited an inscription alongside affirming their loyalty to the King and undertaking to follow their obligations to him. Those named in the inscription were the members of the ruling class. The King on his part invokes the Buddhist Triple Gem and the gods to sanction his command. Royal power seeks religious sanctions for legitimation. What appears from the available evidence is that the denial of the obligation to the King in the form of opposition to him resulted from the conflicts between the members of the ruling class and the King.

(*a*) *Conflict of Duty*: The norm of providing the King with the obligations of *rājakāriya* could confront the subject with some difficulty. In terms of the normative rules a subject might find that one obligation to the King might conflict with another. The simplest instance is that of a landholder who has more than one landholding, each with a separate obligation, such as the man who found that he had to be on military duty and join an expedition to the north of the Kingdom and the same time provide transport. The case went before the King for a personal decision. In case of difficulty of performing the obligation due to the King for the land, the normal practice was to find a substitute. The failure to perform the due obligation might make a landholder liable to lose his claims to the land. That was the last thing he would want to happen, under normal circumstances at any rate. But the conflicts arising from the obligation to the King would not always be due to conflicts of obligation or to personal incapacity. They could arise from the formal obligation to the King and the self-interest of the subject. A landholder might find that though he was required to perform *rājakāriya* the land he held was not commensurate with the obligations that he was required to perform. He could abandon the land, hand it over to another or appeal to the officer of the King who had the jurisdiction to give a decision. In the last instance another norm of fairness was obviously invoked. In one instance the officer empowered to decide such a case, a governor, used his discretion if not his ingenuity to redress the landholder who was beset with this problem. He decided to give the appellant a fair proportion of the uncultivated land of a common estate. As far as the landholder was concerned there was a conflict between public duty and private interest. At the same time it was an appeal to a fair distribution of land of a common estate among co-heirs. Hence the obligation to the King from the point of view of the subject was not a straightforward relation between the King and himself alone. It involved others including kinsmen and co-heirs of a common estate. Indeed the custom was for heirs to divide the performance of *rājakāriya* between themselves and perform it in turns. This was known as *karamaru*—a change of shoulders.

Scanning the history of political conflict in Kande Udarata one finds evidence of a range of conflicts, some more serious than others. An occasional rebellion did take place, rebellion as seen from the King's point of view. Where does the idea of obligation to the King fit into this situation? Would there not be a conflict in the obligation of the subject to the King and the obligation of the same subject to the ruling class? (This is from the point of view of the subjects.)

In a situation of conflict between the ruling class and the King the relation of the dominant ideology to the interests of the parties to the conflict becomes evident. In such a situation the manner of interpreting the subject's obligation to the King shows the sectional interests of the ruling class. The support of the peasants in such conflicts shows an alignment of the ruled with the ruling class. The people's conscious ideas in those conflicts then do not coincide with their class interests. A bold statement of this nature has to be substantiated by an exposition of its implications. This is the point to return to the observation made at the beginning of this paper regarding the models of interaction. Methodologically, this paper starts with a model of social formations consisting of three levels: ideological structure, legal and political structure, and the economic structure. It remains now to show how this approach explains the operation of the ideological structure.

The King's subjects could face a conflict of obligation of a different sort. The conflict could be between the obligation to the King on the one hand and the obligation to the local *vanniya* who might be a local magnate or a chief who had come under the power of the King. The *vanniyas* of the latter type had their territory on the borders of the Kingdom, in the northwest, north, and northeast limits of the Kingdom. It was these semi-independent *vanniyas* who were analogous to the barons of medieval England. The *vanniyas* who were local magnates were evidently holders of estates within the territory of the King in the Province of Sat Korale. They were apparently lesser men, though they had the same title. The landholders in the territory of the semi-independent *vanniyas* were required to pay dues to the King, and the collection of these dues was the responsibility of the *vanniya*. It is apparent that the men called *vanniyas* were in different relations of subordination to the King of Kande Udarata. The King sent his officers to collect the dues imposed on the local population and to administer justice. Evidently the King's officers tried to exert their authority in order to subvert the power of the *vanniyas*. The *vanniyas* on their part tried to exercise their authority on the inhabitants of the region, ignoring the presence or the authority of the officers of the King. The inhabitants could submit either to the *vanniya* or to the King's officer. Where the local inhabitant was faced with a conflict of loyalties he could appeal to the authority who in his opinion was likely to be the more powerful and more effective in exerting his authority. There is a text that shows an official of the King's administration warning a *vanniya* not to indulge in his wily ways (*kupadam*). This could not have been a powerful *vanniya*, but a petty magnate.

Another conflict of loyalty if not obligation of the subject arose in a somewhat delicate situation. This was when local officials, particularly the powerful *mohttalas*, diverted to their private gain the obligations due from the subjects to the King. These corrupt officials occupied the key position of securing the dues from the local landholders who were under the authority of their own chiefs. They could retain the dues without transmitting them for the King's use or employ the landholders to do their private work rather than work for the King. If the landholder was a peasant, what alternative had he? Yet complaints did reach the King, for there are several texts where the King or one of his officers sternly admonished the wayward and grasping officials.

The greatest conflict that a subject had to face in performing his obligations to the King was where the demands of the King overstepped the limits of human endurance. The manner in which a subject can cope with the demands of an oppressive ruler is limited by the political structure of the social formation. Where there is no legal remedy the only way out is flight. In the legal structure of the Kingdom a landholder was free to abandon his land if he wanted to. In practice this was a legal luxury. The alternative was for a peasant to work on the land of another, especially in the estate of a religious establishment. The second remedy was to flee the country. If oppression was widespread, naturally the demand on the lands of others would be greater and the options for the oppressed diminished. For any family, flight from the village where one's relatives lived and one's source of income was more or less assured up to that point would have been a very uncertain alternative. Where discontent was widespread the ruling class could seize the opportunity to foster rebellion unless they themselves were the beneficiaries of oppression.

The obligation due from a landholder to the King might not be met due to a land dispute. The usual procedure in a dispute was to prohibit the use of the land by either party to a dispute—

there could be more than two parties involved, of course. The land could just be abandoned by the party holding it on the grounds that they were not prepared to cultivate it, without another party actually contesting for it, as happened in one case. The matter of obligation of the landholder to the King was the concern of the functionaries and local officials. They were likely to step in or the local village council could be assembled and the conflict resolved. In the alternative the matter could be reported to the competent authority by the local functionaries. Pending the settlement of a land dispute this authority could not get the land cultivated and the King's dues furnished. Where a subject held his lands but had not furnished his dues to the King, he was liable to be punished by the appropriate judicial authorities. This was the fate that overtook a bold man who dodged his obligations with impunity for nine long years until the wheels of the King's administration turned slowly and he was caught and imprisoned.

It is time now to recapitulate this exposition of the obligation of the subject to the King and to relate it to the duty of the subject. The shift in the terms is also a shift in the focus of discussion. I must therefore return to an exposition in terms of duty. You will recall that I began this paper by substituting the term obligation for the term duty.

Taking an Austinian stance one could try to distinguish between absolute duty and relative duty. Absolute duty is owed to none while in relative duty the duty of one is the correlative right of another. In more simple language the duty owed one is the expectation of the recipient of the duty. This again is a juristic start. But the sense of duty might be based on grounds other than legal. Here I have to retrace my steps and go back to the convenient simplification I made at the beginning in defining duty as what one 'has to do' or 'must do' or 'should do'. If an obligation is what one has to do then the question that has to be asked is, Why has it to be done? The explanation is in terms of 'because of'. Here one might follow Weber and distinguish between motive and orientation of action. The latter brings in the notion of normative rules. The next point one has to clarify is to find out the basis of the rules.

As regards the notion of loyalty, subordination, and obedience, this was an expectation of the King and it was also a part of custom. It was considered wrong not to be loyal to the King. To betray the King was a crime.

Rājakāriya was on a different footing. If a man held land he had to do *rājakāriya* for it unless specifically exempted from it. Once *rājākariya* was fixed he had to perform it. If a man continued to hold land without doing *rājakāriya*, when he was found out he was punished for his lapse. In due course he could be deprived of the claims over the land. But when a man performed his *rāja-kāriya* there was the likelihood that he would continue to enjoy the land unless he committed a crime which made him liable to lose the land. If the King decided to take the land away from him there was nothing he could do. There was no legal authority to whom he could appeal. Where it was a command from the King the subject could do nothing against it. In fact the King compensated landholders for the loss of their lands if he had to take over their lands. There is evidence that the King provided maintenance for a landholder when he had to take over his land. There was clearly an expectation on the part of the subject that he would be allowed to enjoy the land provided it was not used on the basis of changing tenure. Hence one could speak of a contractual element in the relationship between the King and the subject. But the relationship was between two persons of unequal status. The relationship was between the King and his subordinate, the subject. It is from the economic point of view that the difference becomes clear. *Rājakāriya* was not just rent paid for the land nor was it just a tax. The relationship between the subject and the King was both economic and political. But this was not all. Some of the subjects considered it an honour to serve the King. For the service that the landholder did identified his caste status and where the service was that of the King, it was the highest according to the scale of values of the Sinhala people of the Kingdom. In this instance the landholder not only derived legal enjoyment from the land but he also derived prestige from performing his obligation.

Notes

[1]H. L. A. Hart, *The Concept of Law*, 1961, p. 27.
[2]*Ibid.*, p. 21.
[3]Von Wright, *Norm and Action*, 1963, pp. 1-14.
[4]Rājādhirājasinhagevata, B. M. Or. 6606 (163).
[5]*Mandarampuvata.*
[6]See n. 4.
[7]N. E. Cooray (ed), Pukāna Goyam Malaya, v. 91, 1972.
[8]Rājādhirājasinhagevata, *op. cit.*
[9]Gadaladeniya Slab Pillar Inscription E2 IV.
[10]*Ibid.*
[11]*Mandarampuvata* v. 397.
[12]*Ibid.*, v. 481.
[13]Sittu R. D. 183.
[14]*Saparagamuve Pärani Liyavidi*, Colombo, 1946, p. 143.
[15]Alutnuvare Slab Inscription E2 IV.
[16]Rev. W. Demenanda (ed.), *Rajavaliya*, Colombo, 1959.
[17]*Mandarampuvata* v. 64.
[18]Gadaladeniya Inscription, *op. cit.*
[19]*Mandarampuvata* v. 384.
[20]*Ket Habevinisa*, B. M. Ms. See also U. A. Gunasekara, Land Tenure in the Kandyan Provinces, B. Litt. Thesis, Oxford, 1959.
[21]Sittu of Saka, 1728. Ker D. 181.
[22]Sanvase of Saka 1642. Ven K. Nahavimala p. 41.
[20]*Ibid.*
[24]*Mandarampuvata* v. 468.
[25]*Mandarampuvata* v. 105.
[26]D. Fergusson, J. R. A. S. (CB).
[27]P. E. Pueris
[28]Tridapata of Saka 1717, p. 140.
[29]*Mandarampuvata*. vv. 522-537
[30]Offering of Saka 1734 Ven K. Nahavimala pp. 82-83.
[31]*Mandarampuvata*. v. 102.
[32]*Ibid.*
[33]W. Penananda (ed), *Rajavaliya*, 1959, p. 15.
[34]*Mandarampuvata*
[35]Penananda, *op. cii.*
[36]Ven K. Nahavimala, 1946, p. 73.

PART II

THE MEDIEVAL AND MODERN PERIOD : MUSLIM, BRITISH AND NATIONALIST CONCEPTS OF DUTY

The Duty of the Sultan (in the Sultanate Period) to Further the Material Welfare of His Subjects

P. HARDY

Humpty Dumpty

However, the egg only got larger and larger, and more and more human: when she had come within a few yards of it, she saw that it had eyes and a nose and mouth; and, when she had come close to it, she saw clearly that it was HUMPTY DUMPTY himself. "It can't be anybody else!" she said to herself. "I'm as certain of it, as if his name were written all over his face!"...

"And how exactly like an egg he is!" she said aloud, standing with her hands ready to catch him, for she was every moment expecting him to fall.

"It's *very* provoking," Humpty Dumpty said after a long silence, looking away from Alice as he spoke, "to be called an egg—*very*!"

"I said you *looked* like an egg, Sir," Alice gently explained. "And some eggs are very pretty, you know," she added, hoping to turn her remark into a sort of compliment...

"Don't stand chattering to yourself like that," Humpty Dumpty said, looking at her for the first time, "but tell me your name and your business."

"My *name* is Alice, but—"

"It's a stupid name enough!" Humpty Dumpty interrupted impatiently. "What does it mean?"

"*Must* a name mean something?" Alice asked doubtfully.

"Of course it must," Humpty Dumpty said with a short laugh: "*my* name means the shape I am—and a good handsome shape it is, too. With a name like yours, you might be any shape, almost."...

"I don't know what you mean by 'glory'," Alice said.

Humpty Dumpty smiled contemptuously. "Of course you don't—till I tell you. I meant 'there's a nice knock-down argument for you'!"

"But 'glory' doesn't mean 'a nice knock-down argument';" Alice objected.

> "When *I* use a word," Humpty Dumpty said, in rather a scornful tone, "it means just what I choose it to mean—neither more nor less."
>
> "The question is," said Alice, "whether you *can* make words mean so many different things."
>
> "The question is," said Humpty Dumpty, "which is to be master —that's all."
>
> (Lewis Carroll, *Through the Looking-Glass*, Chapter VI, *passim.*)

The account of the meeting of Humpty Dumpty and Alice is an account of how two people from different worlds of experience were struggling to find a mutually intelligible language to express their awareness of a sudden and novel encounter. Although we do not all inhabit the same world of awareness, we must for purposes of intelligible communication inhabit at the moment of attempted communication the same world of meanings. Humpty Dumpty attempted to impose his own personal code of meanings upon Alice, to her inevitable bewilderment. The participants in this multi-cultural seminar are not to be bewildered by a *diktat*: they have come together for mutual enlightenment by a free mutual exchange of ideas. Professor Derrett's introduction to his paper has identified most of 'the common ground we owe to our humanity' when we talk of duty; if I go over some of that ground again, it is not in order to reassure myself and others that the Indo-Islamic tradition which forms the subject of this paper is in fact located in that common ground, but rather to discover exactly in what terms that tradition should be seen to be so located.

Implicit in the use of the word 'duty' in the thought world using English as its language, is the notion of preference for and approbation of some courses of action over others, related in the social context to judgements about the quality of one order of social existence in comparison with another. But courses of action, however preferred and approved, which may without censure be taken up or abandoned at will, are not, in English usage at least, spoken of as courses of action constituting one's duty or obligation. Rather, our duty is spoken of as something which, in the language of *The Book of Common Prayer*, is 'bounden' upon us. What strength does 'bounden duty' have that 'preferred and approved action that we should do' does not have?

With H. L. A. Hart's *The Concept of Law*[1] to assist us, we may conclude that the meaning of 'bounden duty' is not exhausted in the context of the criminal law which defines certain kinds of conduct as required ('duty to do') or as to be avoided ('duty to abstain'), and then backs up its requirements by threats of unpleasant consequences for those who defy or ignore those requirements. Many might (and indeed some do) accept that they are not merely 'obliged' not to beat their wives, but are furthermore 'under an obligation' not to do so, even if, as often happens, (the newspapers tell us) they have nothing to fear in the way of detection. By reason of this distinction, it is impossible to equate fully with 'our duty' action into which one has been forced. This is because of being pressed by the opinion, or by the physical threats, of our fellow men.

No definition of duty expressed in terms of 'that which serves, or is intended to serve the doer's interest or self-satisfaction *per se*' (though it may in fact do so) can do justice to usage, otherwise why is there a distinction in usage between saying 'I have an inclination, or desire or a need from the point of view of my own interests to do this' and 'I have a duty to do this'? Indeed, the situations in which a man is described as doing his duty are often those in which he himself would claim that the only reason why he is acting as he is, is that he regards that way of acting as his duty. His 'normal' inclination would indeed be to do something more to his own taste and satisfaction (not that he may not in fact, and as a 'windfall', attain satisfaction after doing his 'duty'). The point is that he would feel more comfortable doing his duty.

'Duty' does not, indeed, by definition mean action against personal inclination or interest. The sense of it, however, is unlikely, in a given society, to have developed into a moral code had not human beings been often if not mostly disinclined to perform certain 'other-regarding' actions—telling the truth when they may be punished for it, supporting relatives when they may lose money by it and aiding the police when terrorists may shoot them for it. As P. H. Nowell-Smith[2] has put it: 'If we only promised to do things that we would do in any case because we enjoy doing them, promise-keeping would not be thought of as a *duty*'.

Duty, then, appears to refer to action taken for a principle other than that of merely serving the actor's own inclination or interest. But what principle? The writer finds acceptable as *the* principle of duty, the principle of minimizing disharmony and conflict among men. The notion of duty can only arise in society, in situations where the actions of one human being may prejudice the position and the welfare of another.[3] The essentially social ground of the concept of duty has been so well put by J. R. Lucas in his *The Principles of Politics* that it is best to quote him *in extenso*:

> It is incoherent to think that one could be a member of a community without having any obligations. For that would be to have all the other members of the community subservient to one's own will: and then they would not be colleagues and equals, but slaves. Therefore one cannot be a *member* of a community without obligation, but only a *tyrant* over it. To have the sole say about what shall happen is to be isolated. An autocrat is cut off from the give-and-take of social life, because for him it is all take and no give. It is logically possible to wish to be a self-sufficient despot: but it is not logically possible to combine that with a social existence.[4]

The central body of thought analyzed in this paper will not be that of Indo-Muslim sultans themselves, but of writers who addressed themselves to sultans or to members of the educated Muslim élite in the pre-Mughal period. From the texture of the evidence for the Mughal period, it is feasible, within a comparatively short period, to uncover the actions, the decisions (and the process of decision) of the rulers themselves and to deduce therefrom their own working code of duty and sense of obligation towards their subjects. The much more limited, stereotyped and circumstantial evidence for the history of the sultanate period would have necessitated forms of detective work to discover the sultans' own sense of duty, which could not be contemplated within the time-scale of this seminar. Nevertheless, it is hoped that the materials consulted (listed *infra*)[5] have been made to yield findings of interest to the seminar.

The advice and exhortation offered to sultans on how they should act to further the material welfare of their subjects (or the panegyrical accounts of what the writers allege particular sultans did in fulfilment of notions of 'duty' which both sultan and subject could join together to admire) bear an integral relationship to the writers' assumptions about the place in human life of the possession and enjoyment of worldly goods. Yusuf Gada in his *Tuhfa-i Nasa'ih*[6] is clear that the exercise of property rights is subordinate to 'duty' and to 'morality.' Following the doctrine of the Hanafi school of Islamic jurisprudence, Yusuf Gada states that it is absolutely obligatory (*farz*) upon the owner of a slave girl not to have his way with her immediately on coming into possession of her, but to wait until after her first menstruation following his acquisition of her. Yusuf Gada advises an owner, in selling a slave girl, to give preference to 'chastity of relationship'—presumably meaning he should not sell her for profit to a lecher. To avoid poverty and to enjoy true riches one should perform a variety of actions both obligatory according to Islamic law and estimable according to custom.[7] The idea that the enjoyment of material goods is both a sign and a consequence of some other grace, rather than a grace in itself, is implicit in Shams al-din Siraj 'Afif's ordering of his account of the abolition by Sultan Firuz Shah (1351-88) of royal regulations (arrived at by means other than reasoning, by analogy from the sources of revelation under the rules of Islamic jurisprudence [*quanunat-i ghair-qiyas*]) being followed by the spread of prosperity among all classes.[8]

Several possible attributes of human kind stand, in the writers' estimation, much higher than those of the possession and egocentric enjoyment of material goods. Fakhr-i Mudabbir places the values of generosity and of hospitality over those of getting and spending.[9] Yusuf Gada calls a miser an enemy of God. The anonymous writer of the *Sirat-i Firuz Shahi* moralizes on the vanity of worldly possessions and recommends 'under-consumption.'[10] Barani in his *Ta'rikh-Firuz Shahi* dramatizes the 'political' dangers of the existence of wealth in the wrong hands.[11]

There is a general attitude of reserve, if not of manifest hostility, towards the free operation of a market economy. The working of the economy is too serious a matter to be left to economic forces. Barani in his *Fatawa-i Jahandari* trumpets (the word is just) his fear of the moral, social and political consequences of allowing supply and demand, as expressed in prices asked and prices paid, to operate as freely as possible. Other writers in a more muted fashion share his fears.[12] Barani repeatedly condemns several occupations for which, one may reasonably conclude, there was an economic demand in medieval India during his time (Barani lived between c. 1285 and c. 1357). He is particularly hostile to bazaar-traders[13] and grain merchants. For Barani the free operation of market forces within society is not conducive to a good or stable social order.

The stable society is one in which there is an enduring hierarchy of occupations in which men should engage for reasons other than that they supply an economic want as ascertainable in the behaviour of a free market. Barani holds that, at the very first appearance of Adam, God the eternal Craftsman imparted to the minds of the sons of Adam the crafts necessary to enable them to obtain a livelihood. All crafts, the honourable (*sharif*) and the dishonourable (*khasis*), were imparted to men's minds and hearts in accordance with the virtues and the vices which had, in their original nature(*asli fitrat*), been made attendant upon their souls.[14] 'Ain al-Mulk Multani presupposes a static order of society, one which owes its system of occupational relationships to the working of principles other than those of market supply and demand. He states that it is appointed (*muqarrar*) that a particular order (*ta'ifa*) has been chosen (*ikhtiyar karda and*) for a particular activity or service: warriors for war and *jihad*, the *'ulama* for instruction and *ijtihad*; the people of the pen and of (economic) capacity and the possessors of ingenuity and intelligence (*ashab-i kiyasat o darayat*), for the collection of revenue (*jibabat-i amwal*).[15] The context of this passage is that of Professor John Hicks' 'command economy' where the collection of revenue (the transfer of resources) from the countryside is organized from above, by the ruler who does not have to fear for the division of labour in the countryside because it is customary and not subject to rapid change, and who can arrange for a division of labour within his own ruling apparatus by a system of appointment and reward.[16] 'Afif's account of the reign of Firuz Shah is based on a similar set of presuppositions. Our authors certainly do not appear to dread any wind of economic change, destructive of traditional occupations, blowing in the society of their time. In advising sons to follow, for moral reasons, their fathers' occupations, the author of the *Sirat-i Firuz Shahi* assumes that it will be possible for a son to obtain a livelihood by following his father's occupation.[17]

In ascending order of generality, the objects of the sultan's 'duty' in the sphere of material welfare are, in the eyes of our authors, his own subjects, the Muslim religious classes, the poor, and the Muslim population at large. Non-Muslims are to be the objects of the sultan's consideration only if they enjoy the status of *zimmis*. One author, Barani, does not wish polytheists to have that *de facto* status under the Delhi sultan or to be allowed to pay *jizya* and *kharaj*; he would have them killed (certainly if they are Brahmins), enslaved and utterly abased.[18] The distinction between the poor and the generality of the sultan's Muslim subjects is at times only a formal one. There are the poor that are always with us even in 'normal' times, that is when there is no famine and dearth, and there are the potential poor who may include the generality of the ruler's subjects, (outside, perhaps, members of the official élite), in times of dearth and famine.

Several writers, members of the class of gentleman-suppliants themselves, declare that the ruler 'must', or 'ought' (*bayad*) to be generous to those in a relationship of actual or potential service of clientage to him. For Amir Khusrau, kingship and giving are inseparable.[19] Barani, 'Afif and the anonymous author of the *Sirat-i Firuz Shahi* are extravagant in their praise of Firuz Shah for his largesse towards the members of the service and military elite. 'Afif's account of Firuz Shah's efforts to find positions for the unemployed in the *muhallas* of Delhi shows that 'Afif praised those efforts as directed towards the sons of the educated classes—potential official material.[20]

'Afif demonstrates how the royal duty to provide for 'the ruler's own' shades into a more general duty towards the poor at large when he mentions the establishment of a *diwan* to provide poor Muslims with financial assistance in marrying off their daughters. Fakhr-i Mudabbir lists seven classes of Muslims to whom the ruler should show liberality—darwishes, the indigent, those to to whom *kharaj* and *sadaqat* are (over) due, slaves unable to find the money to purchase their freedom, those arrested for debt, those without the means of fighting, as they wish, in the way of God, and those in trade who find themselves in want far from home.[21] The sultan is, in effect, being asked to remember that he is but a creature of God just like any other Muslim, endowed with more resources perhaps, but for that very reason needing the more to be reminded of his shared humanity and status as a Muslim. He must ever keep in mind the Day of Judgment, when property and kingship will be of no avail, seek out the company of the poor and avoid the company of the rich, namely, in the

Prophet Muhammad's own words, the dead.[22]

Several writers believe that the ruler best serves the material welfare of the generality of his subjects when he is obedient in the fiscal sphere to the mandates of the Islamic law (*shari'a* or *shar'*). Not only should he distribute alms to the prescribed classes of Muslims, but he should also avoid collecting or levying any dues other than those prescribed by Islamic law, namely, *'ushr*, *zakat*, *khums*, *kharaj* and *jizya*.[23] But even where the *shari'a* is not specifically invoked, there is a sense that the ruler has no *ex-officio* discretionary authority to interfere with property rights or to vary socio-economic relationships in his own interest. The ruler must remember that he is but one element in a properly-ordered polity with no inherent right to extinguish other rightful elements in that polity.[24]

Nevertheless, within the limits of his lawful authority (i.e. lawful in terms of the *shari'a*), and, one may presume, of the general responsibility of the individual Muslim, ruler and ruled alike, to promote the good and to combat the evil (*hisba*),[25] the ruler did have an obligation to use his discretion to alleviate hardship. In time of famine he should reduce (*takhfif*) the rate at which land revenue (*kharaj*) was levied, he should throw open his own granaries to the people and he should control prices (*tas'ir*).[26] As we shall see, however, Barani would go further than this; he regards it as one of the ruler's most imperative duties to control prices, not only of grain but also of cloth and other commodities, both in good times and in bad.

Although royal manufactories (*karkhanas*), financed by royal capital, appear to have flourished under the Delhi Sultanate, our authors in general see the economic function of the ruler as regulative rather than as entrepreneurial. Indeed, Fakhr-i Mudabbir would not have a ruler engage himself in trade.[27] However, Saiyid 'Ali Hamadani would have a ruler build bridges and rest houses for travellers and Fakhr-i Mudabbir would have him develop irrigation. Agreement is moreover general, that one of the abiding duties of the ruler in the sphere of material welfare is to maintain a sound currency.[28]

The purpose of the recommended modes of intervention by the sultan in the economic activities of his subjects is not their material welfare as an end in itself. Subjects' material welfare is indeed both desirable and necessary, but only as the lowest value in a scale of values each step of which underlies the one above to form an ascending curve which ultimately reaches into an extra-temporal world. Material welfare is seen as a good to be served for the reason that its absence makes impossible the achievement of 'higher' goods. More than that, its presence is a sign or symbol that 'all is right with the world' and its absence that all is not. These three overlapping beliefs about the place of material welfare in the general scheme of things are expressed the most explicitly (in descending order) by Barani, Saiyid 'Ali Hamadani and by Fakhr-i Mudabbir.

It may be useful first to note the Persian (or Persian-Arabic) terms which connote 'material welfare' in Barani's tenth 'Advice' (*nasihat*) in his *Fatawa-i Jahandari*, entitled 'On the benefits (*fawa'id*) of the king's (*padishah*) efforts to answer for (*pazirad*) the cheapness (*arzani*) of that which is connected with the readiness of the army and the livelihood of the generality of the people' (or the 'common people' '*amma khalq*). The terms are *asbab-i ma'ash* 'the means of livelihood or subsistence' or *asbab-i ma'ishat* 'means of living',[29] terms which suggest that Barani visualizes a society in which the generality are sufficiently sheltered, clothed and fed for a modest contentment.

Barani opens this *nasihat* with the statement that as the army needs money and low prices for its proper order, so subjects need cheapness of the means of livelihood, or else they will not regard the royal dominions as their refuge and the royal court as the object of their duty (*mubtagha*); consequently they will migrate to regions (*iqalim*) where, they hear, the means of livelihood are easier and cheaper to obtain.[30] (In short, the prestige and power of the king will suffer.)

So, the king must control prices even in times of abundance (*dar aiyam-i khisb*) when all sorts of grain and the fruits of the earth are plentiful. (This passage[31] alone, I think, establishes that Barani does not consider material prosperity a desirable end in itself.) After he has laid down the price control procedures the king should adopt, Barani lists ten advantages to be gained from cheapness of commodities needed by both the army and the King's subjects. They are: the army, that is the 'capital' (*sar-maya*) of kingship, becomes loyal and properly constituted; the royal capital attracts men of every skill and profession and thus becomes a 'universal city' (*misr-i jami'*); the enemies of the king will cease to want to conquer his kingdom; the king acquires a good reputation, and jealousy and anger between his subjects disappear, replacing the urge for vengeance against forestallers and regrators when prices are dear; the royal treasury has to spend less; the king is enabled to perform the greatest purpose (*maqsud-i mu'azzam*) of kingship, namely the securing of justice and equity; the divine command to take from the rich (i.e. hoarders) and to give to the poor is fulfilled—forestalling and regrating (*ihtikar*) is a contagious sin (*gunah-i muta 'addi*); to remove it is of benefit to king and subject alike; price control prevents a transfer of resources from the homes of Muslims (whose honour [*'izzat*] rides pillion [*radif*] with the commands of God and of His Prophet) to the houses of Hindus and Zoroastrians whose property, women and children are, according to several schools of law, lawful and permissible to Muslims—those honourable and respected in the eyes of God should not, through want, become abject and afflicted (*khwar o zar*); lastly securing the cheapness of commodities ensures that each man devotes himself to his own proper occupation and profession—forestallers and regrators and bazaar-traders do not seek after honourable employment and noble men become caravan merchants and caravan merchants desire to become commanders and generals, and so forth. Employment remains according to the established order (*bar qarar* [F. Steingass, *Persion-English Dictionary*, London, 1947, p. 176, 'continuing as heretofore']).[32]

Barani confronts those who argue that cheapness is brought about by plenty and that therefore the ruler should not intervene in the market. On the face of it, Barani says, this is true—but irrelevant. As the passing ages bring men nearer to the Day of Judgment and further away from the time of the Prophet Muhammad, so their virtues are transformed into vices and love of the world, and their lower selves and Shaitan gain superiority. Neither fear of God nor fear of the king (wholly) prevents the rich from forestalling and regrating and selling grain and cloth to the poor at any price the rich find necessary. If the king, who is appointed for the general improvement (*islah-i 'am*) neglects to exert himself in the control of prices, how can he answer for his negligence on the Day of Judgment?[33]

Saiyid 'Ali Hamadani's reasons why the sultan should further the material welfare of his subjects are much less systematic than

Barani's. Hamadani assumes that material welfare is but one consideration in a properly ordered world and that too, a very subordinate one. It is more important for justice to be done and for the mandates and prohibitions of Islam to be given unimpeded currency in a kingdom. He states that at the very first creation of men's nature (*fitrat*), morals and dispositions fell out differently among different men so that their inclinations came into conflict. God in His wisdom has therefore established a just ruler to set men on the right path and, to the limit of practicability, to carry out (*tanfiz*) the mandates of the *shar'*, to maintain the restrictive ordinances of God (*hudud*) and the rules of Islam among all classes. This He did so that the strong may not tyrannize over the weak, that the sensory world should remain stable, the disorder (*khalal*) of oppression and innovation not invade the *hudud* of the *shar'* and the characteristics of brute beasts not manifest themselves among members of all classes.[34]

Fakhr-i Mudabbir in the *Adab al-Harb* also places the duty of the ruler towards the furtherance of the material welfare of his subjects in the context of his general function as the dispenser of justice, the holder of the balance between different sorts and conditions of men, and as the guarantor of the currency of the mandates of the Holy Law of Islam in society.[35]

Before proceeding to a discussion of the ultimate justifications offered for the 'code of duty' placed by our authors before the sultan, it may be useful to raise the question of a possible relationship between the hortatory theories outlined above and the social and political realities of life in the period of the sultanate. Put in one way, reality can arouse uneasiness about what may be one's own duty and what another's duty. Put in the idiom of Clifford Geertz's 'Ideology as a Cultural System',[36] ideology may possibly express either a conflict of interest in a society or a state of social tension, providing an indication of social malfunctioning, of unstable equilibrium between insoluble antinomies.

This is not the place to expatiate at length upon the general political role of the institution of the Sultanate in pre-Mughal Muslim India, still less in the Islamic world at large in that period—how the *sunni* educated classes looked to it to provide the steel frame of an inherently unstable social order riven by conflicts between partially-domesticated nomads and settled agriculturalists, between military adventurers and urban merchants and craftsmen, between Isma'ili 'subversives' and orthodox men of substance or, in India, between immigrant refugees from the Mongols and half-subdued or unsubdued Rajput chiefs. It can be plausibly argued that the insistent call in India (as elsewhere in the eastern Muslim world), for the sultan to do justice is explicable as a call by the educated to unlettered political 'strong-arm men' not to throw their weight about at the expense of, or in despite of, men of learning. On the other hand, it can be argued that since such calls provided the stock-in-trade of Muslim writers on government for centuries on end it is almost impossible to relate particular calls at particular times to particular conflicts of interest or uneasinesses in society.

Be that as it may, I would suggest that there are two of Barani's ideas (on the subject of material welfare) that may refer directly to the political and social realities of his lifetime. First, his proposition that if the generality of subjects find prices high they may migrate to regions where they are lower, and second, his statement[37] that forestalling and regrating (though sometimes indulged in by Muslims), is superabundantly the profession of Hindus and Zoroastrians and the skill (*hurfa*) of the unbelievers and polytheists of the kingdom, and should be put down. The first may reflect the fact that the Delhi Sultanate had no clear and controlled political frontiers and that the migration of cultivators and others did occur. The second shows that (as Barani's well-known account of the reign of Sultan 'Ala al-din Khalji also suggests) one of the chief problems facing any Delhi sultan was the rivalry he encountered with Hindu chiefs, other classes of rural intermediary and Hindu grain dealers for the disposable resources of the countryside and supremacy in the markets for the commodities on which the political and military power of the sultanate depended.

To return to the purpose of the paper: the obligation upon sultans to serve the material welfare of individual subjects or of the generality of subjects appears, as with the question of the purposes of royal action to that end, to form an ascending curve away from a zero of temporal expediency towards a peak of cosmic duty. At zero, Barani puts forward the reason for a ruler to bring about cheapness of commodities that his subjects will decamp if he does not and his army will fall into disarray. The *Chach Nama's* style of construction and exposition is such as to suggest that rulers should regard the productive classes as an integral element in policy to the degree that attacking rulers should enter into mutually advantageous secret compacts with the merchants and agriculturalists subject to enemy rulers, assuring the former of lives and livelihood in return for the yielding of tribute and revenue after the victory of the attacker.[38] Slightly up the curve from zero, we find Barani stating that a ruler is appointed for general improvement (*islah-i 'amma*), with the implication that the ruler should recognize a general obligation to further that end. Slightly further up still, there is Barani holding that the king who does not enforce justice in buying and selling and bringing about equity between the 'seventy-two creeds' cannot be called the shadow of God or considered the legitimate ruler (*ulu'l amri bi-haqq*).[39] The moral code in Barani's world, to which he is appealing, apparently affirms that rulers should be the shadows of God and are seen to be such. Saiyid 'Ali Hamadani seconds Barani with much the same language as the latter uses in the *Fatawa-i Jahandari*. When, Hamadani proclaims,[40] a ruler and king strives in the path of justice and equity and endeavours to establish the *hudud* of the *shar'* and obedience (*niffaz*) to the requirements of religion, then he is the deputy (*na'ib*), the chosen (*bar guzida*), the shadow and the *khalifa* of God: but when he, the ruler, neglects all these things, then he is the deputy of Anti-Christ (*dajjal*), the enemy of God and the Prophet and *khalifa* of Shaitan—and to be all or any of these things offends the moral code of Saiyid 'Ali Hamadani's world too.

In bringing justice to his subjects, a justice which embraces dealings in economic life, the ruler fulfils one of the principal purposes for which his office was instituted. Fakhr-i Mudabbir opens his *Adab al-Harb wa'l Shuja'at* with the exordium that God created man and sent the Prophet Muhammad that the world might be cleansed of malice and polytheism; God created kings for the collection of armies, the seizure of kingdoms, the preservation of realms and subjects from unbelievers, mischief-makers and the enemies of religion—all this that the world may become a place of safety through the royal exercise of manliness and justice. This is in fulfilment of the Qur'anic proclamation (LVII, 25): And we sent down with them the Book and the balance so men might uphold justice. And we sent down iron, wherein is great might and many uses for men.[41]

So in performing his duty in the sphere of a justice that includes the proper promotion of the material welfare of his subjects, the sultan would be acting in recognition of the *raison d'etre* of the office he holds. That act, however, requires a further action of recognition—that God exists and makes certain demands upon men and upon the kings among men.

But some of our writers found the duty of sultans more specific than doing their best to create conditions in which the revelation of Islam and the requirements of Islam are safe for a free run, so to speak, in society. They describe the sultans as having a specific duty to see that the Holy Law, the *shari'a,* is followed in general, and in those areas of life that touch on the material welfare of subjects, for example the bestowal of alms and the levying of taxation. Some of our writers[42] use the technical language (*farz* and *wajib*) of absolute obligation according to Islamic law in this context. Barani indeed speaks of the royal obligation to fix prices and to strive for the cheapness of commodities as the *afraz al-fara'iz*[43]—the obligation of obligations. Moreover, in company with Saiyid 'Ali Hamadani, he invokes fear of the Day of Judgment as a motive for the king to perform his obligations.[44]

Finally, let us turn to the issue which this seminar has presumably come into existence to illuminate—in what sense is the language of 'duty' appropriate to the ideal requirements which our authors have laid down for sultans in the furtherance of their subjects' material welfare? First, it might be, in principle, possible for us to speak of the duty of the Delhi sultan as a legal duty, owed to, because imposed by, a human superior endowed with recognized authority to impose sanctions for breach of that duty. Sultan Shams al-din Iltutmish in 1229, Sultan Muhammad-ibn-Tughluq in 1345 and Sultan Firuz Shah in 1353, 1362-63, 1364-65 and 1370, accepted diplomas of investiture as deputies, either of the 'Abbasid Caliph in Baghdad or of the 'Abbasid Caliph in Cairo. By doing this, or by putting the names of 'Abbasid Caliphs on their coins, it can be said that many Delhi sultans accepted a legal obligation to act according to, or in the furtherance of, the Islamic law. The office of Caliph existed to supply temporal sanctions for obedience to this law. However, the writers that have been examined regard Caliphal authority as in practice dormant (as did the sultans of Delhi themselves) and thus treat Islamic law as actually making moral rather than legal claims upon sultans.

Why should sultans recognize any moral claim, within or without the *shari'a* of Islam? At one level of thought, the claim can be stated in the manner implied by Barani, namely that he, the ruler, is recognizing the purpose of his existence as ruler, to bring about general improvement. In effect, he is being asked to recognize the logic of authority, namely that it exists for other than selfish purposes and is itself a recognition of the claims of others. But, in general, our authors by appealing to external authority—to God—and by acknowledging, as we have seen, the existence of rulers who rule for their own selfish pleasure, admit that for such recognition rulers often need 'external' encouragement. Hence the threat to rulers of having to answer for their actions or their negligence on the Day of Judgment.

Following Immanuel Kant and his hosts of commentators,[45] we may see that fear of the Day of Judgment cannot do more than remind sultans of what they should do. Even if that fear should oblige sultans to act rightly, it cannot, as an appeal to fear, create an obligation to act rightly. Either one's motives for obeying what one believes to be the will of God are moral (i.e. because it is thought 'right' on grounds of principle to do so) or they are not[46] (i.e. they are prudential—if God were not thought of as Punisher one would not consider obedience to Him either desirable or necessary). If they are moral, then God adds nothing to the case (except perhaps a prod, which is beside the point). At one level indeed, Barani, Fakhr-i Mudabbir and Saiyid 'Ali Hamadani do ask for the sultan's recognition of duty on grounds of principle—the principle that unbelief and injustice should not exist and the principle that with their destruction the poor will be served and a due meed of material welfare attained by the generality of Muslim subjects.[47] But why, on grounds of principle, should the sultan subscribe to the destruction (or at least to the curbing) of unbelief? In order to remove any disharmony between God, the creator of man, and man the creature of God. It was to remove disharmony between man and God brought about by failure of man to realize he was God's creature, that God sent His Prophet Muhammad with a reminder of who God is, and who man is, and with a guidance as to how man should show

God his realization of the position of each and of their mutual relationship.[48]

For Barani, disharmony in society is a reflection of the disharmony between Creator and created humanity brought about by man's ingratitude for the good of existence, bestowed by God, and by man's attempts to defy his original nature (*fitrat*) conferred upon him at the moment of creation.[49]

For Barani (and almost equally so for Fakhr-i Mudabbir and Saiyid 'Ali Hamadani, with their repeated stress on the duty of the ruler to do justice and specifically justice between rich and poor) society as he knows it provides a spectacle of finally unresolvable disharmonies which only the action of a right-minded sultan can at best moderate. Whether this sense of disharmony is attributable to awareness of the existence of a large and only partly acquiescent non-Muslim fighting élite, or to awareness of stresses and strains within the Muslim ruling élite or to fear of attack by the Mongols, we need not here discuss, but the fact of a strong sense of disharmony and potential conflict within society impresses itself upon me in considering much of the evidence on which this paper rests.

If one is justified in predicating in our authors a strong sense of disharmony between not only the interests but also the moral codes of those with whom they lived in medieval India, then one is, I conclude, justified in using the terms 'duty' and 'obligation' in reference to the classes of actions our authors recommed the sultan to take for the furtherance of the material welfare of subjects. To hark back to Professor Toulmin's argument[50] that 'the notions of "duty", of "obligation", of "morality", are derived from situations in which the conduct of one member of a community prejudices the interests of another, and are to be understood as part of the procedure for minimizing the effects of such conflicts', it does seem as if the classes of action recommended to the sultan are intended to have the effect of minimizing social (and individual) conflict. (Whether they would do so is another matter.) If therefore we find Professor Toulmin's proposition valid, then we may use the language of 'duty' for the recommended kinds of action we have been noticing.

Where, however, Barani and his fellow Muslim authors would be likely to part company with Professor Toulmin (and perhaps with ourselves), is over the issue whether the removal of social disharmonies should carry with it the harmonious satisfaction of (at first sight) conflicting desires and interests. Barani and his fellows, as Muslims of their time, did not in principle seek or accept harmony or accommodation on an equal footing with non-Muslims. In principle, they sought the disappearance of unbelievers from society or at least their forcible reduction to an unequal status arrived at in the context of a peace of defeat rather than of free mutual adjustment.[51]

Nevertheless, this Islamic element in our authors' thinking should not, within the meaning of duty that has been suggested, inhibit us from speaking of the duty of the sultan to further the material welfare of his subjects, since he, the sultan, is being told that, in situations of disharmony and of conflicts of interest and of codes of conduct among human beings, there are certain classes of action that, as a matter of principle and not just for his own convenience, he should prefer to perform.

Notes

[1]H. L. A. Hart, *The Concept of Law*, Oxford, 1961, especially p. 27 and chapters V, VIII and IX.

[2]P.H. Nowell-Smith, *Ethics*, Harmondsworth, 1954, p. 211.

[3]Stephen Edelston Toulmin, *An Examination of the Place of Reason in Ethics*, Cambridge, 1968, pp. 156-7.

[4]J. R. Lucas, *The Principles of Politics*, Oxford, 1966, p. 49.

[5] (*i*) Fakhri-i Mudabbir, *Ta'rikh-i Fakhru'd-din Mubarak Shah*, (so called) (ed.), E. Denison Ross, London, 1927.

(*ii*) Fakhr-i Mudabbir, *Adab al-Harb wa al-Shuja'at*, (ed.) Ahmad Suhaili Khwansari, Tihran, 1346 (solar); the first work was intended for Qutb al-din Aibak, the second for Sultan Shams al-din Iltutmish.

(*iii*) Amir Khusrau, *Khaza'in al-Futuh*, (ed.) Muhammad Wahid Mirza Calcutta, 1953.

(iv) ———*Rasa'il-i I'jaz*, Lucknow, 1896, (bound in two volumes).

(v) Ziya al-din Barani, *Ta'rikh-i Firuz Shahi*, Calcutta, 1862. Barani, *Fatawa-i Jahandari*, India Office Persian ms. No. 1149, (photostat in possession of history department library, SOAS).

(vi) 'Ain al-din 'Abd-Allah ibn Mahru, *Insha-i Mahru*, (ed.) Shaikh' Abd al-Rashid, Aligarh, n.d. (1959?); an epistolographic work by a prominent official of the reigns of Muhammad ibn Tughluq and Firuz Shah.

(vii) 'Isami, *Futuh al-Salatin*, Madras, 1948.

(viii) Anon, *Sirat-i Firuz Shahi*, SOAS Persian Ms. No. 283116 (found in the Sir Thomas Arnold collection, copied from the unique Bankipur ms.); completed in 1370 and probably read over to Sultan Firuz Shah.

(ix) Shams al-din Siraj 'Afif, *Ta'rikh-i Firuz Shahi*, (so called), Calcutta, 1891.

(x) Saiyid 'Ali Hamadani, *Zakhirat al-Muluk*, India Office Library Persian ms. no. 1130; the author is thought to have had a large hand in the conversion of the population in fourteenth-century Kashmir.

(xi) Yusuf Cada, *Tuhfa-i Nasa'ih*, Peshawar, 1328/1910; an ethical treatise said to have been composed in 1393.

In addition, the *Chach Nama*, the *Khair al-Majalis* of Hamid Qalandar and a partial translation of the *Dastur al-Albab fi 'Iim al-Hisab* by 'Abd al-Hamid Muharrir Ghaznawi have been consulted. It is regretted that a fuller examination of *sufi* material has not been attempted for this paper.

[6] *Tuhfa-i Nasa'ih*, p. 41.

[7] *Ibid.*, pp. 73-5.

[8] *Ta'rikh-i Firuz Shahi*, pp. 98-100.

[9] *Ibid.*, p. 56; *Adab al-Harb*, pp. 53-5.

[10] *Sirat*, folios 114, 151.

[11] Pp. 224, 239, 283.

[12] E. g. *Insha-i Mahru*, pp. 60-61 : 'Isami, *Futuh*, p. 221.

[13] *Ta'rikh-i Firuz Shahi*, p. 298. *Fatawa-i Jahandari*, folios. 92 a-b.

[14] *Fatawa*, folios. 216b-217a.

[15] *Insha*, p. 68.

[16] John Hicks, *A Theory of Economic History*, Oxford, 1969, chapter II.

[17] *Sirat*, folio 52.

[18] *Fatawa*, folios 118b-120b.

[19] *Rasa'il-i I'jaz*, I p. 38.

[20] *Ta'rikh-i Firuz Shahi*, pp. 334-6.

[21] *Ta'rikh-i Fakh u'd-din*, p. 16.

[22] Saiyid 'Ali Hamadani, *Zakhirat*, folios 91b-92a.

[23] Fakhr-i Mudabbir, *Ta'rikh*, pp. 15-16, 33 : *Sirat Firuz Shahi*, folios 124-5.

[24] E. g. *Adab al-Harb*, pp. 4, 37, 73-4, 118-9; the sense of a polity being composed of various elements is particularly strong in the *Chach Nama*, the Persian text of which is dated to 1216-17. See P. Hardy, 'Is the *Chach Nama* intelligible to the historian as political theory?' to be published in the proceedings of the International Seminar 'Sind Through the Centuries' held at Karachi in March 1975.

[25] For an account of *hisba* and of the officer (*muhtasib*) entrusted directly with furthering it during the period of the Delhi sultanate, see the article *hisba* in the second edition of the *Encyclopaedia of Islam*, volume III, section by A. S. Bazmee Ansari, pp. 491-92.

[26] Barani, *Fatawa*, folios 9lb, 179a; Fakhr-i Mudabbir, *Adab*, pp. 97-98, 102, 103.

[27] *Adab*, p. 99.

[28] Fakhri-i Mudabbir, *Adab*, p. 117; Barani, *Ta'rikh*, p. 475; 'Isami, *Futuh*, p. 460.

[29] E. g. *Fatawa*, folios. 91a 92a.

[30] *Ibid.*, folios 91a.

[31]*Ibid.*, folios 91b.

[32]*Ibid.*, folios 93a-96a.

[33]*Ibid.*, folios 96a-b.

[34]*Zakhirat*, folios 75a.

[35]*Adab*, p. 4.

[36]Clifford Geertz, 'Ideology as a Cultural System', a chapter in *The Interpretation of Cultures*, New York, 1973, pp. 201 et seq.

[37]*Fatawa*, folios 94a-b.

[38]'Ali b. Hamid al-Kufi, *Chach Nama*, (ed.), 'Umar ibn Muhammad Da'udpota, Hyderabad, Deccan, 1939, (for example) pp. 34-35, 40, 42-43, 118-20, 204-8, 238.

[39]*Fatawa-i Jahandari*, folios 92b-93a.

[40]*Zakhirat al-Muluk*, folios 82b-83a.

[41]*Adab*, pp. 2-4; A. J. Arberry's rendering of the Qur'anic text is used here.

[42]E. g. Fakhr-i Mudabbir, *Ta'rikh*, p. 15.

[43]*Fatawa*, folio 91b.

[44]Barani, *Fatawa*, fol. 96b; Hamadani, *Zakhirat*, folios 92a-b.

[45]I have benefited from instruction in Kant's ethical philosophy, by S. Korner, *Kant*, Harmondworth, 1955; H. J. Paton, *The Moral Law*, London, 1948; H. B. Acton, *Kant's Moral Philosophy*, London, 1970; C. D. Broad, *Five Types of Ethical Theory*, London, 1934.

[46]With specific acknowledgement to Bernard Williams, *Morality*, Harmondsworth, 1973, pp. 78-9; Professor Williams' point later on that action need not be *either* moral *or* prudential is taken.

[47]E. g. Barani, *Fatawa*, folios 121b.-123a.

[48]I regard this as implicit in the exordium to *Adab*, pp. 2-4.

[49]*Fatawa*, folios 117b-124a, 217b-220b.

[50]*An Examination of the Place of Reason in Ethics*, pp. 156-57.

[51]There is, it should be pointed out, a passage in Barani's *Fatawa-i Jahandari* (folio 91b) where he contemplates as desirable a reduction by the sultan of the rate of *jizya* in time of famine. He does not however refer to the status of *zimm* in this particular passage and as many other passage in the *Fatawa* show, Barani in disinclined to allow Hindus the status of *zimmis*. It is also possible that he may be using, in the particular passage cited, the expression *kharaj wa jizya* to refer generally to land revenue.

Stern Daughter of the Voice of God: Ideas of Duty Among the British in India

T.G.P. SPEAR

Duty was described by Wordsworth as the stern daughter of the voice of God; his reflections in his Ode suggest that it had a definite, if nebulous moral character which included guidance, self-sacrifice and the exercise of reason. Moral philosophers like Moore, Bosanquet and Green have been apt to link the idea with that of station; 'My Station and its Duties' was the title of a famous chapter.[1] By what devious route this linkage may have been derived from Indian thought I will not speculate; but it is certain we have here an approximation to the Hindu idea of *dharma*. Duty had moral overtones but very practical consequences in the here-and-now; it was a limited, fragmented thing, bound up with class and worldly station, an implement for keeping things as they were. As the hymn has it—

The rich man in his castle,
The poor man at his gate,
God made them high and lowly,
And ordered their estate.[2]

In all this one notes a high degree of authority. There was a hierarchy into which one must fit and obedience was an essential part of the concept. But obedience to whom? To Wordsworth (when he wrote his Ode) it was the voice of conscience; later it was the claims of society as expressed in the established order. So the flashings of divine conscience were transformed into the counsellings of an Archbishop of Canterbury; these included obedience to authority, carefully ordered and deliberate change, a respect for things as they are, and moderation in all things.

The more prosaic *Oxford Dictionary* divides the meaning of the term into fiscal (which we may omit here, though indeed it is too much with us), obedience to orders and obedience to the moral law. Here again is the element of obedience and the element of morality or moral principle. So far, so good; but the question is still wide open for we may yet ask—obedience to whom and why? Is it to constituted authority as established by law, or to the inner voice of conscience? The dilemma implicit here was exposed long ago in the *Trial and Death of Socrates*. And if it consists in obedience to the inner voice, how do we know which of the inner voices that beset us from time to time is the authentic one? If we shift our ground and say, 'It is the voice which expresses or reveals the moral law to us', we are still confused, asking plaintively, whose, or what moral law? Is it to be buttressed by an authority like a church or by the cold clear light of reason? But then this, alas, does not conform to the laws of physical light by proceeding in straight lines. It is not the same for all, but bends and twists according to our several idiosyncrasies. If, on the other hand, we submit to an authority, whether an institution like the Roman Catholic Church or a totalitarian state, or a person like Gandhi or Adolf Hitler, or a book like the Bible or Marx's works, how is this to be reconciled with the conscience within? The record shows that the still small voice will not be silenced permanently and has a disconcerting trick of breaking out in embarrassing ways. And if we appeal to reason, is it not another way of appealing to the light within? For what is reason to us is what the conscience says is right and therefore in accord with reason. One person's reason is another's madness. The way of conscience, one might say, leads to anarchy and the way of authority to revolt.

It looks then, as though we shall have to fall back on the English refuge of pragmatism. There must be a 'working' definition of duty as a guide to our classification. Taking then this less adventurous, and pragmatic line, we may ask what are the constituents of a sense of duty, separating the fact of experience from the concept of right. One such would certainly seem to be a sense of obedience. Human nature has within it this tendency, just as it also has the desire to command. There are various motives for obedience, which have much to do with the various concepts of duty. One is because you like it, that is, you feel a natural attraction towards a person or an institution or an idea. Many have felt a kind of mystical attraction towards an idea, like that of holiness or the blood of a race, or to an institution like a church or a secret society, or to an individual. The charismatic leader draws obedience to him; in Toynbeian phrase he 'charms' his followers by his example and his magnetism. This is something to be found equally in many religions and in the mainstream of life. Did not many stormtroopers have these feelings for Hitler as French soldiers had for the young Napoleon and others for St. Francis?

But charm he never so wisely, the leader can't charm everyone. Neither can he live forever. How many promising movements of renewal have withered because the charmer-founder was succeeded by a disciplinarian or a dictator. There must be something more to obedience than this. A second and powerful motive is fear, fear of the consequences of disobedience, whether physical, mental or in the imagination—the concentration camp, the firing squad or merely prison, the thought of disgrace or the apprehension of divine wrath. Whatever the form it takes, fear must be given a large place in promoting obedience. Yet it cannot become the sole motive or be solely equated with duty. For there are many occasions when duty may point one way and fear, respectably dressed as discretion, another. Fear can inhibit duty as well as promote it. Yet it cannot be ruled out altogether, for in some cases it acts as a buttress to a sense of duty. The soldier, for example, accepts the duty of service to his country, of which obedience to his chiefs is a component. The fear of punishment and disgrace, as well as the hope of glory, helps to maintain his duty of obedience in times of difficulty.

Another inducement to obedience in the interest of duty is a sense of the 'rightness of things'. If we are convinced that a regime, a system, a doctrine, broadly represents the nature of things, a mood of acceptance is created. It may pass to resignation; but here we come close to the borderland of apathy, indifference and cynicism. But there is no doubt that this sense of 'rightness', mixed with a tincture of fear and a pinch of hero-worship or admiration, make powerful ingredients for the dish of duty. We live, says the same poet, by admiration, hope and love, and while these do not make up the whole of the pudding of duty, they do constitute essential elements.

But I think something further is needed, the impulse which stirs to action, which leads to decision. One needs a motive force to set the whole process of response to life moving. This motive force must come from within for it to be effective; it must be wholly personal and individual, and also cosmic. It is not 'Thy will, not mine, O Lord', or the Norseman's 'I will die the prop of battle, sooner die than yield an inch'; it is the devotee's 'I am Thine and Thou art mine', the 'Thou art That' (*Tat tvam asi*) of Indian philosophy. It is, in fact, the moral imperative of Kant. Without it, duty is not really duty; it is conformity, time-serving or indifference. This imperative is an internal, not an external thing, for otherwise it would be obedience induced by considerations of fear or convenience. It is moral because the 'ought' which convinces the mind and stirs the will is linked with the inner sense of the rightness of things. The concept of 'rightness' may of course vary greatly with different people. But there must be some such feeling if there is to be any genuine sense of duty. Some, no doubt, have no strong feelings of duty.

There is one further proviso. The sense of duty, to be effective, must be related to others and to society as a whole. It could, one may suppose, exist in isolation, but then it would be sterile. The hermit and the world-renouncing yogi may have a genuine enough inner sense of duty, and be inspiring in themselves; but without social contacts it is a case of saving themselves but not others. We should therefore, perhaps, in clarification, say that the duty we are concerned with is social duty or duty in society.

With these considerations in mind we can now attempt a pragmatic definition of duty for use as a working tool in the discussion which follows. It would seem that the inner sense of 'rightness' is the basic factor, for this gives content to the concept, provides the spur to action, and serves as the regulator of relations with others. This basic concept is in turn modified in its expression by the other factors already mentioned. Hero-worship or loyalty can warp as well as strengthen an idea of duty; loyalty to persons or things can give it meaning and power. The tendency to the acceptance of things as they are can blur and even suffocate it, while fear can modify its expression, inhibit it altogether or stimulate some to more determined action.

In what follows it is proposed to take successive periods of

British Indian history and in each to consider the characteristics of certain individuals and groups. From such a brief survey it may then be possible to get some tentative views about the Indo-Briton's sense of duty. The colourful antics of the eccentric and the portentious diatribes of the didactic must both be avoided. A sense of duty, as shown in men's actions as well as their words, is the goal of our search.

In the eighteenth century one has to distinguish sharply between the pre-political period to 1740 in the south and 1756 in Bengal, and the adventuring period which came thereafter. The pre-political merchants had a fairly clear pattern of behaviour and personal standards. Their business was to make money both for the East India Company and themselves. Their ability to do the latter encouraged their general loyalty to the former. The Company was not to be defrauded in a large way, as happened with the Dutch further east, so long as its servants could prosecute their own fortunes without much interference. Aggression, since the unlucky child war with Aurangzeb, was frowned on. The servants sought what advantage they could from the Indian authorities by arguments, complaints and obstructive devices, but there was no thought of going further. Promoting the interests of the Company, maintaining peace with the country powers and their reputation for commercial integrity, was about the sum of their concept. Within those fairly wide limits, anyone was free to make a fortune if he could.

This mercantilist sense of duty was not a very strong plant; it did not long survive the political transition when glittering prizes came within the reach of many a previously plodding merchant. Then the Company found itself trying to enforce some discipline over its servants, usually with scant success. As a type of the adventuring Company's servant we may take the most successful of them all, Robert Clive, and along with him the servants associated with his and related enterprises down to about 1770. This group, as a whole, was zealous for the Company's interests, whether in fighting the French in the south, or in promoting its wealth and dominion in Bengal. Clive himself, it is true, went beyond the Company and proposed to Pitt the Elder the setting up of a royal dominion in India.[3] But the rest were the Company's men; Clive himself was at the bottom. Gone to the winds were all restraints on the acquirement of fortunes; if it fitted in with the Company policy, so much the better; but the fortunes had to be made in any case. Clive's later claim in Parliament to have been 'astonished at his own moderation' was really a rhetorical flourish.[4] 'Dear self' was the paramount factor until his return to Bengal in 1765. Then his fierce attack on the practices his contemporaries had learnt from him both staggered them by its unexpectedness and was out of character for the group as a whole.[5] This money sense was potent even with supposed reformers like Henry Vansittart, who took a large present from the new nawab he installed in Bengal within weeks of his arrival there[6]. It ran riot in Madras where enterprising servants like Benfield could make fortunes by borrowing at high rates to lend to the Nawab of the Carnatic at still higher ones, on the security of assignments on the Carnatic revenue. Others in Bengal secured the administration of monopolies and commissions on the revenue, and resorted, through agents, to large scale intimidation as vividly described by Warren Hastings.[7] Francis Sykes was known as 'squire *matoot*' because he was supposed to have received the proceeds of a tax of that name[8]. There were those in 1770 who did not refrain from speculating in rice at the time of the great Bengal famine of the year.[9] A sense of duty was lax in the army too; there were frequent threats of disobedience, culminating in the 'White' or Fletcher mutiny of officers suppressed by Clive in 1766. Clive's actions during his second governorship were, I believe, sincere. They represented a sense of obligation to the Company and the State as overriding private profit. But before this is taken as a modification of the previous statements, it must be remembered that at this time Clive was applying to others standards he had not previously applied to himself. He would never consider giving up even the *jagir* granted to him by Mir Jafar to support his title and rank within the official Mughal nobility.

A sense of duty could thus not be described as a virile plant during this period. The next period covers the Warren Hastings years down to the arrival of Cornwallis. Those who look at these years will find an external scene full of action and drama, and an internal one which was gay, factious and corrupt by turns. Internally there was drama too, with Philip Francis, primed with Clive's careful briefing,[10] acting the part of Caesar's ghost at Philippi. In one sense it could be considered a continuation of the previous period in a minor key. Financial grand slams were no longer possible, but sizable tricks and rubbers could still be won, specially at Courts like those of Murshidabad and Lucknow. The curbs were greater but the appetite remained. The discipline of fixed salaries had yet to come and the main body of the servants were not content with the top-class-favouring commissions in the revenue which had replaced Clive's brief Society of Trade. But this admitted, I think that some change in attitude could be detected. In the Bengal presidency both civilians and soldiers, perhaps stimulated by Hastings himself, showed a higher sense of public obligation, which in turn produced better performance. Incidents like Popham's march across Central India, the rescue of Bombay from the Marathas and of Madras from Haidar Ali, revealed qualities not observable before in anyone except Clive and Eyre Coote and perhaps Major Lawrence. On the civil side there was a beginning among the new district officers of a sense that they were there to protect the people as well as to enrich themselves. Men like Shore and Charles Grant were beginning their careers, though still overshadowed by the Barlows and the Middletons. In Hastings himself we can detect a wider view of public affairs and a larger range of cultural appreciation. Indian life and culture was for him something to be studied and even admired rather than a fecund cow to be milked. This could perhaps be expressed by saying that while money-making was important and justifiable, there was a provision that you should not be found out; an incident like Clive's *jagir* was now unthinkable. All this goes for Bengal only. Bombay had not yet emerged from its traditional parochialism while Madras, at least up to 1780, was proceeding merrily, though surreptitiously, with the game to 'make what you can while you can with the help of the Nawab of the Carnatic'. The Nawab of Arcot's debts are less known and condemned in British Indian history than the Bengal presents only because they lacked the publicity of a parliamentary enquiry and were so complicated that they have not yet been fully unravelled.

With the coming of Cornwallis in 1786 a new era begins which may be taken to extend to about 1830. Cornwallis himself described his immediate predecessor's government as a 'system of the dirtiest jobbing';[11] with his reputation for integrity, with his assured position in England, and with the steady support of the then Prime Minister, he was independent of the Company in London and its local servants alike; he was both willing and able to enforce his ideas of public duty. No longer was it the kettle which called the pot black. Early suspensions, dismissals and reproofs, reinforced by a generous salary system and the separation of commerce from public administration, changed the Bengal atmosphere almost overnight. But this change in the authoritarian concept of duty, salutary though it was, might have been a seven years wonder ending with his reign, like Clive's second governorship measures after his departure. Without support from the Company's servants his measures could not have lasted. But Cornwallis had the advantage of Clive. He found a new generation of Company's servants to whom public service was more important than fortunes, for whom public duties were moral duties, for whom the idea of justice extended to the Indians in their charge. Cornwallis's part was not only to set a pattern of public behaviour, but also to encourage by promotion those Company servants to whom such patterns were already a matter of conscience. His example and his actions introduced the period which may be called that of public duty *par excellence*.

From this time there were in the public service two streams of opinion and two views of duty. The first began with the men Cornwallis promoted like John Shore and the Grants. It continued with men like Holt Mackenzie, who might almost be described as an administrative monk, Mountstuart Elphinstone and Charles Metcalfe, for whom personal integrity was something of a fetish. There was the unattractive Barlow who was nevertheless high-minded and devoted. There were the Bengal civilian councellors, like Stirling and Edmonstone and John Adams, disliked by the more forthright men in the country like John Malcolm, but who had the moral capability of standing up to a governor-general as powerful as Lord Hastings. In the army we similarly find a group of officers for whom public duty had become paramount. John Malcolm was free-handed with government money, but it was not his own pocket which was filled. There was no doubt of his integrity and devotion to the public service. Then there was Thomas Munro with his years of solitary work in the Madras hinterland. There was, in fact, a new set of men with a new set of values.

Another element in this new outlook must now be noticed.

It appears when we ask, what was the motive force of this new outlook? To some, as is found to be in a good deal of Charles Metcalfe's writings,[12] it was a combination of stoic endurance and persistence in the face of difficulty, and of deistical moralism—the cosmic clockmaker, the great law-giver, the disposer of events. To this group belonged Mountstuart Elphinstone and Holt Mackenzie,[13] though the principle was covered in their case with a coating of Utilitarianism. Holt with his cheerfulness was on the sunny as Metcalfe was on the shady side of the hill of difficulty. To this group, duty, based mainly on reason and 'natural law', included a sense of moral responsibility to themselves and to the people in their care. It was expressed in such things as Mackenzie's search for an equitable land settlement and insistence on village rights, in Metcalfe's crusade against highly patronized corruption in Hyderabad State and Elphinstone's settlement of the Deccan and later educational measures. Here was a new sense of duty coming from *within.*

The other group of this class sailed, as it were, on a parallel course but used a different tack, or perhaps we should say, a different motive power. This was the religious, emerging in its dynamic but yet hardly popular, form of Evangelicalism. Evangelical influence is usually dated from the despatch of the Evangelical chaplains to Calcutta in the 1780s.[14] The outward signs were a new decorum in the behaviour of Calcutta society and a new taste for attendance at church. Among an increasing number of the Company's officers these phenomena concealed the movement's typical inner revolution; first the worldliness, often exaggerated in retrospect, then the conviction of guilt and the fear of death—dark night of the soul which lead to the glory of redemption by grace and faith, and finally the certainty of salvation. But the process did not end there; it involved not only a personal amendment of life, but also a sense of responsibility towards others, a longing to pass on the good news to them. Men were souls and souls were to be gained or lost. Conviction of sin was the prelude to the converting of souls. Further, some understanding of the truth was a precondition of conversion, a thought which explains the Evangelical enthusiasm for education.

This spiritual progression was well known among the early Evangelicals, from William Wilberforce onwards, and is often described in their letters and memoirs. Those in general sympathy with the movement, but who never sank into the pit of despair which presaged the new life, like William Pitt or Lord William Bentinck, rarely rose to the heights of conscious salvation and the urge to prosletyze. But they formed the penumbra round the shining cloud of salvation, a circle of ministering spirits round the central band of the elect, who helped to spread the influence of the movement far beyond the main corps of devotees. The Evangelically inspired were the *satyagrahis* of British India. In India we have early examples in John Shore and Charles Grant the elder, both of whom went through what may irreverently be called the mystery ritual. It was no accident that John Shore on retirement helped to found the Church Missionary Society, formed largely because Parliament had refused the official promotion and support of missionary activity; or that Charles Grant in his influential *Considerations*. . .[15] saw no hope for Indian society save in its conversion to Christianity, with English education as a necessary preliminary.

A feature of this movement was that it was more dynamic than the stoic-deist creed of men like Charles Metcalfe. Such men could save themselves but others were content just to admire (or reprobate) them. Lesser men touched with the Evangelical fire were not only unable to rest themselves, but had a magnetic power within which they drew others to their causes. So western education—was it not sponsored in Parliament by William Wilberforce himself?—gathered momentum in their hands. Concern for social welfare took the form of campaigns against *sati*, infanticide and child marriage as well as against heathen idolatry and the Company's patronage of Hindu ceremonies and festivals. The refugees from the City of Destruction could not abide the spectacle of the Company as the Churchwarden of Vishnu. The movement had an intellectual in young Charles Trevelyan, an august patron in Bentinck, home patrons in Charles Wynn and Charles Grant the younger, an enthusiast in James Havelock who preached the Gospel in city bazaars when off-duty, its gadflies in Henry Martyn, Alexander Duff and some of the Baptists, and its crusader in the Madras general who resigned his post rather than take part in ceremonies which seemed to honour heathen gods.[16] In the list of new departures and achievements of those years—missionary activity, the development of western education, the reform or curtailment of social abuses within Hindu society, the break with the age-old tradition that the government of the day countenanced and patronized all law-abiding religions—one sees the influence of the Evangelical movement, whether working through the conscience of individuals, by the force of attraction, by the hope of reward or the fear of the thunders of Exeter Hall.

It is not our purpose to take sides, to praise or blame, but rather to record a development. By and large, the Evangelical religious movement added a new dimension to the Indo-Englishman's sense of duty, or, one might say, a fresh facet to the hitherto rather dull jewel of duty within the lotus of the soul. Moral causes, concern for welfare, promotion of education and western values were now a part of man's duty. This development underlay much of the moral and material programme of the British in nineteenth century India. The great irrigation projects, the efforts to achieve social justice by equitable land settlements, the promotion of education all owed much to this motivation in individuals and the ring of influenced helpers who surrounded them.

This side of the picture of British ideas of duty in early nineteenth century India has been stressed because, as it seems to me, the religious factor has been largely confined by historians to individuals, as if an assurance of salvation and attendance at church were the end of it. This influence was social, ubiquitous and profound. But it was not the only influence. Here the contrary pitfall must be avoided of supposing that the 'old-timers' and their influence disappeared overnight. They were very much there; perhaps even a majority of heads could have been counted among them. But they were no longer a positive, thrusting force as they had been in Clive's and Hastings's days. Their outlook was now negative; they stood for the old ways; their argument was to let things be, that change was dangerous. They stood for obedience to the Company's orders and the promotion of its interests; those interests were conceived mainly in terms of power and prestige rather than those of reform and improvement. They would willingly join in the suppression of the Thugs, because they regarded them as an Indian thorn in the Indian flesh, a home-grown ulcer, as it were, which any good ruler, Hindu or Muslim, would wish to suppress. But their zeal would stop short of suppressing *sati* or infanticide. Discourage, yes, but do not otherwise interfere with established customs, even if they are distasteful to a westerner.

This position sprang from their attitude to Indian society; they were restorers and conservers rather than reformers; they would therefore give government countenance to Indian religions, promote traditional authority where possible, leave education as it was, and let the revenue collect itself through local agents. The Permanent Settlement of Bengal, establishing the *zamindars* as the local rulers, was much to their taste; Holt Mackenzie's and Bentinck's interfering ways were not. They willingly presided over fairs with their religious overtones and temple connections; they frowned on missionaries as being both dangerous and undesirable. They were for the maintenance of chiefs and princes whenever possible.

The dividing line between the best of this class and the reformers may well have seemed blurred, and from the point of view of action indeed it was. But the division can be seen as a distinction in motive. Charles Mecalfe, for example, was very cautious in action; the British dominion was frail; India might rise at any moment.[17] But he was a reformer in motive and carried out reforming measures like the suppression of *sati*. Elphinstone was similarly a conserver in the Deccan, but his rule in Bombay evidenced his practical steps towards grafting western concepts on an eastern world—a very untraditional stance. The Evangelically-minded were bolder, for they had the fear of the Lord to spur them on.[18]

The traditionalists were divided on a point of personal behaviour. One section accepted not only the obligation of obedience to authority and attention to official duty, but also the standard of personal probity introduced by Cornwallis. John Malcolm could be mentioned as an example of this class. But there was another section who thought—or so rationalized it—that the former easy financial relationships were part of the Indian scene and should therefore be retained. Favours, presents, grants and loans, and archaic payments were legitimate perquisites as long as they did not go beyond traditional Indian limits. Clive and his generation went too far, perhaps, but that need not be a reason for giving up a well-understood (and profitable) practice altogether. This class was considerable, for a number of them attained high office. We know of this class from the cases which came to light where the practice *did* go too far, usually under some sort of financial duress. There was James Todd of Rajasthan, Russell of Hyderabad, whose activities as Resident were unmasked by his successor Metcalfe; there was Ricketts, of Lucknow, said by Bentinck to have been 'overwhelmed by temptation'; and there was the classic case of Sir Edward Colebrooke at Delhi, the details of whose activities were neatly docketed by the young Charles Trevelyan. After his exposure (1829-30) cases still occurred, but they were individual and sporadic (like that of Charles Beames) and not representative of a class.

The major part of the traditionalists were men of integrity and devotion who saw their duty as the promotion of Company interests and the conservation of Indian society. On the humanitarian side they tended to be fatalists, an attitude perhaps imbibed from their Indian surroundings. Amongst them may be mentioned Major Scott-Waring, the agent and champion of Warren Hastings, General Palmer, Hastings's friend and correspondent in later years, and 'King' Collins. Palmer and Collins were both concerned with Maratha and Rajput affairs. Eminent among them was the boisterous and likeable Malcolm, the friend of princes and chiefs, the generous pensioner of the defeated Maratha Peshwa, the subject of the term 'Malcolm riot', who could not bear Bengal civilians and believed only 'in gradual change'. There was Sir David Ochterloney,[19] soldier and diplomatist, the hero of the Nepal war, and later Sir John Low, the opponent of Dalhousie's annexation policy. Meadows-Taylor, author of *The Confessions of a Thug*, belonged to this group, and so did that individual who 'settled' areas in Rohilkhund galloping full speed on horseback over a dusty plain.[20]

To these various concepts must be added, before the revolts of 1857, a mutation of the reforming species. This was the Punjab school. It had in it traces of Evangelical moralism. Montgomery, John Lawrence's successor as Lieutenant-Governor of the Punjab, was much occupied with thoughts of conversion and supported the Church Missionary Society. But more important was the covenanting spirit of Ulster with its fighting zest, its stern sense of justice, its feeling of destiny and mission, its severity and occasional ruthlessness. The Lawrences, Montgomery, and John Nicholson all came from Ulster, and they stamped their image on the school of administrators whom they trained. The Punjab civilians had a more intense sense of duty and urgency to action than was felt elsewhere; their sense of justice was keen but somewhat narrow; they were buoyed up by a conviction of righteouness which made their opponents seem wicked; so strong was their inner conviction of rightness that discipline was sometimes bent at the behest of conscience; they were decisive in action and ruthless in war; in peace they were do-gooders in forceful ways. At their best they were vigorous paternalists like John Lawrence himself; they could also be sadists and killers. Their moment of glory was the 1857 crisis in the Punjab, their achievement the material development of the Punjab, their toll of doom the Amritsar shooting and their legacy the Punjab massacres of 1947. To the general concept of British-Indian duty they added self-righteousness, an intenser sense of duty and commitment, resolution verging on implacability and a conviction of moral superiority. They loved the Punjabis and were admired in return. But they could never capture more than a personal loyalty or integrate the Punjab communities into a nation.

The Mutiny and Revolt of 1857 was a traumatic experience for the British in India; it affected their motivation as it also affected their outward policy. To British eyes India was never quite the same again as it had been before. But it wasn't only shock that was altering attitudes. It came at a time when new influences were beginning to play on the British in India, some of which had begun to spread their rays before the actual crisis. These factors tended both to unify their outlook and to modify it.

First we may list the introduction of the examination system for entry into higher government services from 1853 in place of directorial nomination. In itself it might not have greatly altered the composition and outlook of officialdom. It is known that many of the old families managed to secure entry by examination as they had formerly done by nomination. But the development which was linked with it had important consequences. This was the Charles Trevelyan-Benjamin Jowett conspiracy to link the new examination with the old universities and so secure a university or 'educated'[21] cadre. The proposal involved the closure of Haileybury and the adjustment of the age of entry. In this the planners were successful, and their success had another effect. In general the universities were fed by the new public schools which were then proliferating. The ICS entrants were therefore provided with an ethos or set of values by the new schools. The universities introduced them to the world of intellect and of men. They were relatively mature by the time of their selection and their values much less liable to erosion during their first Indian years. India became for them their field of activity rather than the provider of a finishing course in their early service and impressionable years.

Another new influence was the opening of the Suez Canal in 1869. Journeys which formerly took (by sail round the Cape) anything from four to fifteen months, could now be made regularly in a month and gradually less. Many officers like Holt Mackenzie (25 years), Elphinstone (24 years) and Metcalfe (37 years), had spent the whole of their service lives in India; now it became common to take periodic leave in Britain and so be so much more open to current British influences. The new travel facilities encouraged the increase of British families, reducing the sense of exile by prospects of leave, and making it possible for wives to return home with their families.

In addition to these considerations there was the traumatic effect of the Great Revolt. It dealt a heavy blow at the former feeling of security and self-confidence, both of which had grown strong. The former warnings about 'the frailty of the British dominion' were then dismissed as creakings. Also dismissed was respect for Indian institutions, as obscurantist in an age of progress. The post-Revolt generation never felt fully secure again, a fact demonstrated by the average reaction to the events in the Punjab in 1919. In addition, the previous faith in Indian willingness to reform its society, so buoyant in the thirties, disappeared. To touch Indian institutions was now considered as dangerous as fiddling with a faultily insulated electric power cable. The British had received a great shock but did not quite know which part of the wire it came from and where another might come if the fiddling continued. So positive social measures were dropped and the moral duty to improve confined to things like railways, roads and irrigation. Indian society was incorrigible and one could only spread a western veneer over it, not change it.

With fear went disdain; race feeling was markedly strengthened. It had been growing, it is true, for the previous thirty years or more. Some would argue that it had been present since the mid-eighteenth century, but I think this view arises from a confusion between the attitude of 'my civilization is better than yours and therefore I shall do better than you', and 'I and my civilization are inherently superior to you and your culture and always will be'. The implication of the first statement is 'reform your civilization and draw level'; there is here a basic concept of equality. The implication of the second is, 'I am your ruler, your guardian, your instructor, your corrector; it is for you to obey and be thankful'. The transition from the one to the other state of mind can be seen by comparing the outlook of the men of Wellesley's day with that of the younger generation from Bentinck's time onwards. Racialism replaced mere arrogance and self-confidence.

We can now turn to consider the effect of this shock and these influences upon the average British official. The new system of entry provided not only a number of new entrants outside the Directorial circle, but also successive sets of people conditioned in a new and uniform way. Your family connections with India might go back to the eighteenth century, but you had to submit with the rest at least to the curriculum imposed by the examination and probably to that of a public school and university as well. So we find a new uniformity in the service outlook. It extended to others as the men of commerce and the men and women of religion, for they were all, or nearly all, exposed to some or all of these influences. This uniformity, thus induced, spelled the end of the 'old-timers' as a significant group within the whole body of the British. Their survivors were regarded as eccentrics. Those who continued to have conservative views of Indian society and its values, like many members of the Political service, did so from a new angle of superiority. 'Yes, it might be good for them because it keeps them quiet, but not for *us*, because we belong to a higher culture'. The appreciation of Indian culture by men like Warren Hastings, James Forbes and James Todd in the late eighteenth and early nineteenth centuries, the accommodation with Indian manners and customs, became things of the past. They were left to the scholars like H.H. Wilson, James Prinse and Max Muller, and then usually confined to the uncontroversial field of Ancient India. The new conservatives made few concessions to Indian institutions or Indian personalities. To the former their attitude was one of guardianship, not admiration or interested enquiry; as to the latter Lord Northbrook remarked in the seventies that no Englishman seemed to think that an Indian could do anything.

There was another influence that faded from about this time. This was the Evangelical. The Revolt was not the cause, for it rather stirred Evangelical feelings at the time, feelings reflected in men like Robert Montgomery and finding expression in revived demands for government support of Christian missions. Rather it stemmed from Britain, where Evangelicalism, though still powerful, was no longer the thrusting dynamic force which it had formerly been. The movement was reaching a state where it could still obstruct but could no longer impose its will on others. This tendency was helped by a widespread feeling that missionary activity had been at least an irritant in the Indian body-social. Missionary activity, still largely motivated by Evangelicalism, came to be variously regarded by the average Englishman in India with feelings ranging from tepid approval to conviction of futility and a belief that it was an unnecessary interference in Indian life. No longer the demanded reform, the denunciation of abuses, the personal propagandism, the raising of the Christian banner on political issues. The command 'Feed my sheep' tended now to be rated as highly as the injunction 'Go out into the highways'. Propagandism went on but the movement had lost its cutting edge. But if Evangelicalism faded as an 'ism', it continued to exercise indirect influence as a moral force.

From this basis we can consider the content of the concept of duty among the British in India between 1858 and 1914. The conventional ideas of duty were there as before, perhaps somewhat strengthened by the new conditioning of school and college. Haileybury was more important for providing a haven for Malthus than a philosophy for Indian officials. There was respect for authority, devotion to the task in hand in district, court and secretariat. There was a heightened sense of responsibility, a new emphasis on the concept of the Indian empire. India was no longer a place you governed, no longer a political accident, but an empire and a world providentially entrusted to the British as part of their mission of empire to the world. These feelings strengthened as the idea of empire spread and with it the idea of mission. They found their embodiment and most eloquent expression in Lord Curzon.[22] One must not overpress this aspect or forget that salaries continued to be as important as service to most officers. But a glimpse of the change can be obtained by noting the differing attitudes taken up by the biographers of Clive. The first approval of him as a successful adventurer gave way in the mid-century to moral disapprobation. This changed again in the late nineteenth century to praise as an empire-builder; Clive was the founder of that mystical entity, the Indian empire, and this muted all criticism. This can be seen in the two biographies of Colonel Malleson, the one (1882)[23] blaming and other (1893)[24] defending and praising.

The schools inculcated self-reliance and discipline; were not their products said to be 'good for the colonies'? Insofar as this marked change, it was chiefly a strengthening of the sense of discipline; the Company's officers were noted for their self-reliance in any case. But self-reliance moves towards leadership and leadership involves relations with the led. It is here that the new generation showed a marked deviation from the old. They were now members of a superior race and a superior civilization. Their destiny was to lead and to govern, their privilege to reflect a new light on a benighted world. They did this by their character and example rather than by direct interference. 'An Englishman is just; he does not take bribes; he does his duty without fear or favour; he is punctual, etc'. Such an attitude in itself might have turned India into a warren of little dictators, a kind of nineteenth century King Stephen's England. But it was controlled by the moralism which still flourished and surrounded its possessors in the schools, the universities and middle-class society. Duty was still moral duty. So the superior leader found himself a paternalist in outlook and a guardian by profession. His charges were his children, not his cattle as in the nomadic ideology, whether as individuals or groups in a district, or in the abstract in a province as a whole, or in all India. A paternalist has severity, but it is kept in reserve; he has benevolence in intention and feels guilty if there is no smiling countenance behind a frowning providence. This outlook provided the hallmark for the British administrators in the later nineteenth century. They combined a sense of authority which ran to pomposity with some and more occasionally to severity, a sense of involvement with their charges and a concern for their welfare, and a feeling of loyalty to the government with a special sense of guardianship of a mystical entity called the *Raj*. All this was often concealed beneath layers of simulated cynicism or indifference. The lucky ones had canal settlements to organize, others the grimmer stimulus of large-scale famine relief; the majority matters of revenue settlement, district improvements and fighting for their charges' interest against the higher authorities. And the higher authorities themselves often withstood the London rulers from the same motives. For a detailed picture of all this we have the absorbing pages of *The Guardian*;[25] it is here sought to suggest how this particular breed of overseas Englishmen came about.

To balance this picture we have to note two other ingredients in the middle and late nineteenth century Indo-British consciousness. The first I would call clannishness, the feeling of belonging to a group for mutual advantage to the exclusion of others. It may be equated with the spirit of the corporation where individuals organize themselves for a common purpose, commercial, industrial, professional. The fellowship within is matched by the exclusiveness and aloofness without. This quality among the British in India owed much to the normal spirit of the corporation; it was perhaps sharpened by isolation in a large alien population of strange habits and thoughts. It may have been further strengthened by the pervading sense of clannishness in Indian society itself, exemplified in the ubiquitous caste system as well as in much surviving tribalism. How easy to excuse exclusiveness (to oneself) on the ground that the British rulers were a sort of white Brahmins, a kind of super-caste. Distinctions multiplied and were sharper than in Britain—the *boxwallah* (upper and lower, business-man and shopkeeper) and the official; the twice-born and subordinate services (the two European families in a country station who cannot meet or dine together because they belong to different services); the Eurasian and the European. Amongst the officials it was exemplified in the steady resistance to the admission of Indians to the higher services, not merely from racial motives, though the Ilbert Bill controversy showed that these existed, but also on monopolistic grounds. More jobs for Indians meant fewer for Europeans, thus reducing the opportunities open to their relatives and friends. Juggling with the examination age-limit and the attempt to create a less 'higher civil service'[26] are examples of this attitude, which delayed a real break-through on Indian appointments until the Lee Commission's report in 1923.

There was a further point. The duty to work *for* Indians did not extend to working with them on an equal footing. The paternalist attitude, were it never so benevolent, stopped short of dealing with one's charges on equal terms. So, when it came to the new western-orientated Indian who wanted a share in the administration, and an opportunity to talk on equal terms, there was a failure in understanding and in relationships. So the District-Officer *raj* of work and benevolence began to turn sour towards the end of the century as Indians began to insist on talking to and even criticizing their official and racial 'betters'. There was incomprehension and irritation, indignation and fear of an unknown quantity leading to harshness. The D.O. could not abide the local lawyers and distrusted the political leaders; there were the snide jokes about the Bengali *babu,* the talk of 'wogs' and inefficiency. Hence the sad breach between the Government and the Congress, leading to repression of the left wing, to boycotts and bombings.

There remains the final period which I have dated from 1919-47. But perhaps it should be put back to 1910, the year of Lord Hardinge's arrival in India, for then the Government began to practise co-operation with Congress in place of its former estrangement, and the higher authorities to encourage just those attitudes which so many of its officers found so distasteful. With the Montagu regime (1917-22) this became settled policy; there was to be co-operation towards the goal of full partnership. The new Indian was adolescent; the British were no longer to be parents or guardians; they were to be senior friends, wise uncles or elder brothers. The assumption of wisdom and the offer of guidance might seem irritating; the manner of its giving heavy and patronizing, but underneath was the implication of equality lightened by a vision of partnership.

But did the British as a whole accept it? A great many did not. The resignations from the Services in 1921, the resentment of many more who stayed on, the groundswell of support for General Dyer's action at Amritsar, are evidence of this. But there is also evidence of a new generation of officials who came to India with these concepts already accepted, as well as some senior ones who now came to the front like Sir Malcolm (later Lord) Hailey and Sir William Morris. These new men were willing to work with and under Indians and saw their duty as including the promotion of ultimate self-government. Sir Evans Jenkins, Sir Frederick Puckle, Sir Jeremy Raisman and Sir Penderel Moon were men of this kind. There was again a division amongst the British about the content of the idea of duty as there had been before the Great Revolt. It was really the same division between the old-timers and the new-lookers, though the subject of difference of course varied. It was a particular rather than a general change of outlook, and a division of opinion which steadily weakened with each annual contingent of recruits. The influences blowing from India were now so strong that there could be no question of the final outcome. For these reasons I would call this final period a kind of appendix to the major post-Revolt period which preceded it.

I am conscious that a number of important categories of the British in India would appear to have been omitted from this survey. First there are the women, nearly a half of the total British resident population (excluding British army units temporarily stationed in India). In general they identified themselves with their husbands and had been conditioned to the same general concepts, either before leaving Britain or soon after arrival in India. Their attitude to Indians was perhaps more aloof because the Indian social system and languages prevented free intercourse with Indian women. People like the Indian Civilian's wife who inveighed against the British as oppressors in India, as they were in Ireland, were the exceptions which proved the rule. But there was an area where their sense of values and duty was distinctive. It was that of compassion. The suffering and ignorance of India moved them much more strongly than they did the men. The first British non-missionary schools for Indian girls were founded by the influence of Lady Bethune in 1849.[27] In later years there is a long record of medical and educational achievement; Vellore (founded by an American lady) and Ludhiana in the north pioneered medical work for women; the Kinnaird College in Lahore, the Women's Christian College in Madras, and others, educational work. They planned and manned government services for women with the Lady Hardinge Medical College at its apex. Professional women were to be found in schools, colleges, and institutions like the YWCA; they were specially prominent in the missionary field, where they often took the lead (for example in Delhi) in medical and educational work.

There was another aspect of their influence. Their presence, their behaviour, apart from the positive impact made by a few official and many non-official women on Indians and Indian society, had an important effect. They both tended to divert their own men's attention towards Britain more than had formerly been the case, and also to mellow their attitudes in India itself. By Indians they were seen and heard. Some disapproved; more wondered, admired and sought to emulate. The movement for the freedom of Indian women was undoubtedly stimulated by the example of these women as they went their ways.

Then there were the missionaries. The urge to convert was of course strong among them. They had little sense of obligation, during the nineteenth century, to understand the religions they were attacking. In early days Lord Hastings likened one of them to a man firing a pistol into a gunpowder magazine.[28] As the century turned those attitudes softened. The urge to convert was supplemented and gradually replaced by the pastoral desire to conserve and build up the church. Zeal was reinforced by knowledge which bred in its turn, respect and tolerance. Old-timers remained who still saw a world of heathen darkness, and they were reinforced by Dr Kraemer's thesis[29] in the thirties. But most preferred preaching the Gospel to denouncing heathenism and quite a few could see good in Mahatma Gandhi.

Next, there was the large European business community. Their main duty, as they saw it, was to make money. This granted, their values were not unlike those of the officials, perhaps accentuated by a greater sense of insecurity and lack of the public servants' corporate discipline. Their loyalty was to themselves and their firms rather than the Indian state of the British. Thus the Mutiny panic and the revenge hysteria in Calcutta were an index of this sense of insecurity, as was also the support for General Dyer. In race relations they were divided between the aloofness and hostility of Calcutta and the cosmopolitanism of Bombay; outside these two there were many scattered through the country whose relations with Indians were easy and natural. Businessmen more easily came to terms with the westernized Indian than the official, because they had never been their superiors. In the final phase, when it became clear that the continuance of business depended more and more on Indian goodwill, they showed imagination and foresight in cultivating good relations. It became the businessman's duty to be friendly and forthcoming with

Indians.

Finally, there comes the Indian Army. The regimental officer corps constituted a world of its own, secluded from both the British civil and the Indian world. Their life has only recently been described by Philip Mason in his *A Matter of Honour.*[30] The army underwent a radical change after the Great Revolt. Duty became not only obedience to superior officers and the leadership of men in battle, it now included the understanding and almost parental care of their men in camp and cantonment. Thus arose a special compartmentalized sense of duty—'My men (Sikhs, Gurkhas, Pathans etc.) are splended fellows—of course I don't know about the others'. Since the army was so much a world of its own, it cannot be wholly integrated with a general review of the British in India. We leave them here in the skilful hands of Philip Mason.

In this survey one cannot but be struck by the correspondence of ideas of duty between the British in Britain and in India. Even the mercenary outlook of the British in mid-eighteenth century India had some British counterpart. In general it can be said that the British idea of duty in India was British in origin, but modified by local circumstances. That modification was large in the eighteenth century for various reasons; it grew steadily less thereafter though there were lags, throw-backs and overlaps through various circumstances. With Lord and Lady Mountbatten even the viceregal throne found in its last occupants a pair of thoroughly modern-minded Britons.

Notes

[1]F. H. Bradley, *Ethical Studies*, London 1876.

[2]From 'All things Bright and Beautiful', by Mrs, C. F. Alexander. In most modern hymnals, e. g. *Songs of Praise* from the 1931 edition, this verse is now omitted. See her *Hymns for Little Children*, 25th edition, London, 1876.

[3]The full text is given in G. B. Forrest, *Life of Lord Clive*, London, 1918, vol. II, pp. 412-14, and relevant extracts in P. Spear, *Master of Bengal*, London, 1975, pp. 102-4.

[4]Forrest, *op. cit.*, vol. II, p. 394. The remark was made before the Select Committee of the House of Commons in May 1772.

[5]Forrest, *op. cit.*, vol. I, p. 228, and Spear, *op. cit.* p. 58-59. The letter of Clive to a friend, 1754.

[6]See P. E. Roberts, *History of British India*, 3rd Edition, Oxford, 1952, p. 150-51.

[7]Warren Hastings to Vansittart, 25 April 1762, from B. M. Add, MSS. 29096. Quoted by Forrest, *op. cit.*, vol. II, pp. 227-28, and Spear, *op. cit.*, pp. 113-14.

[8]Mathute tax, see H. H. Wilson, *Glossary of Revenue & Judicial Terms. etc.*, London, 1855, p. 334, *Mathaut* etc.

[9]W. W. Hunter *Annals of Rural Bengal* (4th edition) London, 1871, p. 38. A. Majed Khan, *The Transition in Bengal, 1756-75*, Cambridge, 1969, pp. 217-20, 222-3.

[10]Spear, *op. cit.*, p. 192-23; A. M. Davies, *Clive of Plassey*, London, 1939, pp. 489-90.

[11]*Correspondence of Charles, First Marquess Cornwallis*, (ed.) C. Ross, 3 vols. London, 1859, Vol. I, p. 371.

[12]E. Thompson, *Charles, Lord Metcalfe*, London, 1937.

[13]P. Spear, 'Holt Mackenzie, Forgotten Man of Bengal', *Bengal Past and Present*, July-December 1967 (Jubilee no.) Vol. 86, Part II, serial no. 162 Calcutta, pp, 24-36.

[14]See Charles Simeon, *Memoir of Rev. D. Brown*, London, n.d.

[15]C. Grant, *Observations on the State of Society of the Asiatic Subjects of Gt. Britain*, Gen. App. I of vol. I of the Report of the Select Committee of the House of Commons 1832. Also published by Parliament 1833.

[16]See J. W. Kaye, *Christianity in India*, London, 1859.

[17]See e. g. J. W. Kaye, *Papers of Lord Metcalfe*, London, 1955.

[18]See J. W. Kaye, *Christianity in India*; and K. Ingham, *Reformers in India*, Cambridge, 1956.

[19]See J. Pemble, *The Invasion of Nepal*, Oxford, 1971.

[20]E. I. Brodkin, *Rohilkhund from Conquest to Revolt, 1773-1858*, Ch. 2, unpublished Cambridge Ph. D. thesis, 1968.

[21]R. H. Moore, *Abolition of Patronage in the I. C. S. and the Closure of Haileybury College*, Cambridge Historical Journal, vol. 7, no. 2, pp. 246-57.

[22]See e. g. Lord Ronaldshay, *Life of Lord Curzon*, 3 vols. London, 1928; vol. II; Sir T. Raleigh, *Curzon in India* (Speeches), London, 1906.

[23]G. B. Malleson, *Lord Clive*, London, 1882.

[24]G. B. Malleson, *Lord Clive*, (Rulers of India), Oxford, 1893.

[25]P. Woodruff, *The Guardians*, London, 1854.

[26]The Statutory Civil Service of 1879. P. E. Roberts, pp. 457-59, *Cambridge History of India*, Vol. VI, Cambridge 1932, pp. 361 and 365.

[27]S.S.S. O'Malley (ed.), *India and the West*, Oxford, 1941, pp. 454-56, ch. 12, 'The Progress of Women', by Mrs. H. Gray.

[28]E. D. Potts, *Baptist Missionaries in India, 1793-1837*, Cambridge, 1967, p. 200.

[29]H. Kraemer, *The Christian Message in a non-Christian World*, London, 1938.

[30]P. Mason, *A Matter of Honour*, London, 1974.

British Rights and Indian Duties: The Case of Sir William Lee-Warner

KENNETH BALLHATCHET

Great and manifold were the blessings which the British thought that they were bestowing upon the people of India through the spread of education—or, as they were apt to call it, the dissemination of western knowledge. This, at least, was an expectation widespread among officials, missionaries, and a variety of other persons connected with India in the early nineteenth century. Education would encourage the growth of Christianity, prosperity, morality and loyalty. But this optimism was gradually undermined. Converts were few, deterred no doubt by obscure obstacles; prosperity was slow to come, postponed by various unexpected calamities; morality and loyalty were difficult to measure, but the educational system did not seem to be designed to promote them. Clearly, some adjustments were desirable. More attention should be paid to character and conscience, less to intellect and memory. Since the British government spent so much money on education, it had the right to ensure that Indians were taught to understand their duties: such, at least, was the dominant train of thought in the official mind. But their attempts to define the duties of Indians involved the British in difficulties similar to those raised by attempts to provide undenominational ethical instruction in nineteenth-century Britain, while their attempts to control the educational system met with resistance at every level.

Moral training seemed to the British to be linked with loyalty not merely, or even primarily, because of the need to provide a philosophical basis for political obligation, but because the tendencies which they most disliked in schools and colleges had political implications—'tendencies unfavourable to discipline and favourable to irreverence in the rising generation'.[1] Various explanations were attempted: the education supplied was merely 'intellectual'; it was divorced from religion; it was too western. Various remedies were formulated: the provision of sporting activities, on the assumption that boys accustomed to keep to their places in teams would continue to do so in the outside world; the development of habits of discipline through the infliction of punishments similar to those suffered by English schoolboys; finally, the inculcation of principles of morality and citizenship through lectures and text books. The control of text books is the concern of this paper: for some years it attracted a growing amount of official attention, and it was an important motive behind Curzon's attempts to control universities.[2]

In 1873 the Government of India called for the appointment of local committees to examine and report on the books used in state-supported schools: special attention was to be paid to the relevance of text books to pupils' understanding and experience.[3] There was a dutiful chorus of approval. From the Panjab, the Director of Public Instruction wrote promptly to demonstrate how well he understood the government's wisdom: 'a Native boy of fourteen' could not well understand 'an account of the discovery of America by Columbus, or a biography and criticism of Benjamin Franklin'; such subjects fostered the 'dissociation of phrases from things and of language from actual life' that was the bane of Indian education.[4] On the other hand, the provision of books on Indian themes might involve difficulties. Saiyid Ahmad Khan, as Secretary to the Committee for the better diffusion and advancement of learning among the Muhammadans of India, had recently addressed a lengthy protest to Government against Shiva Prasad's text book on Indian history, as objectionable to Muslims. Several lines of defence were erected by Kempson, Director of Public Instruction, NWP. Muslim rulers may have been portrayed as licentious or tyrannical, but this only showed how preferable were their successors. Moreover, history could not be properly written without bias: he cited Gibbon and Lingard. Such reasoning might not have commended itself to Muslims, however, and Kempson subsequently referred with satisfaction to a protest he had received from 'the Pundits of Benares' against Shiva Prasad's book: 'This at least shows the author's impartiality'.[5] But some changes had to be made.

It soon became apparent that books on Oriental themes were attracting adverse comment from the various text book committees. The Berar Committee found the *Arabian Nights* objectionable: it contained 'many indecent passages', and was therefore 'unsuitable for boys'. Instead, the Director of Public Instruction recommended a text book written by the Deputy Educational Inspector of Mirat—'an allegory in which knowledge and ignorance enter into a dispute and appear before wisdom, who decides in favour of knowledge'.[6] Even the *Prem Sagar* aroused anxiety. Special precautions were taken in Oudh. The Director of Public Instruction carefully explained: 'The passages objectionable on the score of indecency are omitted. In each book directions are given to the teacher to omit whole pages and chapters'. He would have preferred Bowdlerization, but economics provided a decisive argument against it: 'It was unfortunately necessary to publish the book as a whole, or it would not have been bought; every boy would have preferred to buy his own unabridged edition in the bazaar'.[7] One official urged that special precautions be taken to shield Indian boys from temptation: '...books that are innocuous to the comparatively pure and healthy morals of English boys may not be so to the more inflammable minds of Indian boys'. He was also worried about the *Arabian Nights*—'full of adventures of gallantry and intrigue, as well as of the marvellous. The latter is what the English boy's mind fastens on, but the Hindu, and especially the Muhammadan youth... gloats quite as much on the former, to his own moral harm'.[8]

When the text book committees had submitted their voluminous reports, the Government of India characteristically appointed a central text book committee to consider them and make recommendations. Among the innocuous proposals that emerged was the recommendation that every series of primary school readers should include some moral instruction, including 'reverence for God, parents, teachers, rulers, and the aged; a simple sketch of the duties of a good citizen, and universally admitted principles of morality and prudence: cleanliness of habits, politeness of speech, kindness of conduct to other human beings and the brute creation'. No one was likely to object to the inclusion of reverence for rulers in the midst of such an assembly of unexceptionable exhortations.

The Government of India duly considered them, and eventually commended them in a Resolution.[9] Further approval was conferred upon them by the Indian Education Commission under the chairmanship of W.W. Hunter, which emphasized two significant points. First, 'there was no necessity to restrict aided schools to the use of the text-books authorized for Government institutions. Any such interference with schools under private management would be inconvenient, and was clearly opposed to the general educational policy of Government'. Secondly, it was recommended that 'the text-book Committees in the several Provinces include qualified persons of different sections of the community not connected with the Department, and that to these Committees be submitted all text-books both English and vernacular, that it is proposed to introduce into schools, and all text-books now in use that may seem to need revision'.[10] These two points were to be ignored by Curzon.

The Hunter Commission also recommended the preparation of a moral text book, based on 'the fundamental principles of natural religion', and the delivery of lectures in every college on 'the duties of a man and a citizen'. These recommendations were rejected by Ripon's government:'...strongly as it may be urged that a purely secular education is imperfect, we cannot believe that a text-book of morality, sufficiently vague and colourless to be accepted by Christians, Muhammadans and Hindus, would do much, expecially in the stage of collegiate instruction, to remedy the defects or supply the shortcomings of such an education'. This resembled the Roman Catholic and High Anglican objections to undenominational ethical instruction in Britain, and we may suppose that Ripon's religious convictions had something to do with it. However, as a decisive argument against the delivery of lectures on the duties of a citizen, Ripon's government cited the objections of Kashinath Trimbak Telang.[11]

Telang had written a dry and witty minute of dissent:

> If the Professor's lectures tend to teach the pupils the duty of submission to the views of Government without a murmur of dissatisfaction, there is sure to come up a set of liberal irreconcilables who will complain that Government is endeavouring to enslave the intellect of the nation. If the Professor's lectures

> lead in the opposite direction, there will be some Tory irreconcilables ready to spring up and say, even more loudly and quite as erroneously as they are saying it now, that the colleges supported from State revenues are hotbeds of sedition.

His other darts were also shrewdly aimed:

> In a primary school, lectures on the duties of a man would probably be useful; in a secondary school they would probably be innocuous; but in a collegiate institution they would probably be neither useful nor innocuous.

Was it not the aim of education to encourage a critical mind, at least at that stage? He recalled the story of the Cambridge student whose first doubts about Christianity had been roused by studying Paley's *Evidences*. Telang also supported his arguments against a moral text book with a reference to the painful incident when Whateley, the Anglican Archbishop of Dublin, resigned from the National Education Board because a textbook of his, which the Board had formerly approved, was rejected in compliance with the views of a new Roman Catholic Archbishop, who happened to be less tolerant than his predecessor. Telang helpfully provided a reference to Jane Whateley's *Life and Correspondence of Richard Whateley, D.D.*[12] No doubt Ripon took due note of these home truths.

With a new Governor-General and a new Secretary of State, the matter was reopened. Cross sent Dufferin some moral text books used in Britain, with the suggestion that something similar might be used in Indian schools.[13] The official machinery was duly set in motion: a lengthy Resolution was drafted on discipline and moral training in schools and colleges, and local opipions were sought.[14] Dr John Murdoch, a redoubtable missionary in Madras, commented sourly: 'It does not seem very consistent for the Government of India to issue a resolution on moral discipline and permit the works of Zola to be sold at all the principal stations of the State Railways from Calcutta to Peshawar'.[15] But he recommended recourse to Samuel Smiles and welcomed the idea of a moral text book. R. G. Bhandarkar suggested that in addition to a moral text book teachers should also make moral remarks at appropriate points in lessons on history and literature.[16] Justice Ranade hoped that Government-aided Hindu schools would be established, where religious and moral instruction would be combined.[17] One enthusiastic official advocated a whole series of moral text books, 'to suit all classes'. His idea of the contents would have appealed to many: 'short biographical sketches of eminent men, fables, parables, extracts from sermons, speeches, and from the sacred books of the East and the West, inculcating such moral principles as form the common platform of all nations'.[18] But was there such a common platform, even within Hinduism? Shriram Bhikaji Jatar, Director of Public Instruction, Hyderabad Assigned Districts, denied it. 'The masters of the Hindu indigenous schools in the province are too ignorant to attempt any religious instruction; and as the State schools admit boys of all castes from the highest to the lowest, and as the masters do not always belong to the higher castes, such instruction is impracticable even out of school hours in these institutions'. All this boiled down to two points: first, different castes had different moral duties; secondly, moral teaching should be handled by Brahmins. Of course he advised against any attempt to prepare a moral text book.[19] His official superior, A. P. Howell, was furious. He dismissed Jatar's 'jaunty reply' as 'superficial', and Jatar himself as 'the direct product of our own system'. But Howell himself had been advocating moral teaching and moral text books for more than a decade.[20] Even so, nothing new or significant seems to have resulted from his lengthy cogitations. The most incisive comment came from Sir Lepel Griffin, Political Agent for Central India: 'The idea that any moral laws have such universality that all intelligences regard them as binding has been long rejected by scientific and accurate thinkers'.[21] The upshot of these various deliberations was that the preparation of a moral text book was again shelved, while official approval was conferred on other proposals—physical training, the moral influence of teachers, the use of books likely to have a beneficial effect upon conduct, and so on.[22]

The next step was taken by William Lee-Warner, a civil servant in the Bombay Presidency. As long ago as 1874, so he later recalled, Macmillans had asked him to write a school book 'to teach the Indians something about their country'.[23] Twenty years later, at a time when nationalist feeling seemed stronger in Maharashtra than elsewhere, he wrote to the Home Department of the Government of India about the book he wanted to write. He was advised to concern himself with Bombay, and the

Bombay Government welcomed the idea. Shortly afterwards, Sir Alexander Mackenzie took over the Home Department portfolio and urged Lee-Warner to write 'a work of an Imperial character, and not restricted to Bombay'.[24] In 1896 the Government formally approved a Home Department Office Memorandum in which the political advantages of such a text book were clarified: 'They think that the power possessed in the control of education is not at present sufficiently utilized, and they would like to see a good text-book drawn up with the object of teaching the pupils in Anglo-Vernacular Schools something of the nature, methods and objects of our government and administration'. Lee-Warner's words were quoted with approval: 'avoiding all appearance of didactic instruction or of moral education', the book would 'place before the Indian lad the bare facts of the situation in which he lives in such a manner as to promote a better spirit in society and a common interest in life'. The political value of such a book seemed clear enough: 'The general lessons to be drawn from the book should be that life in India is worth living, that the scheme of Government provides a sphere of helpful work for all, that a definite programme of India for the Indians has been laid down...' and so on.[25] Lee-Warner had retired in 1895, to become Secretary to the Political and Secret Department at the India Office, and the Government of India invited J. S. Cotton to write the book. He had been born in India (his father was an old East India Company servant); he had taken a first in Greats at Oxford, and he had helped Hunter in the compilation of the *Imperial Gazetteer of India*. He had also written a short treatise on India as part of a series published by Macmillans on *The English Citizen: His Rights and Responsibilities*.[26] This monograph might be the basis, although Cotton's 'general observations and conclusions ...would obviously be out of place'.[27]

In fact, Cotton's monograph contained much vigorous criticism of British policy in India. For example: granted that the aim of policy was benevolent, nevertheless 'ignorant good will may produce as much mischief as calculated selfishness. "Let us educate our rulers" should be the cry of every Indian who desires to promote the practical interests of his countrymen'.[28] Again: 'Competent authorities, indeed, are of opinion that the condition of the lowest orders has become worse under British rule'.[29] There was even some criticism of the vested interests of the

ICS, and some strong argument in favour of the appointment of Indians to posts of greater responsibility.[30] Small wonder that the Home Department thought that some of Cotton's ideas would be 'out of place' in a text book for Indian schools. That Cotton was chosen at all may well seem enlightened. A strong point in his favour was that he was not an official.

There had recently been a minor turmoil in the Home Department over text books written by J. C. Nesfield, Director of Public Instruction. The first hint of a scandal had come in March 1894, when Babu C. C. Mittra rose in the N.W.P legislative council to ask for details of all the text books used in government schools which had been written by members of the Education Department.[31] Wedderburn was quick to follow suit in the House of Commons in April. Fowler, as Secretary of State, did his best to obscure the issue by replying that the matter could best be pursued in the local legislature.[32] Thereupon Babu Sri Ram asked more specific questions in the N.W.P. legislature. How many works written by Nesfield had been introduced in courses prescribed by the Education Department?[33] The Home Department also began to ask questions, and the N.W.P. Government hastily produced a series of answers, some more convincing than others. Nesfield had indeed compiled a number of books, in fact three series of Readers—'Primary Readers', 'Middle Readers' and 'Entrance Readers'. But he did so when he was merely an Inspector of Schools, and the aim was to comply with the Government's wish for teaching with 'a direct bearing on morality and personal conduct', based on appropriate passages for reading. Of course, the Lieutenant-Governor, Sir Charles Crosthwaite, realized that 'Mr Nesfield's ownership of text-books prescribed for use in schools under his control was not in keeping with his official position, and was productive of criticism'. But Nesfield had been appointed Director of Public Instruction before Sir Charles became Lieutenant-Governor. Also, the books were already in use. To have withdrawn them would have 'thrown the school work of the Province into confusion and would have entailed serious loss on the publishers'. Nesfield was also about to retire. So 'Sir Charles Crosthwaite thought it sufficient to prohibit him from compiling any new text-books or new editions of existing text-books'. He added that 'a strong Provincial Text-Book Committee' would in future have full powers to decide what text books should be used in government and aided schools. Officers in the Education Department had been expressly warned not to have 'a pecuniary interest' in text books. Also, Nesfield had now retired, so the incident might be considered closed.[34]

Lee-Warner was undeterred by and was possibly unaware of the Nesfield scandal. From his new vantage point in the India Office he let it be known that he considered Cotton an unsuitable person to write the text book that he, Lee-Warner, had proposed. He also let it be known that he suspected that the appointment of Henry Cotton as Acting Secretary to the Home Department might have something to do with the choice of his brother as the author of the proposed book. He also let it be known that he was still available. The Government of India promptly told Lee-Warner that he should go ahead, and asked J.S. Cotton to forget all about it. But Cotton would not forget. He spoke of compensation, and the awful prospect of a law suit stirred the bureaucracy into rapid activity. What, after all, had he been offered? In the Home Department's Office Memorandum, he had been advised to settle terms with Macmillans. To encourage him, it was stated that if his book were deemed satisfactory, it would be recommended by the Government of India to Local Governments as a suitable text book: 'there can be no doubt, therefore, that the demand in India would be considerable'.[35] The Legal Adviser was reassuring: '... the Government was not to be an employer. It was to acquire nothing, to pay nothing, to guarantee nothing. All that it gave was a vague promise that the Government, if satisfied with the book when published, would recommed it to Local Governments'.[36] Cotton had no grounds for a legal claim. The Secretary of State's Private Secretary and the Viceroy's Private Secretary nevertheless conducted an anxious correspondence on the subject. A scandal would be unfortunate, even if Cotton lost his case. Of course, Cotton's brother had nothing to do with the Home Department's decision in the first place. Cotton should not have relied on the Government's 'vague promise'. But perhaps something could be arranged. Perhaps it would be generous to compensate an author for his natural feelings of disappointment. Would Mr Cotton like to write the Quinquennial Review of the Progress of Education in India (suitable terms being arranged by the Secretary of State)?[37] Cotton wisely closed with this offer.

Lee-Warner meanwhile set to work, and it was agreed that Sir P. Hutchins, Secretary to the Judicial and Public Department at the India Office, should act as referee. In due course, Hutchins reported favourably: 'I think it should go far to dissipate, in the minds of the rising generation, most of those false ideas of the intentions and mind of the Government, which ignorant or disloyal writers in the Press have been sedulously spreading for several years past'.[38] The book was published in 1897, entitled *The Citizen of India.* It was profusely illustrated (and included, of course, a picture of Queen Victoria), but it was full of unnecessary detail, and schoolboys must have found it indigestible.[39] Its main argument was that with the growth of education and improvements in communications a citizen's interests and loyalties should extend from the village to the whole of India. When the citizen understood the benefits he received from membership of the wider whole, he would realize his duties. Most of the book was devoted to a tedious exposition of the administrative system: Lee-Warner's implication throughout was that every right-minded citizen would want to co-operate with the system as soon as he understood how complex and wonderful it was. His duty was to understand and obey.

The Government of India recommended the book very warmly to Local Governments. Macmillans were prepared to publish translations in Indian languages if they could be assured that local Departments of Public Instruction would sanction it, and opinions were therefore invited. But Lee-Warner was soon mortified to learn that his efforts were not as widely appreciated as he had expected. The Panjab Government acted with characteristic promptitude and decision, and placed an 'embargo' on *The Citizen of India.*[40] In Madras, the local text book committee gave it what the Governor described as 'supercilious treatment'. The Governor asked for a further report; but it proved to be of 'much the same tenor as the former one'.[41] There was similar opposition elsewhere. At one point Lee-Warner was reduced to citing the approval of the Principal of the Rajkumar College at Rajkot, on the ground that 'the Chiefs are a class of students whom it is politically desirable to train in a belief as to the benefits of British rule'.[42] He also noted that Macmillans were 'a bit disappointed at the paucity of copies sold'.[43] In fact, many criticisms were merely to the effect that the book was too difficult for schoolboys.

There was also a feeling that, as a missionary put it, the book was 'calculated to provoke hostile criticism by its perpetual chorus of praise' for British rule.[44] The *Civil and Military Gazette* made a similar point: 'the work in its present form reads too much like a counterblast to speeches made in the National Congress'. Lee-Warner had argued that the British government employed many natives in its army and administration, unlike the Russians in Central Asia, who employed none: the *Civil and Military Gazette* commented that this was to ignore the fact that Central Asia, unlike India, had no large educated class from which a civil service could be recruited. Lee-Warner had argued that the vigour of the British in India was maintained by the supply of fresh recruits from Britain: the *Civil and Military Gazette* commented that this was 'a doctrine calculated (one would think) to excite rather than appease racial jealousy'.[45] The Government of India forwarded these and other criticisms to Lee-Warner, and added a few of its own: for example, he had justified the Government's annual move to Simla by enlarging upon its need to detach itself from local influences, but he was told that he should have been franker about the advantages of a cool climate in the hot season.[46] Lee-Warner professed his willingness to amend future editions of his book, the Panjab Government was persuaded to withdraw its embargo, and encouraging news meanwhile arrived from other authorities. With unconscious irony, Bombay's Director of Public Instruction reported that he had bought copies of *The Citizen of India* with money from the Dakshina Fund—a fund which had its origins in gifts made by the Peshwa of the Maratha Empire for the support of Brahmin scholars.[47]

But the early reactions to his book had already provoked Lee-Warner into drawing up a lengthy 'Note on the Responsibilities of the Indian Governments in the Matter of Text-books'. In it he argued that the text book Committees had usurped powers to which they had no right: it had always been intended that they should be merely advisory bodies.[48] In the Secretariat Luson drily noted that Lee-Warner was forgetting one of the recommendations of the Hunter Commission, of which he had been a member.[49] Lee-Warner went on to urge that the system should be changed. The Committees should recommend, and the Government should decide. In Government schools, all text books should be prescribed. Aided schools might be allowed to choose from a range of authorized books, but must not use any that had not been authorized. He also stated that some committees were too large and were dominated by non-officials.

Lee-Warner found some support for his views among his colleagues at the India Office, although Lyall noted that the Nesfield scandal was a warning against leaving the selection of text books entirely to officials, who would anyhow be incapable of examining the large number of vernacular books published every year.[50] Lee-Warner's 'Note' was duly considered by the Government of India. Curzon himself thought that the influence of *Babus* on the text book Committees was the reason for the difficulties experienced by *The Citizen of India*.[51] An enquiry was instituted into the composition and functions of the Committees, and in due course a Resolution was issued by the Government of India.[52] Its aims were to establish uniformity and to ensure Government control, and Lee-Warner's proposals were closely followed. Clearly, there were great local variations. In some provinces, the Director was the Chairman of the text book committee, in others not (in Bengal Justice Guru Das Banerjea was the Chairman). Henceforth, the Chairman was always to be the Director of Public Instruction, or failing him, an Inspector. The committees would be small, without too many non-officials. Some committees were prescribing books. Henceforth, they would merely recommend; the Government would decide. Moreover, the Government reserved the right to prescribe a book which had not been recommended by a committee. Although *The Citizen of India* was the book which had prompted the change of policy, the Resolution cited as an example of a book which might be so prescribed Dr Cunningham's *Sanitary Primer*. For Government schools, text books would be 'absolutely prescribed'. Some choice would be allowed to aided schools, but no grant would be paid if an unauthorized book were used. Even unaided schools were brought under State control: 'the Government has a direct interest in the course of instruction in schools which do not seek its aid financially, and, in the opinion of the Governor-General in Council, the condition may fairly be made that candidates from an unaided school are liable to be excluded from any public examination, for passing which a certificate is given, or from competition for a Government scholarship, if text-books which are disapproved by Government are in use in the school in question'. The safeguards provided by the Hunter Commission were thus ignored.

The Citizen of India had been criticized as too difficult for schoolboys. But it was also criticized in the universities. Lee-Warner knew that difficulties had been raised in the Senate of Calcutta University over a proposal to include his book among those prescribed for the entrance examinations. As he pointed out in his 'Note', it was the universities and not the text book committees which controlled the curricula in the highest or 'entrance classes' of schools and colleges. He also deplored the loss of European influence in the Bombay University Senate. Curzon was soon looking into the general question. He told the Chancellor of Calcutta University that some of the books prescribed there were not 'desirable'; Burke's *French Revolution*, for example. 'No one will deny that the book is a model of English style, but the matter of it might be harmful even to some young English readers, and it is certainly dangerous food for Indian students'.[53] The Chancellor advised caution, in view of the constitution of the Senate: 'The Native vote in that body is greater than the European, and there is an important section of the Native members—the more radical and militant section—which is strongly opposed to anything like Government interference in such matters. . . .'[54] But Curzon's reconstitution of University Senates is another problem.

After all, Lee-Warner had little to complain about. His book was duly amended and duly authorized. It was reprinted time and again. We may accept as evidence of its success the fact that Macmillans, ever faithful, even published an *Authorized Guide to Lee-Warner's Citizen of India*.[55] But he could not leave it alone. He asked if the Government would go through a revision he had prepared before he published it?[56] By then, Curzon had become impatient with him as an author: his contribution on the Native States for the revised *Imperial Gazetteer* was 'most disappointing'.[57] Hamilton explained that 'he apparently was so pleased that he sent it off before it had been edited or revized'.[58] Lee-Warner was told firmly that it was up to him to revise his *Citizen* as he thought fit.[59] He tried again in 1906, hoping that a new Governor-General might be persuaded to support a new edition of the book. Dunlop-Smith told him that Lord Minto regretted that his Government could not 'take any action in the way of recommending it as a text-book for schools. Lord Minto feels that, particularly in the present state of pubic feeling, it would not be advisable for the Government of India even to appear to give official sanction to the book'.[60] Lee-Warner tried yet again. Dunlop-Smith was polite but firm: the Government's attitude was 'one of benevolent neutrality'. He added kindly: 'Both Lord and Lady Minto have ordered copies for themselves'.[61]

Notes

[1]Govt. of India to Local Govts., 31 Dec. 1887, J & P 1959/1898.

[2]Curzon's ideas about the political implications of education have been examined in Aparna Basu, *Growth of Education and Political Development in India, 1898-1920*, O. U. P., Delhi, 1974.

[3]Home Ed. A, 29 Mar. 1873, 43.

[4]J. G. Cordery, Memo., 9 May 1873, Home Ed. A, Apr. 1877, 27.

[5]Syed Ahmed to N. W. P. Govt., 14 Sept. 1872; M. Kempson, Note. 19 Sept. 1873, Home Ed. A, Sept 1873, 44 ff; M. Kempson to N. W. P. Govt., 31 Mar. 1874, Home Ed. A, Apr. 1877.

[6]R. E. Candy, 4 Oct 1873, Home Ed. A, Apr. 1877, 24.

[7]C. Browning, 27 June 1873, Home Ed. A, Apr. 1877, 21.

[8]L. Garthwaite (Inspector of Schools, Sixth Division) to D. P. I., Madras, n. d., Home Ed. A, Sept. 1889.

[9]Resolution, 10 Jan. 1881, Home Ed. A, Jan. 1881, 46.

[10]Paras 377, 389.

[11]Govt. of India to Sec. of State, 12 May 1884, J & P 1008/1884.

[12]Telang, Minute, 27 Sept. 1883, J & P 1008/1884.

[13]Sec. of State to Govt. of India, 29 Sept. 1887, J & P 1477/1887.

[14]Govt. of India to Local Govts., 31 Dec. 1887, J & P 1959/1887.

[15]J. Murdoch to D. P. I., Madras, n. d, Home Ed. A, Sept. 1889.

[16]R. G. Bhandarkar, 20 Jul. 1888, Home Ed. A, Sept. 1889.

[17]M. G. Ranade, 31 May 1888, *ibid.*

[18]G. V. Subbarayudu (Inspector of Schools, First Division) to D. P. I. Madras, n. d., *ibid.*

[19]Jatar Commr, Hyderabad Assigned Districts, 8 May 1888, *ibid.*

[20]A. P. Howell (Offg. Resident, Hyderabad), Minute, 25 June 1888, *ibid.*

[21]Griffin Govt. of India, 7 Mar 1888, *ibid.*

[22]Resolution, 17 Aug. 1889, Home Ed. A, Sept. 1889.

[23]Lee-Warner, Note, 7 Apr. 1897, MSS Eur F. 84, vol. 32a, 32-33.

[24]Mackenzie to Lee-Warner, 8 June 1895, MSS Eur F. 92/9.

[25]Office Memo., 31 Aug. 1896, Home Ed. A, Aug. 1896, 48.

[26]J. S. Cotton, *Colonies and Dependencies: Part I India*; E. J. Payne, *The Colonies*, London, 1883.

[27]Office Memo., 31 Aug. 1896.

[28]P. 3.

[29]Pp. 68-9.

[30]P. 85.

[31]Proceedings of the Legislative Council, N. W. P. & Oudh, 21 Mar. 1894, Home Ed. A, Dec. 1894, 23 ff.

[32]Hansard, H. C., 4th Ser., XXII, 1447-8, 5 Apr. 1896.

[33]Proceedings of the Legislative Council, N. W. P. & Oudh, 23 July, 1894, Home Ed. A, Dec. 1894. 23 ff.

[34]N. E. P. and Oudh Govt. to Govt. of India, 25 Oct. 1894.

[35]Office Memo., 31 Aug. 1896.

[36]A. Wilson, Note, 13 Apr. 1897, MSS Eur F. 84, vol 32a, 32.

[37]H. Babington Smith to Richmond Ritchie, 28 July 1897, MSS Eur F. 84, vol. 22.

[38]Hutchins to J. P. Hewitt, 15 Oct. 1897, J & P 1166/1897.

[39]Macmillans, London, 1897.

[40]J. Sime (D. P. I., Panjab) to Macmillans, Bombay, 23 Dec. 1898, Home Ed. A, June 1900. p. 6 ff. Sime himself used the word "embargo".

[41]Havelock to Godley, 22 Mar. 1899, J & P 818/1899.

[42]Lee-Warner to Fraser, 31 May 1899, Home Ed. B, June 1900, 25.

[43]Lee-Warner to Hewitt, 8 July, Home Ed. B, June 1900, 25.

[44]Rev E. M. Macphail to D. P. I., Madras, 24 Oct. 1902, MSS Eur F. 92/9.

[45]*Civil and Military Gazette*, 9 Feb. 1900, Home Ed. A, Jun. 1900, 6 ff.

[46]Govt. of India to Lee-Warner, 2 May 1899, Home Ed. B, June 1900. 25 : H. H. Risley to Lee-Warner, 12 Feb. 1903, MSS Eur F 92/9.

[47]D. P. I. Bombay to Bombay Govt., 8 Jul. 1898, Bombay Ed. A, 1898, 242.

[48]Lee-Warner, Note, 18 Apr. 1899, Home Ed. Deposit, Feb. 1900, 2-3.

[49]H. L. Note, 23 May, *ibid.*

[50]Lyall to Godley, 26 Apr. 1899, J & P 818/1899.

[51]Curzon to Lord George Hamilton, 23 Mar. 1899, MSS Eur F. 111, vol. 158.

[52]Resolution, 8 Feb. 1900, Home Ed. A, Feb. 1900, 36.

[53]Curzon to Sir F. Maclean, 14 Feb. 1900, MSS Eur F. 111, vol. 201.

[54]Maclean to Curzon, 23 Apr. 1900, *ibid.*

[55]By the Rev. A. Tomory, Duff College, Calcutta, Macmillans, London, 1900.

[56]Lee-Warner, marginal note on Risley to Lee-Warner, 20 Mar. 1903, MSS Eur F. 92/9.

[57]Curzon to Hamilton, 8 Apr. 1903, MSS Eur F. 111, vol 162.

[58]Hamilton to Curzon, 30 Apr. 1903, *ibid.*

[59]Risley to Lee-Warner, 13 May 1903, MSS Eur F. 92/9.

[60]Dunlop-Smith to Lee-Warner, 27 Apr. 1906, *ibid.*

[61]Dunlop-Smith to Lee-Warner, 15 June 1906, *ibid.*

Concepts of Duty Held By Indian Nationalist Thinkers

DAVID TAYLOR

The problem of the origin of political obligation and duty has been the starting point for many of the most influential theories in the western tradition of political thought.[1] In India similarly the notion of *dharma* has provided the key to successive theories of state and society, and was used as an appropriate ideology for the various strands of activity which eventually made up the nationalist movement. Within the western tradition the distinction between duty and obligation is tenuous, and no single differentiating principle can be established. Obligation belongs primarily, however, to contract theories of the state, and rests on an instrumental basis of exchange. In one meaning duty is a plural term referring to legally enforceable norms of behaviour, but for the political or moral philosopher it refers to the responsibility of each individual to fulfil a particular set of expectations as to his conduct. The source of this responsibility varies. For the utilitarians duty is no more than one's self-interest in a mutual fulfilment of obligations. For Kant true freedom can only come through obedience to a moral law which we prescribe to ourselves. Duty can also be derived from the long tradition of natural law, either from religious sanction or from a consideration of man in a state of nature. Duty corresponds to man's highest natural instincts, and could even become a substitute religion for the atheist: George Eliot is reported to have said 'God is inconceivable, immortality is unbelievable, but duty is peremptory and absolute'.

While obligation has usually been discussed within the narrow limits of formal theories of the origins and powers of the state, duty has been a much wider concept. Previously, it served to integrate political thought into the more general concerns of moral philosophy; nowadays, it provides sociologists and psychologists with a word to describe the feelings of altruism and unselfishness which are engendered by social living. Most ideologies contain elements of obligation as well as duty, but the latter is the more likely to induce people to make substantial sacrifices for a nation or a cause. Nevertheless, once duty had become detached from its roots in revealed religion, the problem of ascertainment became of crucial importance. Merit derived from the motive behind the performance of duty—duty for duty's sake—and the nation or the state was by no means the only object of service. Only within a Hegelian idealism could duty be subordinated entirely to the service of the state.

For the Indian nationalist movement, obligation led into a blind alley. Over the greater part of India the British had replaced not indigenous Hindu states but Muslim rulers, only a degree or two less alien than themselves. Obedience might be due to the British for such benefits as they had brought in the past or might be persuaded to bring in the future, but it was a passive and subject sort of obligation. At what point did the evil consequences of British rule outweigh the good, and how was the importance of self-rule to be assessed? Even if the balance were to be in favour of passive obedience, and for Gandhi at least it was difficult to find an acceptable halfway house between active loyalty and active disloyalty,[3] the colonial context of obligation provided little opportunity for participation in the service of the community. Exploration of the meaning of duty or its analogue *dharma* provided a better foundation.

For some nineteenth-century Indian writers, western concepts of duty, derived for example from Green, had an immediate attraction. Gokhale, whose concern was primarily political, founded the Servants of India Society in 1905 as a means for Indians to dedicate themselves to the performance of secular duty, and the early generation of social reformers and politicians was strongly influenced by western ideas. Nevertheless, dependence on them had to be discarded, and autochthonous theories developed. Western ideas were attractive for their apparent coherence and their nation-state orientation, but the bounded and finite world of interdependent rights and duties did not appeal. The idea of making fulfilment of duty an ultimate end appealed to some writers, but was seen by others as an aspect of *māyā*. Western concepts of duty seemed also to be too uniform. But if ideas developed in Europe were not always appropriate, neither were current formulations of *dharma*. Classical theories had distinguished between differentiated duty—*varṇāśramadharma*—and general duty—*sādhāraṇadharma*. The latter, however, had never been more than a preceptual tradition, and by the eighteenth century the former had frozen into the customary law of a static society. Such reinterpretation of *dharma* as took placew as almost always within the limits of the existing system, while ideas of *rājadharma* hardly guided the actions of the builders of petty kingdoms who had succeeded Shivaji, the last great figure in the purely Hindu kingly tradition. What was needed was a redefinition of *dharma* which would introduce a dynamic element and would simultaneously reconcile *dharma* and duty.

None of the writers to be considered here ever questioned the moral basis of duty, but from the beginning of the nineteenth-century Bengal renaissance, the content and character of *dharma* was a topic for debate. Along with Derozio and David Hare, Rammohun Roy inspired the rationalist and critical mood in which Hindu custom was henceforth approached. The campaign to abolish *sati*, for example, was only part of a wider movement to improve the status of women, in which the male prerogative of property inheritance and the religious justification for banning widow remarriage were brought into question. The argument was twofold. First, Sanskrit scholars such as Ishwar Chandra Vidyasagar went back to the original sources of Hindu law to show that they did not necessarily say what they were assumed to say. The original rules were then shown to be in conformity with a sort of intuitive ethical code. For Rammohun, each individual was to rely on his own conscience, guided by the precepts—not commandments—of the world's religious teachers.[3]

It is true that despite their success in persuading the colonial government to pass legislation, the Brahmo Samajists and other reformers were unable to make much impression on actual behaviour, but what they had succeeded in doing was to establish the separate moral identity of the individual. The importance of *dharma* was in no way lessened, but it had in some way to be self-imposed. The relationship between *sādhāraṇadharma* and *varṇāśrama-dharma* had to be reinterpreted. The problem remained, however, of defining the link between the individual and the community, and thus eventually of rooting nationalist activity in *dharma*. Rammohun himself, as one would expect in the early years of British rule, attached importance to personal rather than national freedom, while later Brahmo Samajists were to develop different strands in his thought, to the point of contradiction. The tradition of reformist social service continued, but it was in competition with the quietistic devotion of Debendranath Tagore, which posed no challenge to the authority of the state, and with the New Dispensation of Keshub Chandra Sen, which seemed to point the way to a supra-national federation of faiths. Ultimately the Brahmo Samaj produced in Bipin Chandra Pal one of the apostles of militant nationalism.

Bankim Chandra Chatterji, who was not a Brahmo but came from a Vaishnava background, represents in many ways the intellectual synthesis that had been achieved in the late nineteenth century. His article 'Samya', for example, which constantly refers to *dharma*, in fact bases its arguments for social equality mainly on the writings of liberals like J.S. Mill.[4] He looks on the requirements of *varṇāśramadharma* largely as products of a particular stage of social evolution. As the structure of society changes, so do the duties of its members. His writings on Hinduism are a restatement of what he believes to be the orthodox faith, but he meets criticisms of it by limiting its scope to a narrow range of theological principles.[5] It does nevertheless provide him with a strong sense of abstract duty, and the chief importance of Bankim Chandra lies in his identification of the Hindu community as the object of service. 'That which leads to the welfare of all Hindus is my duty'.[6] The service of the Hindu people is a means of service of the divine power embodied in the Motherland, and thus a means of fulfilling *dharma*.

Of all nineteenth-century Bengali writers, Swami Vivekananda, while he did not have the immediate importance of Bankim Chandra, has had the widest impact. His contribution to the development of nationalist thought, however, is not a simple one. He was one of the outstanding figures of neo-Hindu revivalism, and he left a tradition of nationally-oriented service and missionary work to his followers, but the idea of duty did not occupy a central place in his thought. That was given to *karmayoga*. Although the essence of *karmayoga* was the performance of useful work without attachment to any of its rewards, Vivekananda emphasized that it was ultimately on a par with other *yogas* as a means of killing the desire that binds men to *māyā*. The *karmayogi* has to recognize that his actions are ultimately valueless, in that nothing can be changed in the world of *māyā*. 'A wave in the ocean' he wrote 'must be at the expense of a hollow elsewhere'; 'the world will go on with its happiness and misery through eternity'.[7] It followed that fanaticism in the performance of action, the consequence of European definitions of duty, was incompatible with unattachedness, though we are also told that it is a great error to confuse sloth or *accidie* with calmness. 'One must pass through activity to perfect calmness'.[8] Ultimately, then, actions are justified in terms of the spiritual motive behind them. This has important consequences for the ascertainment of duty in a particular situation. The individual conscience is the ultimate guide to what is right or wrong, and Vivekananda specifically states that duty and morality vary according to circumstance and from individual to individual.[9] This means in particular that the rigid rules of *varṇāśramadharma* are not applicable, and Vivekananda provides a functional explanation of the emergence of caste and other social customs that is reminiscent of Bankim Chandra.[10] At the same time, however, he argues that some sort of hierarchical ordering of society is necessary, and of course the requirement of non-attachment implies that a man will normally fulfil those duties that are closest to hand, that is those that pertain to his station in life. National service is then only one form of useful action, but Vivekananda is remembered as one of the inspirers of self-sacrificing action on behalf of the nation. The key to this narrowing of focus at the same time includes a redefinition of the nature of Indian nationalism. One form of work with which Vivekananda was particularly concerned was the recovery by India of its spiritual heritage. Once it had been recovered, it could then be diffused to the rest of the world.[11] Although this naturally implied India's political independence, as spiritual regeneration would be inhibited by alien rule, it also meant that, despite Vivekananda's practical concerns with educational and economic improvements, national service need not necessarily be political.

Vivekananda had succeeded in integrating self-sacrificing action into neo-Hindu revivalism, but he had worked during a period of political quiescence. Immediately after his death, Bengal was convulsed by Curzon's partition proposals and the militant agitation that followed. The new intellectual leaders, notably Aurobindo Ghose and Bipin Chandra Pal, went beyond his formulations to insist on the overridingly political character of *dharma*. Like their predecessors, they drew their ideas both from the Indian tradition and from contemporary Europe. In particular, Aurobindo took up the idea of evolution (more in a Comtean than Darwinian sense) and integrated it into a purely Indian idealism to produce the idea of the superman.[12] Before mankind could achieve this self-transcendence, each nation would have to achieve its fullest self-development. As he wrote in 1909.

> Nationalism is our immediate practical faith and gospel not because it is the highest possible synthesis, but because it must be realized in life if we are to have the chance of realizing others.[13]

Like Vivekananda, Aurobindo believed that India had a specific heritage of spirituality which it was her mission to impart to the world. Indeed, it was only by India's willingness to fulfil her mission to the world that the nationalist movement could be distinguished from 'collective selfishness'.[14] For the individual there was thus a hierarchy of objects of service. The individual had to subordinate himself to the family, the family to the group, the group to the nation, and ultimately the nation to mankind.[15] Before his withdrawal to Pondicherry in 1910, however, Aurobindo had effectively broken the chain at the level of the nation, by directly equating its service with the fulfilment of the *sanātana dharma*. For him the Motherland was 'more than a stretch of earth or mass of individuals'. Rather it was a 'great Divine and Maternal power'.[16] Rather than subordinating religion to nationalism, nationalism is absorbed into religion, so that duty becomes a means of religious sacrifice. In the famous Uttarpara speech in 1909, he concluded

> I say no longer that nationalism is a creed, a religion, a faith;

> I say that it is the *Sanatan Dharma* which for us is nationalism. This Hindu nation was born with the *Sanatan Dharma*, with it it moves and with it it grows.[17]

Although he pays formal homage to the division of duties within society, he redefines the Brahmin *dharma* as a sort of civic virtue, and calls for it to become general throughout society.[18] Aurobindo also raised the question of whether non-violence was to be regarded as an absolute end, and came to the conclusion that provided the motive was pure and unattached to the fruits of the action, violent action was justifiable.[19] This was in contradiction to Vivekananda's expressed view on the subject, although the line of argument was similar.

All the writers who have been considered so far have been Bengali, and several of them were not actively involved in the nationalist movement. In India as a whole, Bal Gangadhar Tilak and Mahatma Gandhi were perhaps the more influential figures. In their different ways, both were significant philosophically, but they were of greater importance in their ideological roles. They have rightly been seen by many commentators as advocating opposed political moralities. It may be worthwhile, however, to start by pointing to some of the similarities which set them apart from, for example, Gokhale, Tilak's Maharashtrian rival whom Gandhi had at one point called his political guru, or even from Vivekananda. Both based themselves primarily on the *Bhagavad-Gītā*, and both were insistent on what Tilak called its 'energistic' interpretation.[20] Gandhi freely acknowledged the intellectual debt he owed to Tilak's massive and scholarly *Gita-Rahasya*. Compare these summaries of their views on the central message of the *Gītā*. In Tilak's words, the *Gītā*,

> After showing that there is no conflict between Knowledge and Action, expatiated on the Karma-Yoga doctrine that Jnanins must, notwithstanding that they have destroyed desire, perform all Actions, purely as duties, for universal benefit.[21]

Gandhi had endeavoured

> to show that its message consists in the performance of one's duty with detachment.[22]

Both Tilak and Gandhi proclaimed themselves to be monists in search of *mokṣa*, but there are substantial differences between their position and that of Vivekananda. Tilak and Gandhi clearly envisage lifelong activity, while for Vivekananda withdrawal is ultimately possible for the man who has destroyed desire, and fanaticism in the performance of duty only leads to fresh ensnarement. They accepted that renunciation of the fruits of action often led to those fruits becoming richer, but they taught that a man should accept them with indifference rather than decline to act. Like Vivekananda, Tilak distinguished between pure and applied *Vedānta*, but for Tilak performance of duty was an inevitable consequence of the search for release. Indeed, in the *Gita-Rahasya* he states specifically that he has used the term *dharma* instead of *kartavya* for what in the English translation becomes 'duty', because of its link with *mokṣa*.[23] Tilak and Gandhi were also basically at one in their interpretation of the *Gītā's* admonition to follow one's own *dharma*, whatever it might be, rather than another's. This was of course implied in the idea of non-attachment, but neither considered that the obligations of *dharma* justified the caste system as it actually existed. Gandhi held that a man should earn his living within the *varṇa* of his father, but that he might follow other socially desirable occupation if he did so without desire for their fruit, while Tilak interpreted the *Gītā* to mean only that one should not abandon one's *dharma* for someone else's before the task had been fulfilled. The service of the community in any case transcended the categories of *varṇāśramadharma*, so that Tilak, for example, considered that under some circumstances Brahmins should take up arms.

Gandhi and Tilak's disagreements came over the practical content of duty—in particular over the question of the status of non-violence and the use of deceit and falsehood in dealing with an enemy. Shortly before Tilak's death in 1920 the issue was discussed in an exchange of letters in the context of the non-cooperation movement against the British,[24] but the divergence of opinion is equally clear in their separate writings. Gandhi's position on non-violence is well-known. Although *ahiṃsā* was not the ultimate goal of the *karmayogi*, it was in Gandhi's view an essential precondition of a person attaining the ideal of *anāsakti* or unattached action.

> Let it be granted, that according to the letter of the *Gita* it is possible to say that warfare is consistent with renunciation of fruit. But after 40 years' unremitting effort and endeavour fully to enforce the teaching of the *Gita* in my own life, I, in all humility, feel that perfect renunciation is impossible without perfect observance of *Ahimsa* in every shape and form.[25]

For Tilak the literal words of Kṛṣṇa at Kurukṣetra were enough. He did not see violence in a good cause as incompatible with renunciation. Like Aurobindo he equated nation and religion, so that independence was itself a prerequisite of renunciation. 'Our life and our Dharma' he wrote 'are in vain in the absence of Swarajya'.[26] There were differences also in their treatment of the principles of social organization, although here it was more a question of emphasis, since neither was content with existing arrangements. Gandhi devoted much of his energy to reforming the position of the Harijans, while Tilak was only prepared to consider social reform after independence, and then too, if there was a mass demand for it.

One source of Tilak and Gandhi's disagreements over the precise meaning of duty can be traced to their fundamentally different approaches to the exegesis of the *Gītā*. For Gandhi it was divinely inspired but was not to be taken literally. It had also to be treated as a work of literature with its own requirements and conventions. Thus, in considering whether Kṛṣṇa's advice to Arjuna to continue the fight can be taken as a definitive argument against his own position on non-violence, Gandhi suggests that Kṛṣṇa's advice has to be understood as a response to the 'pretentious wisdom' of Arjuna, and that it would be 'profitless to conjecture what would have happened if non-violence...had suddenly really possessed him'.[27] Generally, Gandhi suggests that there are infinite layers of meaning in the *Gītā* which only reveal themselves gradually and to the reader who approaches it in the right frame of mind. In this he takes the same view as, for example, Aurobindo. Tilak's approach, as befits the Sanskrit scholar, is more textual. Although he does in fact argue that the arrangement of society into castes as described in the *Gītā* is not necessarily applicable to all phases of Hindu society, he nevertheless considers not simply the central message of unattached action but also the manifest ethical principles of the *Gītā*, for example justified violence, to be part of its essence.[28] He is concerned to defend the *Gītā* not only against its modern traducers, but also against the quietistic interpretation given to it in the *advaita-vedānta* school of philosophy. In contrasting the two exegetical approaches, the title of Tilak's commentary, *The Esoteric Import of the Gītā*, might more aptly be applied to Gandhi's interpretation.

With the partial exception of Rammohun, all the writers considered here derived their ideas of duty from a study of the Hindu tradition in the light, on the one hand, of European rationalism, and on the other, of the practical requirements of the nationalist struggle. Despite the wide divergence of outlook between, say, Vivekananda and Tilak, or between Bankim Chandra and Gandhi, certain common themes emerge. Duty is simply an operationalization of *dharma*, and has therefore to be determined and judged primarily in terms of the effect that it has on the individual. Because duty is assimilated into the wider context of *dharma*, it becomes a means to achieve *mokṣa*. What is of primary significance is the attitude of the actor to the result of his actions, and what is right for one man may not necessarily be right for another, although to some extent an individual's ability to fulfil his *dharma* depends on other people's fulfilling their's. What is new, however, is the way in which duty is linked to the concept of the nation and the nation-state. National identity is not, as in Europe, a way of asserting the rights of a particular group of people, but a way for them to fulfil their *dharma* and to convey to the rest of the world their special gifts. Only Tilak unambiguously demanded independence as his birthright, and he too saw it as essentially a religious matter. National independence was necessary, but it was only a step on the road to a higher form of human association. In classical Hindu political thought, the state had been seen as the upholder of its subjects' *dharma*, and a specific *rājādharma* had been recognized, but now the nation itself had a *dharma* to which individuals and groups had to subordinate their own.[29]

An important feature of the new formulation of *dharma* was that apparently conflicting individual or class interests could be harmonized in the service of the nation. As Bipin Chandra Pal put it, Indian democracy would be one in which 'all interests will be harmonized, all rights...shall be resolved or dissolved in duty'.[30] Although nationalism did not necessarily imply democracy, it was closely associated with it, whereas existing theories of *varṇāśramadharma* had implied monarchy or aristocracy. The underlying principle of *varṇāśramadharma* was not abandoned, but the traditional classification of duties was replaced by one which drew its rationale from the needs of the nation. In its service all could achieve a new Brahminhood.

Notes

[1]For a general treatment of the problem, see, for example, E. F. Carritt, *Morals and Politics*, Oxford, 1935.

[2]Raghavan N. Iyer, *The Moral and Political Thought of Mahatma Gandhi*, London, 1973, p. 257.

[3]Rammohun Roy, *The English Works*, (ed.), K. Nag and D. Burman.

[4]Translated by M. K. Haldar in *Bankim on Equality*, Nedlands, 1974, (University of Western Australia Working Papers in Asian Studies, No. 5).

[5]'Letters on Hinduism', Vimala-Chandra Sinha (ed.) *Bankim Pratibhā*, Calcutta, 1938-39.

[6]Quoted in Jayanta Kumar Das Gupta, *A Critical Study Life and Novels of Bankimcandra*, Calcutta, 1937, p. 138, fn. 2.

[7]Swami Vivekananda, *The Complete Works*, vol. iii, 11th ed., Calcutta, 1973, 214; vol. i, 14th ed., Calcutta, 1972, p. 77.

[8]*Ibid.*, vol. i, p. 40.

[9]*Ibid.*, vol. i, p. 64.

[10]*Ibid.*, vol. v. 9th ed., Calcutta, 1970, p. 145.

[11]*Ibid.*, vol. iii, pp. 221-3.

[12]Sri Aurobindo, *Birth Centenary Library*, Pondicherry, 1972, vol. xvi, p. 275-81.

[13]*Ibid.*, vol. ii, p. 42.

[14]*Loc. cit.*, p. 109.

[15]*Loc. cit.*, pp. 107-8.

[16]*Ibid.*, vol. xvii, p. 347.

[17]*Ibid.*, vol. ii, p. 10.

[18]*Loc. cit.*, pp. 11-12.

[19]*Ibid.*, pp. 118-123.

[20]The *Gītā* is the central source of nationalist ethics. Besides Tilak and Gandhi, Aurobindo, Vivekananda and Bankim Chandra all discussed it in their writings. Lajpat Rai also published a commentry, and more recently Vinoba Bhave has written extensively about the *Gīta*'s meaning.

[21]B. G. Tilak, *Giṭa-Rahasya*, 2nd English edition, Poona, 1965, p. 689.

[22]M. K. Gandhi, *The Search for Truth*, Ahmedabad, p. 182.

[23]P. 92.

[24]G. P. Pradhan and A. K. Bhagwat, *Lokamanya Tilak*, Bombay, 1959, pp. 374-5.

[25]M. K. Gandhi, *Gita—My Mother*, (ed.), Anand T. Hingorani, Bombay, 1965, p. 50. Gandhi believed, of course, that those who disagreed with him on this had the right to use violence.

[26]Quoted in Theodore L. Shay, *The Legacy of the Lokamanya*, Bombay, 1956, p. 100.

[27]Gandhi, *op. cit.*, p. 56.

[28]Tilak, *op. cit.*, pp. 36-7.

[29]Echoes may be found of the older tradition. Gandhi's ground for asserting India's right to independence on 26 January 1930 was the harm done to India by British Rule rather than an inherent right to independence. For a suggestive comment on the attitudes of the 'service castes' to British rule, see C. A. Bayly, *The Local Roots of Indian Politics*, Oxford, 1975, p. 7.

[30]Bipin Chandra Pal, *Writings and Speeches*, vol. i, Calcutta, 1958, p. 168.

The Semantic Fields of Dharm and Kartavy in Modern Hindi

SIMON WEIGHTMAN and S.M. PANDEY

1.a. This short and exploratory communication seeks to offer a view of the relative range of contexts in which the two words that express the concept of duty occur in modern Hindi. Both experience and the dictionaries tell us that these two words are *kartavy* and *dharm*. The English word *dyuutii*, although it may be used by an English-speaking Indian in search of a word to express the concept in an inadequately controlled Hindi, is, on the whole, restricted to such phrases as *raat kii dyuutii*(night duty), and other usages covering this particular connotation of the English word. Also excluded are what may be termed 'Urdu' words like *farz* which have cultural and religious implications that would take us far beyond our present restricted purposes.

1.b. Although we describe below just how limited should be our expectations of what semantics and semantic field-theory can offer in general, particular difficulties arise from the state of what we have termed modern Hindi. Modern Hindi is, in one sense, a young and developing language. While its grammatical structure is now, to all intents and purposes, fully stabilized, the same cannot be said of its vocabulary or of the relative position of any lexical item with regard to any other. Every language when it is used by society generates many different styles and registers which are dependent upon the context of situation. The context in turn determines which words are appropriate to a given occasion. But with Hindi there is a further problem. Someone born in the U.P., or coming from an area which the linguistic map designates as 'Hindi-speaking', will most probably have as his mother-tongue a local sub-dialect of a regional dialect like

Braj Bhaaṣaa, Avadhii, Bhojpurii, Bundelii or the like. Modern standard Hindi in the sense of *Kharii Bolii* Hindi will be something acquired or studied at school. There is reason to believe that this is changing and that some families prefer to speak Hindi at home to their children, either as the sole language or the equal second language. In addition the widespread use of Hindi in education is having a considerable effect. The pressure for Hindi to be used as an official language means, however, that it is being studied and learnt by people from other language states of India for whom it will never be a mother-tongue. What all this means is that, while there may be some hundred million people who can speak Hindi in some form or style, there cannot be said to be, as yet, a Hindi-speaking community of the kind that maintains and regulates a reasonably consistent socio-linguistic usage of the language in speech. It may well require two or three generations before there can be said to be a Hindi speech community.

I.c. It would not be unreasonable, given the absence of a coherent speech community, to look to the written word to supply the normative influences whereby stability is brought to lexical usage, and words are able to acquire a semantic field of force through their contextual distributions. In India, however, illiteracy and social and educational differences seem to produce, to a far greater degree than elsewhere, a wide divergence between the spoken and the written word. It is no part of this paper to develop this theme further, but it cannot be ignored because it means that newspapers, the radio and novels are too 'learned' to have any marked effect on speech habits. Not only are they unable to have a standardizing effect on speech, but they too in fact reflect this very same lack of standardization in their vocabularies and styles. Of course, every writer, as with every speaker, has his own idiolect, and his style is also modulated by his particular creative aspirations, but to compare the way that different Hindi newspapers treat of the same material reveals the lack of a norm in both style and vocabulary that goes far beyond what may reasonably be attributed to personal idiosyncracy.

1.d. Nothing that has been said so far should be taken as implying that Hindi is not capable of acting as a medium of communication between millions of people—it already does just that—nor that there is anything inherently wrong with the language which somehow makes it impossible for a speaker to express whatever he wishes so that others may understand his import. It is not the language nor its potential word power that is responsible for the present lack of cohesion in its usage and hence in the semantic ordering of its lexicon. Hindi has been represented as the linguistic answer to the aspirations of a united India, but what we find in reality is a language that has yet to find a cohesive speech community in which it can develop to its full potential. As we have said, this may be a matter of only a few generations and it would be reasonable to expect that one of the first signs that this is happening will be the coming together of the spoken and the written word.

2.a. The situation just described regarding modern Hindi usage might suggest that it would be impossible to arrive at any definite conclusions regarding the semantic field of force of any given lexical item, but this would be altogether too negative a view. Fluid and unordered as it may be, modern Hindi is a recognizable *état de Langue*, a contemporary slice through Indo-Aryan speech which has been evolving over many hundreds of years. Certainly it makes the investigation more uncertain, but probably no more difficult than it would have been anyway. Some acquaintance with the theory of semantic fields and structural semantics must be taken as given. The golden procedural rule is that 'one should know a word by what a man does with it, not by what he says about it'. It has also been stated, 'accept everything a native speaker says *in* his language, but treat with reserve anything he says *about* his language until it has been checked'. Perhaps one of the most rigorous studies of this kind is *Structural Semantics* by John Lyons in which he analyzes part of the vocabulary of Plato by examining the distribution of certain lexical items and their linguistic environments and thus establishing the relationships that hold between these items to establish their respective fields of force. Lyons worked from established texts, but the present exploratory study is not based on a given identifiable corpus but seeks to discover semantic fields through establishing the normal distributions of the chosen words in social discourse, that is to say, in usage. It is clearly not possible to treat usage with the same rigour as a corpus of texts since usage is the totality of speech conventions and permits considerable freedom.

2.b. If we take usage to be the speech conventions of a speech community, it is necessary to realize just how great is the permissible freedom. Except in highly formal and conventional situations, we convey our intentions by means of usage, not necessarily within it. That is to say that much speech is in fact unconventional particularly when, in specific situations, speakers use words to imply something quite different from that which they would normally be understood to imply. This is particularly true of figurative language. It would be hard to find occurences in lierature or elsewhere of the collocation 'gossipy windows'; indeed, it might well be rejected as an impossible or, at least, an unacceptable collocation by the very discovery procedures we are using here; yet such a use of a transferred epithet speaks volumes about many a suburban street. Thus individual speakers have quite considerable freedom in their use of speech conventions, although, if they become too eccentric, communication breaks down. 'A word can mean exactly what I want it to mean', is true to some extent and indicative of this freedom, but it must always be a qualified freedom if others are to understand. From the standpoint of the present investigation then, it must always be accepted that we are seeking norms and it will always be possible to find examples or to construct situations that appear to disprove our assertions.

2.c. It is perhaps unnecessary to stress that rarely does a single word convey exactly the same thing to any two speakers. On the whole, our procedures will be unaffected by personal differences, but there is an area where there is a genuine difficulty. A Sanskrit loan word will almost certainly carry with it different associations for an illiterate peasant and for a scholar of Sanskrit, yet they may use it in much the same way. Now these associations may be so different for two speakers that to all intents and purposes they are talking about two different things. In this case it is clear that the words evoke for each speaker an experience that is different in *kind*. Such a situation where there is a problem of communication can be resolved by the speakers testing other words that they regard as synonymous until they arrive at shared vocabulary for their particular purposes. The problem arises, however, when we find words that are regarded as synonymous in given contexts, and agreed to be so by general consent, but when one is felt somehow to be a 'stronger' word. That is to say that the words evoke an experience that is similar in kind but different in *depth*. One must be alert for such situations, and respect in this case what a speaker says about a word as well as how he uses it, for such differentiations will perhaps never show in distributional analysis.

2.d. The criterion by which we judge whether a sentence is an authentic usage is to see whether it is found acceptable to native speakers. In this preliminary investigation we have tested hundreds of sentences, but certainly nothing like enough, nor have we exposed our sentences to a wide enough spread of speakers to enable us to claim that our findings are, in any sense, authoritative, even given our limited expectations. Furthermore we have concentrated perhaps too much on the relation of synonymy, whereas a fuller study would have to take note of other types of relations. In spite of all this, however, what emerges is of interest and perhaps one of the most significant aspects of this is that it is quite different from what was expected at the outset of the enquiry.

3.a. Turning from general considerations of modern Hindi and semantics to the 'concept of duty' and the two words *dharm* and *kartavy* in particular, we shall do well to remember that 'duty' is a fairly abstruse concept, perhaps a 'learned' concept even in English. It is doubtful if it would show up very highly placed in any word frequency tables of representative English discourse. There would be no reason therefore to expect the two chosen words which convey this concept in Hindi to be any more frequent in representative Hindi discourse. They are both Sanskrit loan words and carry with them a certain prestige on account of their origins. In fact, of course, as in English, the various shades of 'should', 'must', 'ought' and the like are most commonly and subtlely expressed in Hindi by means of verbal forms and sometimes whole phrases. To explore how this is done, however, would require a highly complex study. What best can be seen from our examination of how *dharm* and *kartavy* are used in modern Hindi is the kind of semantic shifts that have taken place over the centuries and it is particularly hoped that this will be of interest to those who are aware of the earlier uses of these words.

3.b. Of the two words, *dharm* occurs in a far wider range of contexts than *kartavy*. It is therefore with *dharm* that we begin, treating each usage or set of contexts separately. Although we have tested many sentences to reach our conclusions, we shall only give here representative samples to illustrate our point since to do otherwise would greatly add to length of this paper. Our findings indicate that there are three main sets of contexts in which *dharm* occurs and it is the third of these that shows *dharm* and *kartavy* to be distributionally related. This will not complete the study, however, because one is obliged to ask whether we have here a single lexeme that is used in three totally unconnected ways, or a single concept that takes on a different force in the three different sets of contexts.

4.a. The first set of contexts in which *dharm* occurs are those that show it to have a distributional relationship of restricted synonymy with the words *svabhaav* and *prakṛti* (nature, disposition, inherent character). Examples are :—

Animates

i. *gaay kaa svabhaav hɛ duudh denaa.*
gaay kii prakṛti hɛ duudh denaa.
gaay kaa dharm hɛ duudh denaa. (It is the 'nature' of a cow to give milk.)

ii. *saap kaa svabhaav hɛ kaatnaa.*
saap kii prakṛti hɛ kaatnaa.
saap kaa dharm hɛ kaatnaa. (It is the 'nature' of a snake to sting.)

Inanimates

iii. *baadal kaa svabhaav hɛ paanii barsaanaa.*
baadal kaa dharm hɛ paanii barsaanaa. (It is the 'nature' of a cloud to rain.)

iv. *aag kaa svabhaav daah hɛ.*
aag kaa dharm daah hɛ. (It is the 'nature' of fire to burn.)

v. *per kaa svabhaav hɛ chaayaa denaa.*
per kaa dharm hɛ chaayaa denaa. (It is the 'nature' of a tree to give shade.)

It would seem with inanimates that *dharm* is restricted to those that appear to be capable of 'self-initiated' action or to those that can be represented figuratively as being so. This can be shown from the following two examples.

vi. *caaquu kaa svabhaav hɛ kaatnaa.* (It is the 'nature' of a knife to cut.)

vii. *gaarii kaa svabhaav hɛ calnaa.* (It is the 'nature' of a vehicle to go.)

In these two examples *dharm* is not an acceptable synonym for *svabhaav*, but *viṣeṣtaa* [attribute, peculiarity, characteristic] would be. We find, however, no examples where *viṣeṣtaa* is synonymous with *dharma* in connection with inanimates. This then represents the restriction at the lower end of the scale. The upper restriction to the synonymy of *dharm* and *svabhaav* occurs the moment they are used with reference to human beings. When used of human beings, *svabhaav* indicates something like 'character in the sense of temperament', and *dharm*, as we shall see later, indicates something quite different from this.

The above delimitation of the range of contexts in which *dharm* occurs as a possible synonym of *svabhaav* appears to cover those 'meanings' of *dharm* which the notoriously unreliable dictionaries give as (property, attribute).

4.b. The second set of contexts in which *dharm* occurs is by far the largest in frequency if not in range, from which we could say that this usage is the principal usage of *dharm* in modern Hindi. If you ask the following question :—

viii *un kaa dharm kyaa he* ? (What is their *dharm*?)

the answer would most probably be of the form :—

ix. *ye hinduu, muslim, iisaaii, yahuudii, log. he*. (They are Hindus, Muslims, Christians, Jews...)

The word *dharm* in Hindi has an almost totally identical application to that of the English word 'religion', which has, of course, an enormous semantic spread, and it would seem highly probable that the English word and concept is the major determinant factor in the Hindi usage. The adjective *dhaarmik* which is formed from *dharm* has likewise a similar application to the English adjective 'religious'. Further examples of this usage are found in the collocations *dharmgranth* (scripture) *dharmpracaarak*, (missionary) and *dharmaandhaa* (fanatic). Although we cannot claim 'religion' as a Hindi loan word from English, in that characteristic mode of discourse amongst educated people where sentences are sometimes begun in Hindi and finished in English, or English words are scattered freely throughout, or a Hindi sentence is sometimes repeated afterwards in English, we do find 'religion' to be synonymous with *dharm.* With regard to major religions or creeds such as *hinduudharm* (Hinduism), *boddhdharm* (Buddhism), *iisaaiidharm* (Christianity), *vɛṣnavdharm* (Vaishnavism) and *ṣɛ-dharm* (Shaivism), we find the word *mat* (doctrine, dogma, tenet, belief, etc..) to be synonymous and equally common, giving us *hinduumat*, *boddhmat*, *isaaiimat*, *vɛṣnavmat* and *ṣɛvmat.* Sometimes both are found together as in the phrase *vɛṣnavdharm or mat ke anusaar* (according to Vaishnavism). There is, of course, a major restriction here because to ask:—

x. *un kaa mat kyaa hɛ* ? would be to ask what their opinion is, not what their religion is.

The word *dharmṣaastr* refers to the specific Sanskrit texts but is also sometimes used in a more general sense of 'theology' or religious jurisprudence. Dictionaries often give the meaning 'law' in the entry for *dharm* but the Hindi words for law are *qaanuun* and *niyam* and, although we are not conversant with the specialized usages of legal discourse, we would doubt very much if *dharm* is ever used with the connotation of law other than when used in reference to the *dharmṣaastr.*

4.c. It might be of interest to insert here between the second and the third usages of *dharm* a 'negative' fact. We do not find any relationship at all in terms of semantic force fields between *dharm* and *niiti* [ethics, morality]. They appear to be totally independent concepts each with its own fields of force and having no semantic interaction.

4.d. The third set of contexts in which *dharm* occurs are those that indicate a distributional relationship with *kartavy.* It is here that we meet with the 'concept of duty'. In these contexts we find the relation of hyponymy to hold between *dharm* and *kartavy.* To say that *dharm* is a hyponym of *kartavy* is to say that, in these contexts, *dharm* will generally be understood to be synonymous with, or better, to imply *kartavy*, but that *kartavy* does not imply *dharm.* The same relation holds between scarlet and red. Scarlet is said to be a hyponym of red, for, while scarlet will generally imply redness, red does not imply scarlet. Consider these examples:—

xi. *patnii kaa dharm hɛ pati kii sevva karnaa.*	(A wife's duty is to look after her husband.)

xii. *adhyaapak kaa dharm hɛ parhaanaa.* (A teacher's duty is to teach.)

xiii. *patnii kaa dharm hɛ vrat rakhnaa.* (A wife's duty is to fast etc..)

In each of these contexts *kartavy* would be acceptable, even in the the last one, although it would be felt that a certain force had been lost. In the next examples, however, *dharm,* would not be found acceptable :—

xiv. *adhyaapak kaa kartavy hɛ thiick samay par klaas mĕ aanaa.* (It is the duty of a teacher to come to class on time.)

xv. *patni kaa kartavy hɛ ghar mĕ sab se pahle uthnaa*) (It is the duty of a wife to bethe first to arise in the household.)

We find *kartavy* to be the general word in Hindi to convey the concept of duty implicit in the English word. In fact it seems probable that the English word and concept has acted on the usages of *kartavy* as the word religion has acted upon the usage of *dharm.* It is *kartavy* that occurs in the Hindi version of the Constitution of India. There we find phrases like *naagarikō kaa kartavy,* (the duty of citizens). The word *dharm* is used for 'linked duty', that is to say the duty implicit in being what one is : it could be occupation- or relationship-linked duty, for example. On examining the force that is lost in example xi, it seems to be that *dharm* is a duty with all the sanctions of religion. This however arises from the fact that marriage is a religiously sanctitioned relationship and we must not conclude from this that *dharm* is equivalent to 'religious duty'. It is so only in cases where the relationship or category of person is essentially a religious one. The force that is lost is that *kartavy* does not convey in the same way as *dharm* that the duty is somehow inherent to that particular class of people. This is why we say that *dharm* is a hyponym of *kartavy* since *dharm* certainly implies duty, but *kartavy* can be imposed on on one 'from outside' and does not contain the inherentness of *dharm.*

We conclude this analysis of *dharm* and *kartavy* by noticing two adjectival collocations. *Kartavy-paraayan patnii* is the Hindi for a dutiful wife, but *dharm-paraayan patnii* is the Hindi for a religiously inclined wife.

5.a. The question now arises whether or not there is a central concept of *dharm* which is modified by the contexts in which it occurs so that it appears to have three separate 'meanings', or whether we simply have one word which is used in three quite unconnected ways. The situation we have uncovered so far can best be represented in the following diagram where the circle may be taken as representing the semantic space that *dharm* marks off as its own, or better, in which *dharm* is present and the semicircles that intersect as the three usages we have established by our analysis of overlapping usage.

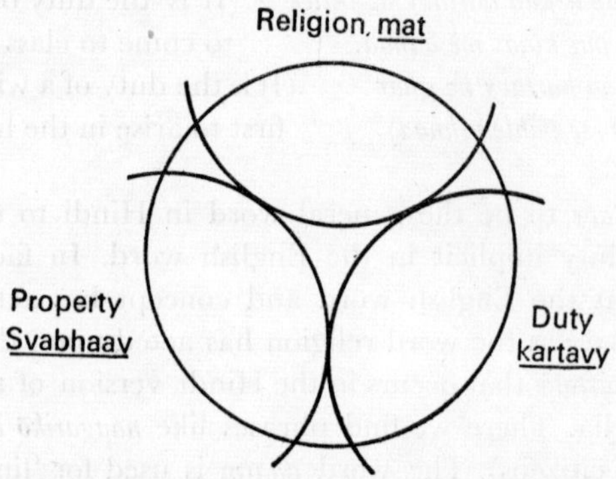

The words used here are merely to indicate the three types of usage discussed in paragraphs 4.a, 4.b and 4.d and no more. An examination of the contexts in which these usages occur suggests that the three sets are mutually exclusive. Broadly we can say that *dharma* conveys the notion of religion when used of people treated as individuals, of duty when used of people viewed as members of classes, and of property or nature when used of animates or certain inanimates. This adds weight to the proposition that there could well be a central concept from which each of these 'meanings' is derived. There is further support for this from:

xvi. *cor kaa dharm hɛ corii karnaa* (The *dharm* of a thief is to steal).

where *dharm* is taken to imply *apnaa dharm* or *svadharm* and the nearest synonym is *aacaran* (mode of behaviour, way of life). Also we have sentences like

xvii. *us ne jhuuth bolnaa apnaa dharm banaa liya.* (He made lying his *dharm.*)

which again takes us to a central concept for *dharm* which we would now state as 'the inherent mode of behaviour proper to a..'. That to which it is proper supplies the context and hence the sense in which *dharm* is to be understood. This central concept is rarely directly apparent but is implicit in and influences all usages of *dharm* in modern Hindi. Our final representation is thus.

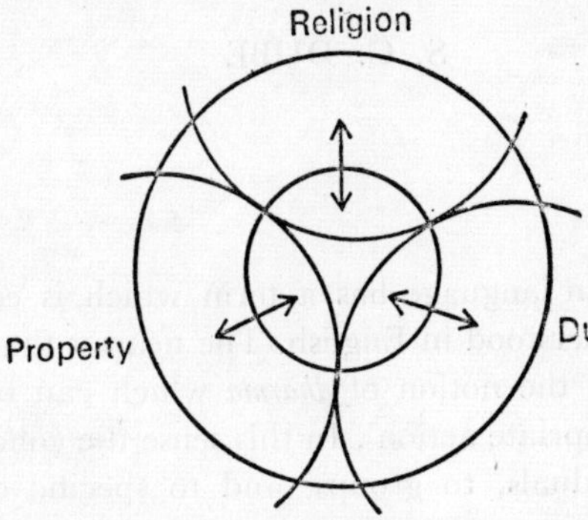

In this diagram the central concept is represented by the inner circle.

Changing Norms in the Hindu Joint Family

S. C. DUBE

Perhaps no Indian language has a term which is equivalent to 'duty' as it is understood in English. The nearest that we can get to the concept is the notion of *dharma* which can be translated roughly as 'appropriate action'. In this sense the concept of duty applies to individuals, to groups, and to specific categories of persons and positions. One can speak of *dharma* for particular castes, for the lineage and the family, and for different categories of relationships including those encompassed in the network of kinship. The elements of *dharma* are believed to be space- and time-bound and are modifiable in relation to *desa* (country) and *kala* (time). Thus the notion is not inflexible: it can be adapted to different contexts and situations. Certain core values, especially those defining relations between man and the supernatural, man and man (particularly with those with whom one has kin or affinal ties), and man and the wider society have had a degree of continuity over time. But the winds of change have made a powerful impact on the notion of *dharma* and this has resulted in considerable reinterpretation and redefinition of the thought and behaviour patterns implicit in the norms determined by it.

Sacred texts elaborately prescribe the *dharma* relating to the lineage and the family as well as to different statuses within these units. They do take some account of the diversities in different regions as well as in different castes and classes. However, there is considerable variance between what the sacred texts say and what the people actually believe. The native categories of thought make a distinction between the ultimate norms—which one should strive to achieve but many of which in practice are not easily achievable—and the proximate norms which determine the patterns of behaviour and deviation from which invites strong social censure and often leads to conflict and fission in the family. The prescriptions of the holy texts and ancient law givers can be viewed, thus, only as broad indications of what is ideal. Our concern in this discussion will be mainly with native categories of thought regarding the concept of duty in the context of the joint family and the patterns of adjustment and adaptation they are undergoing in a period of rapid social change.

The Hindu family is a social, economic, and ritual unit. These three components are inextricably interwoven in the norms that govern behavioural patterns of its members. The Hindu marriage, as is well known, is not a contract : it is believed to have a measure of continuity life after life. This at any rate is the desired ideal. Most married Hindu women observe at least one fast during the year to ensure that in subsequent births they get married to the same person to whom they are married in this life. Maintaining the continuity of the family first by marriage and then by begetting children (especially a son or sons) is itself a part of *dharma*. If no sons are born, it is said, 'there will be no one to give water to the ancestors' (only a son could discharge the necessary ritual obligations to ensure incorporation of the dead among the ancestors). Having no children or having only daughters was considered a calamity and put both the husband and the wife under considerable emotional stress. Polygyny was justified in the interest of the continuity of the family.

The living members of the family are tied together in a complex set of relationships. Each dyadic relationship within the family involves a series of obligations and expectations. There are prescriptions in regard to what one must give to the other members of his family and structured expectations in regard to what others will do for him. The relationships are patterned on the principles of repayment of social and ritual debt (*ṛṇa*), sentiment, loyalty, service, and obedience. While discharging its obligation to the wider society, a family should organize its internal relationships in such a way that it faces the outside world as a close-knit and united unit. Dissensions within are expected to be suppressed so that they do not become a matter of public knowledge. Discreet mediation by elders and close friends can be sought so that the causes of discord within the family can be sorted out and rectified. In some cases this is not enough and severance of ties appears to be better than continuing a relationship that cannot endure.

Rights and duties are determined by one's status in terms of generations, age, sex and position in the scale of kinship. What one owes to others is determined by these criteria. So also are the respect that must be shown, the distance that must be maintained, and the obedience that one must render. When we view family as a process and take account of its developmental cycle there are visible changes in the system of obligations and expectations: the core remains unchanged but on the periphery the changes are significant.

What is the joint family?

The definition of joint family has been a subject of controversy and debate for the last three decades. Sociologists have argued for and against different sets of attributes considered essential to constitute a joint family. There has been some discussion also on the degrees of 'jointness'. For the present discussion we shall take the joint family to mean a co-residential and commensal unit consisting of closely related male patrikin and their wives and unmarried daughters. Commonly it is a two- or three-generation group; in rare cases four generations may be found living together. We shall also consider interlinked households of male patrikin, whether co-residential and commensal or not, who retain close social and ritual ties. Households within this unit, though they have a separate identity and considerable independence, are governed nevertheless by some of the traditional norms of the joint family. Though they are separate residential and commensal units they are expected to have a degree of closeness and have to abide by norms of sentiment, loyalty, and limited obligations. In crises they have to stand by each other. They also join together in a few select ceremonials and rituals. The norms determining obligations and expectations between such linked or allied households are quite different from those governing relationships between households having no such ties. The role configuration of households which contain, besides the nuclear unit, relatives like a widowed parent and/or siblings of the husband is indeed complex and has its basis in the norm relating to the care of the aged and the young belonging to the joint family. Such households will also be considered in looking at the changing norms. In a broad sense they constitute an incomplete joint family.

It is generally believed that India is the land of the joint family. Census data, however, unmistakably brings out the fact that a sizable proportion of families in the country are nuclear in character. The joint households consist of parents, their unmarried children, and married sons with their wives and children. Two or more brothers and their wives and children may also be living together in a joint household. Ownership of corporate property cannot be regarded as the sole test of a joint family. There are numerous examples, especially after the introduction of land reforms, of persons holding property separately but living in a co-residential and commensal household. On the other hand, one can also find some clusters of households which may hold substantial property in common but may be living separately. The role configurations of the members in the two cases are similar in many ways although the system of obligations and expectations within the joint household is much more demanding.

Factors of change

The forces of change operating in Indian society have not left the joint family and joint-family-like groups unaffected. Individualization and secularization have been two important features of post-independence India. The first has adversely affected the group orientation of the joint family and loosened its coherence. The second has weakened the ritual norms which contributed so much to the unity of the joint family in the past.

A number of factors account for this. The rapid spread of education has contributed to the widening of the mental horizons of those who have passed through the portals of institutions of learning. Between the first generation literates and their illiterate parents the gulf has widened. This disturbs the normal rhythm of joint living as parents and their children are often not on the same wavelength. Girls are also going to school and even to institutions of higher learning in increasing numbers, although their proportion is still small compared to that of the boys. An educated girl cannot easily conform to the ideal norms of a docile wife and submissive daughter-in-law. The near anomic conditions prevailing in the educational institutions, and the general erosion of confidence in the instititions of society, has created a new psychology which is carried also to the home and manifests itself as an unsettling influence.

Alongside of education we have also to consider the impact of mass media. Newspapers reach only a small segment of the society but they do open to the readers a window on the outside world. International styles are adopted quickly by the élite, and those who look upon this group as their reference model are not slow to catch up with them. Literature also makes an impact and brings about certain attitudinal and value changes which are not in conformity with the norms of the joint family. The cinema is perhaps the most important single source of changing certain patterns of behaviour and modes of thought. Styles of dress and make-up that were frowned upon until a few years ago have now penetrated even into the villages and are grudgingly and ungrudgingly accepted. The change is not confined to these alone. Patterns of interpersonal relations are also influenced. The new style, in some ways, is remarkably different from the old one.

Consider also the new structure of economic opportunity. This has encouraged geographical mobility. Obviously the entire joint family cannot move out together. Those who leave the joint family retain relatively close connections with it for a few years but geographical separation over a period of time creates a definite distance between the joint family and the migrating unit. Occasional visits, gift giving, and participation in important rituals does not bind a seceding unit with the larger group in the same way as joint living. Women are now joining the work force in fair numbers. The woman working out of the home becomes a separate category and has to resolve the dilemmas of her two roles. She is often under great psychological stress and physical strain because the impossible is expected of her : in addition to a full time job which earns a regular income for the family, she is also expected to do all the work which a traditional wife should do in the joint family. However, with rising levels of aspiration and increasing cost of living a woman working outside the home is not unwelcome. In fact the trend is encouraged even by parents-in-law and husbands. But the earning woman does demand recognition of her individuality and contribution to household economy. Her work brings her in association with many of her co-workers. Obviously she cannot maintain the conventional seclusion. The older generation does not often see eye to eye with her and this gives rise to friction. Intra-family conflict leads to the establishment of independent homes. Cases have been observed, however, where nuclear families with working wives deliberately move towards a limited jointness. A mother-in-law or some other relative is a welcome member of the household if she/he is willing to take care of young children when the wife is away at work.

Growing demographic pressures do not make for joint living. They at least affect the degree of jointness. Disparities in the earnings of different members of the joint family are also an important cause of tensions and discord.

Trends of change

Because of these factors the joint family today has not remained a viable unit. However, a 'we feeling' between close kin still persists, and if there are no major clashes of interest they still demonstrate their solidarity on ceremonial and ritual occasions. On a diminishing scale some people still continue to fulfil their social and economic obligations to close kin. But the structure and functions of the joint family are undergoing perceptible changes. Joint household units are tending to be smaller, the cut-off points in the developmental process are shortened, and brothers often do not hold together for long after the death of the parents.

According to the traditional norms group-orientation in the joint family was stressed. It was expected to be a close-knit group with a strong sense of solidarity. Ideally the individual was required to subordinate his interest (as also the interests of his wife and children) to the collective interest of the household. Incomes were to be pooled and the share of each member in consumption was more or less equal. Neither education nor higher income entitled a member to ignore his obligation to the other members in terms of their generation, age, or kinship status. The situation is changing rapidly. Group-orientation is getting narrowed. The incidence of joint families is perhaps not statistically lower than at the turn of the century, but the collateral spread of the household is definitely narrower. For example, it is rare to find adult cousins living together. The limits of obligation and responsibility are being sharply delimited in relation to one's parents, children, spouses, and real siblings. Education and income matter significantly and can reduce one's expected behaviour towards others in terms of their generation, age, and kinship status to token acts.

Another significant change is in the status of women. In several communities, especially in the upper castes in rural areas and in middle classes in urban areas, women had to live in relative seclusion. In North India they were not allowed to expose their faces to elder male members falling in certain prohibited categories of kinship within the family; outsiders were not expected to see them. As a general rule they had to maintain the required degree of social distance as enjoined by custom. Within the family, apart from looking after the normal domestic chores they had to render certain personal service to certain categories of relations. A daughter-in-law was expected to anticipate the needs of the elders and offer to do things for them. After the day's household chores she was expected to massage the body of her mother-in-law or other female relations in the same class, and of the husband. In respect of property rights her position was one of subordination. The situation has altered dramatically. The seclusion of women is breaking down. Covering the face before the father-in-law and other members of the family, more or less in the same class, tends to be notional. The requirements of observing social distance are less stringent. The expectation of personal services is being diminished. Law has given women the right to property and has thus taken a positive step to change their subordinate status. Polygyny is viewed with disfavour. Educated women play a crucial part in the education of their children. Working women can withdraw, to a certain extent, even from traditional responsibilities. The pace of change in the rural areas in somewhat slower: the upper castes and the rich from the lower castes in villages regard it a mark of respectability to adopt the conventional modes of behaviour that were considered appropriate. However, even in this group education is making a difference.

According to traditional norms authority was vested in men and the older people were invariably the decision-makers. By and large the society continues to be male-dominated, but the educated segment of the women is asserting itself more and more in the decision-making processes. The older people cannot claim an unquestionable right to obedience from the younger members of the household. They get respect from the latter only in so far as they do not legislate their lives and make unreasonable demands on them. As before the young have to learn to live with the elders but the elders now find it imperative to adapt and adjust to the new generation. Thus the norms of deference and obedience are undergoing change. An uncle and a nephew, if they are more or less of the same age, are more likely to behave as friends than to be governed by their respective kinship statuses. Greater freedom is being demanded and generally given in the choice of a mate or an occupation. There is an overall decline in the extent to which parents deem it their duty to regulate the lives of their children with respect to social habits, dress, friendship, education, morals, and marriage. This is specially in evidence in the middle, upper-middle, and upper class families.

Many of the task-oriented roles of the family are undergoing change too. For example, some of the socialization functions of the family have been taken over by the school which takes the children outside the orbit of the family for an important part of the day. The new open structure of economic opportunity has, in a substantial measure, changed the economic functions of the family. Hereditary occupations may either be discarded by all members of the younger generation or they may be pursued only by one or two. Training in crafts and other ways of making a living within the family has thus lost much of its importance.

The conventional joint family was an important ritual unit. Religious ceremonies, tasks undertaken to earn merit, and rituals connected with the life cycle played an important part. With increasing secularization of outlook and deteriorating economic conditions ceremonials are being underplayed. Rituals connected with marriage and death are still considered important and draw almost all members of the extended family who continue to perform their traditional obligations, though on a somewhat restricted scale. But on the whole the character of the family as a ritual unit is becoming feeble.

Division of labour within the family is slowly undergoing change. The earlier emphasis on service as a manifestation of asymmetrical relations is declining. The notion that obligations of personal service maintain and sustain the joint household is being diluted. The changes in the pattern of division of labour are introducing parallel changes in the pattern of responsibility towards parents and siblings.

The power of kinship obligation has been substantially eroded. Poor and low status relations do not often get the treatment which their kinship position entitles them to. People interact with such of their kin as are equal in status and make a special effort to forge links with upper status relations. Settling sons in life and arranging decent marriages for daughters (with payment of substantial dowries) continue to be major parental obligations. Other than these, interests rather than ties of kinship are emerging as a major determinant of close personal interaction. The boundary for compulsory fulfilment of kinship obligations has shrunk substantially. There is evidence of the weakening of the principle of patriliny: close bilateral ties tend to receive greater recognition.

The traditional ethos promoted the ideal of 'one for all, all for one' and emphasized collective interest. Contemporary social legislation in respect of inheritance of property, separation, divorce, and adoption is all in the direction of an emphasis on individual self-interest. In actual practice not many seem to take advantage of the law at present but the trend likely to emerge is unmistakable. It appears that more and more people in the future will assert their legal rights. This will further erode the legitimacy of the surviving conventional norms governing the joint family.

It is difficult to generalize for a country of enormous cultural diversity such as India, but one can say that the joint family is mostly an upper middle class and middle class phenomenon. These are the segments which are increasingly taking advantage of new educational and economic opportunities and have been the most exposed to the influence of mass media. As such they have been vulnerable to the powerful currents of change. The traditional concept of duty has not been totally eroded but it has certainly been diluted.

Index

Adam, 152
Adharma, *xtv*, *xix*, 3, 7, 10, 37, 99
'Afif, Shams al-din Siraj, 151-53
Agni (*see also* Fire), 6-7
Agnihotra, 86, 88-89
Altekar, A. S., *vii-ix*
Āpaddharma, 68
Āpastamba, 27, 29, 38
Arabian Nights, 192
Arjuna, 68, 97, 100, 213
Artha, 16, 26, 66-79
Arthaśāstra, *xv-xvi*, 33, 47, 52-53, 64, 69-77, 93, 96
Arya Samaj, 93
Ascetic, 66, 96-98, 104
Aśoka, *xvii*, 111-13
Āśramas, 66, 71, 96
Asuras (*see* Demons)
Aśvins, 5
Ātman, 8, 10, 92
Aurobindo Ghose, *xvii*, 210-11

Bali, 103-4
Banerjee, Surendranath, *xviii*
Bankim Chandra Chatterji, *xix*, 12-13, 208-9
Barani, 151-56, 158-63
Baudhāyana, 34-35
Bhagavad Gītā, 9, 16, 41, 97, 99-101, 112, 211, 213-15
Bhakti, *xviii*, 13, 97, 99-101, 104-5
Bhīmasena, 68, 72
Bodhisattva, 12, 15
Brahmā, 8, 69, 103
Brahmacārin, 66
Brahman, 92
Brāhmaṇas, 81-82, 85, 91-92
Brahmins, 8, 26, 28-31, 35-36, 39-45, 58, 61, 72-74, 78, 80, 86-91, 97, 99-101, 105, 109-12, 153, 195 211-12, 215
Brahmo Samaj, 207-8
Bṛhaspati, 30, 39, 69, 70
British (individual references, plus pp. 166-215), *ix*, *xv*, *xvii-xix*, 45, 47, 50-51, 54, 63, 77-78
Buddhism, *xi*, 5, 10-12, 14-15, 52-53, 97, 100, 104, 107-18, 122-23, 132-34, 224

Caste, *ix*, 29, 31, 35, 37, 45, 48, 63, 74, 101, 123, 130-33, 136, 184, 213, 228
Ceylon, 114, 119-43
Chariot, 88-90
Christianity, *x-xi*, *xix*, 41, 45, 54, 77, 115, 166-89, 190, 193, 223, 224
Clive, Robert, 170-73, 176-77, 183
Conscience, *x*, *xix*, 21-22, 59, 166-67
Constitution, Indian, *viii-ix*, *xi*, 19, 45, 50, 225
Cornwallis, 172-73, 177
Cotton, J. S., 196
Curzon, 182, 193, 201-2, 210

Demon (*Asuras*), *xiv-xv*, *xix*, 88, 96-106, 107
Devas (*see* Gods)
Dhamma, 4-5, 53, 111, 113-14, 122
Dhammapada, 108
Dharma, *passim*
Dharma, personified, 5

Dharmaśāstra, *x*, *xv-xvi*, 5, 25, 27-29, 33-39, 46, 49-50, 61, 66, 72, 112, 119-20
Dissent, *xvii-xviii*
Diti, 104
Draupadi, 28, 34
Dunlop-Smith, 202-3
Duty to husband/wife, *x*, 224, 229, 234
Duty to mankind, *ix*, 13
Duty to one's country, *vii*, *ix-x*, *xvii*, 13, 192, 208
Duty to one's parents, 8, 48, 123, 192, 234-35
Duty to oneself, *x*
East India Company, 170-71, 175-76, 196
Education, *x*, *xi*, *xv*, 190-204, 231-33
Eightfold Path, 107
Élite, *ix-x*, 150, 153, 162
Elphinstone, Mountstuart, 173-74, 177, 180
Enlightenment (*see also Nirvāṇa*), 113-14, 117
Evangelicalism, 174-78, 182
Evil, *xiv*, *xix*
Expiation, 96

Fathers (*pitṛs*), 27
Fire (*see also* Agni), 86-88
Forest-dweller, 66

Gada, Yusuf, 151
Gajendragadkar, P. B., 45
Gandhi, M. K., *xv*, *xix*, 14, 41, 79, 167, 187, 206, 211-14, 216
Gautama, 10, 34
Gītā (*see Bhagavad Gītā*)
Gods (*devas*), *vii-xiv*, *xv*, *xix*, 6, 10, 13, 72, 82-83, 88-89, 98-99, 104, 111, 152-53, 156, 159, 161, 166-89
Gokhale, *xviii*, 206, 211
Golden Age, 103
Grant, Charles, 173, 175
Great Tradition, *xvii*
Greeks, 50, 52
Guest, 87-90, 111

Hamadani, Saiyid, Ali, 154-56, 159-62
Harikeśa, 101
Hariśchandra, 87
Hastings, Warren, *xviii*, 171-73, 176, 178, 181, 187
Hegel, 77
Hesse, Hermann, 67
Hierarchy, 18
Hitler, Adolf, 167
Householder (*gṛhastha*), 66, 74, 90, 97, 101, 109-10, 111
Hunter, W. W., 193, 200, 202

Indra, 7, 69, 97, 104, 135
Islam, *xi*, *xviii*, 24, 40, 41, 45, 147-65

Jainas, *xviii*, 45
Japan, *ix*, *xi*
Jayaswal, 30
Jews, *x*, *xii*, 40, 223
Joint family, 228-36
Jones, Sir William, *xviii*

Kabir, *xvii*
Kali Age, 34, 103
Kali, incarnate, 103
Kāma, 66-79
Kāmasūtra, 68, 69, 71-74, 76-77
Kandy, 119-43
Karaṇiyam, *xiv*
Kārma, 9, 12-14, 99, 132, 209, 211-12
Kātyāyana, 29, 39
Kauṭalya (*see Arthasastra*)
King, duty of (and to), *xv-xvi*, 30-31, 33, 38, 43, 53, 61, 66, 69, 72, 75-76, 85-86, 93, 111-112, 119-43, 147-65, 192, 207, 214
Kṛṣṇa, 9, 97, 100, 213
Kṣatriyas, 58, 68, 86, 88, 96, 111
Kullūka, 32
Kūṭadanta Sutta, 112

Land grants, 124-25
Land tenure, 127, 129, 133, 136-43
Lannoy, R., 17
Lawrence, J., 172, 178-79

Layman, Buddhist, 107, 109, 113, 115, 124
Lee-Warner, Sir W., 190-204
Lingayats, *xvii*, 45
Liquor, 73
Lokāyatas, 70

Mackenzie, Holt, 173-74, 177, 180
Mahābhārata, 28-29, 56, 67, 69, 72, 75, 89, 97
Maharashtra, *vii*, *xvii*, 211
Malcolm, John, 173, 177-78
Mann, Thomas, 79
Manu, 27, 29, 31-32, 34, 36, 38-39, 45, 50, 69, 82, 84, 90, 132-33
Marriage Laws, *xi*, 22, 28, 34, 55, 72, 74, 97, 132, 229, 235-36
Marx, Karl, 66, 77-78, 167
Māyā, 207, 209
Mees, G. H., 17
Merchants (*see also* Vaisyas), 29, 66
Metcalfe, Charles, 173-75, 177-78, 180
Mīmāṃsa, 4, 10, 17, 36, 38, 50, 80, 82-83
Minto, Lord, 202-3
Mītāksara, *x*, 50
Mitra, 5, 7
Mitra-miśra, 35, 52, 54
Mokṣa, 9, 67-69, 212, 214
Mongols, 162
Monks, Buddhist, 109, 113-17, 123, 133
Mudabbir, Fakhr-i, 151, 153-55, 157, 159, 161-62
Mughals, 157
Muslims, *x-xi*, *xv*, *xvii*, *xviii*, 46, 48, 54, 55, 150ff, 176, 193, 206, 223

Nāgārjuna, 17
Nārada, 29
Nationalism, *vii*, *xiv-xv*, 13, 205-16
Nature (*see also Svabhava*), *xvi-xvii*, *xix* 7, 11, 101
Nazism, 79
Nehru, J., 13-15, 79
Nesfield, J. C., 197-98
Nirvāṇa, 107-8, 111

Non-injury, 96, 100, 102-3, 112, 212
Non-violence, 97, 211-13
Number (of authorities), 30-32
Nyāya, 10-11

Orthopraxy, *xviii*

Pal, Bipin Chandra, 208, 214
Pali canon, 4, 11, 107-18, 133
Pañcatantra, *xvi*
Panchayats, 45-46, 48, 51
Pariṣad, 30-32, 47
Pitāmaha, 36
Prahlāda, 105
Prajāpati, 69
Prāṇāgnihotra, 89-90
Praśastapāda, 10
Pratt, T. B., 7, 15
Prem Sagar, 192

Qur'an, 41

Radhakrishnan, 9, 44
Rahula, Walpola, 4-5, 107
Rājakāriya, *xiv*, 137, 142
Rāmāyana, 57
Rammohun Roy, *xix*, 12-13, 207-8
Renou, Louis, 80
Revolt and mutiny of 1857, 178-80, 186-87
Rg Veda, *xiv*, 5-7, 42, 73, 87
Ṙights, *ix*, 20, 55
Ripon, 193-94
Rta, *xiv*, 6-7, 11

Sabhyas, 28-30, 39, 46, 53
Sacrifice, 6, 10, 40, 72, 81-92, 97-101, 112
Sādhāraṇa dharma, 30, 96, 107-8, 207-8
Śaivas, 45, 224
Samantu, 27
Sāṃkhya, 9, 11
Saṃsāra, 9
Sanātana dharma, 4, 13, 96-97, 99-102, 211
Śaṅkara, 16, 31-32, 69, 70
Sanskritization, 94

Śāstra (*see dharmaśāstra*)
Sati, 175-77, 207
Sāyaṇa, 6
Sect, *xvii-xviii*
Seers (*ṛṣis*), 82-84
Shah, Firuz, 152, 160
Shore, John, 173, 175
Sigālovada Sutta, 109, 111, 113
Śiva, 66, 69, 101-4
Smṛti, 35, 38, 40-42, 50, 54, 81, 83-84
Soma, 73, 80, 88-90
Špiro, M. E., 14
Śrauta rituals, 80, 86-87, 90-94
Śruti, (*see* Vedas)
Śūdras, 42, 58, 79
Sukeśin, 102-4
Sultan, 147-65
Śunaḥśepa, 87
Śūnyavādins, 11
Svabhāva (*see also* Nature), *xvi*
Svadharma, 4, 7-9, 13-14, 30, 92, 96-105, 107-8, 112

Tapas, 66, 71, 82
Tathāgata, 11-12
Taxation, 112, 142, 154
Telang, Kashinath Trimbak, 193-94
Ten duties of a king (*see also* King, duty of), 133, 135
Text books, 191-204
Tilak, Bal Gangadhar, 211-14
Torture, 74-75
Trevelyan, Charles, 175, 178-79
Trivarga, 67-69, 71
Truth, 8, 96, 100, 103, 212

Ulster, 178
Underworld, *xiv*
Upaniṣads, 6, 8-9, 16, 100, 104
Utteramerūr, 52, 54-55

Vaiśeṣikas, 10
Vaiṣṇavas, 45, 224
Vaiśyas (*see also* Merchants), 58
Varṇa, 30, 35, 66, 71, 85, 92,96, 109, 212
Varṇāśramadharma, 4, 7, 9, 30, 36, 102, 107, 207-8, 212, 215
Varuṇa, 5
Vātsyāyana (*see* Kamasutra)
Vāyu, 7
Vedanta, 4, 11, 13, 97
Vedas, (*see also* Rg Veda), *xiv*, 4-5, 8-10, 30-31, 34-36, 38, 40-42, 44, 57, 61, 73, 80-93, 101, 103, 105
Vijñāneśvara, 30, 38
Village, *ix-x*, *xvii*, 38, 90, 114, 125
Viṣṇu, 88, 103-4, 175
Vivekananda, *xvii*, *xix*, 208-9, 211-12
Vrata, 6
Vṛtra, 7
Vyavahāra, 28-29, 36, 39, 49

Weber, Max, 12, 14, 127, 134, 141
Werblowsky, Zvi, 14
Western tradition, imitation of, *vii-viii*, *xviii-xix*, 40-41, 43, 47-50, 135, 139, 185, 205-9, 214
Widengren, G., 7, 15
Women, *vii*, 23, 74, 110, 186-87, 207, 231-34

Yajamāna, 86-87, 90, 92
Yama, *xiv*, 32
Yudhiṣṭhira, *xiv*, 57, 68, 97

Zoroastrians, 156, 158